IMAGES
of America

FRANCO-AMERICANS OF MAINE

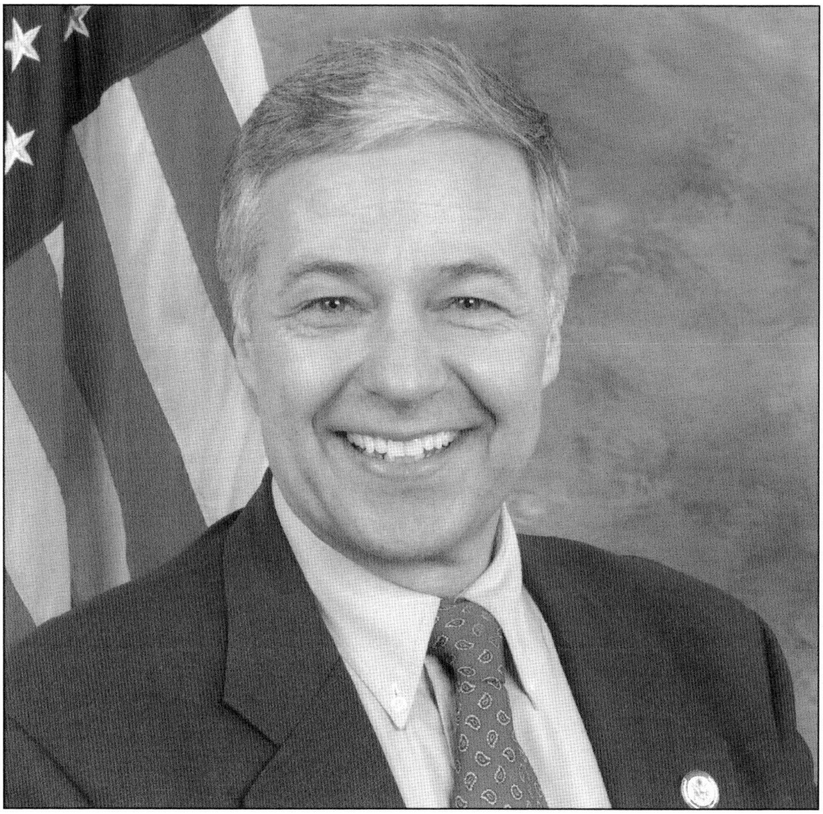

The growth and prosperity that America has enjoyed has been fueled in part by the energy and resourcefulness of immigrants. This has been especially true in Maine, where those of French Canadian descent came south in large numbers in the 19th and 20th centuries and have made a great contribution to this state. Many started in the textile mills, shoe shops, brickyards, and factories and worked hard to develop lives for themselves and for their families. The large rugged buildings where they worked can be seen throughout the state today, often beside a river that provided the power to drive production. Other Franco-Americans, known as Acadians, worked on the land and in the fields of northern Maine. Goods from Maine, be it textiles or farm produce, have became known for quality and value throughout the country. These newcomers to Maine, the Franco-Americans, displayed a strong work ethic and an unshakable devotion to family and culture as they built their communities. I know how much went into developing a life in Maine, because my own family came to the Medway area from Québec years ago. As for myself, having worked in the pulp and paper industry, I have experienced what it's like to work both the day and midnight shift, and I've been on strike. Franco-Americans have always been hard workers, and they overcame many obstacles as they became contributors to their new environment. I am proud to be of Franco-American heritage, and I honor the brave and hardworking families that arrived before us. The immigrants who came to this area helped Maine to become the great state it is, and their contribution will be forever appreciated.

—Congressman Mike Michaud (D-Second District)
Courtesy of the Office of Congressman Mike Michaud

ON THE COVER: Pictured here is the Dufour-Gosselin wedding at SS. Peter and Paul Church in Lewiston in 1957. (Courtesy of the University of Southern Maine, Lewiston-Auburn College Franco-American Collection.)

IMAGES
of America

FRANCO-AMERICANS OF MAINE

Dyke Hendrickson

ARCADIA
PUBLISHING

ISBN 978-0-7385-7280-2

Published by Arcadia Publishing
Charleston, South Carolina

Printed in the United States of America

Library of Congress Control Number: 2009910313

For all general information contact Arcadia Publishing at:
Telephone 843-853-2070
Fax 843-853-0044
E-mail sales@arcadiapublishing.com
For customer service and orders:
Toll-Free 1-888-313-2665

Visit us on the Internet at www.arcadiapublishing.com

*Franco-Americans have a great appreciation for family.
I dedicate this to my immediate family, all lovers of
books: wife, Vicki, and children, Leslie and Drew.*

Contents

ACKNOWLEDGMENTS

I have always felt that librarians are the kindest and most generous of people. After seeking out photographs and information for this book for close to a year, I feel more than ever that this is true.

I would like to thank the staff at the University of Southern Maine's Lewiston-Auburn College Franco-American Collection in Lewiston. Dan Philbrick, Robyn Holman, Maureen Perry, and Donat Boisvert were tireless in making available images from their large and impressive collection.

I would also thank the staff of the Franco-American Heritage Center in Lewiston at the former St. Mary's Church. Rita Dube was very helpful, and she and her team are part of a growing historical community in Lewiston that is creating a rich resource for Franco-American studies.

The staff at McArthur Public Library in Biddeford provided great assistance, especially Renee DesRoberts, Sally Leahey, and director Dora St. Martin. As a former resident of Biddeford, I enjoyed revisiting that valuable resource.

The Maine Historical Society offers hundreds of photographs to review on www.mainememory.net. Dani Fazio at Maine Historical was helpful in guiding me through the process.

My appreciation also goes out to reference librarians in Sanford, including Jason Fenimore, Bob Morse, and Michelle Kaddy. I want to thank Solange Thibodeau Lamontagne and Gerald Lamontagne of Sanford, who were kind to lend their family photographs for use in this book.

Also helpful were Rick Spear of the Lewiston Public Library, Annette Vance Dorey of Museum L-A in Lewiston, and Deanna Bonner-Ganter at the Maine State Museum. My thanks also go to Ray Gaudette, head of the Biddeford Historical Society and the Franco-American Genealogical Society; Rick Morris of the Lewiston Historical Society; and Millicent MacFarland, clerk of the House of Representatives in Augusta.

No discussion about the French in Maine would be complete without paying close attention to the Acadians in northern Maine. Lise Pelletier and Anne Chamberland of the Acadian Institute at the University of Maine at Fort Kent were very helpful. And providing great photographs and good advice was Ken Theriault of the Madawaska Public Library and the Madawaska Historical Society.

I would also like to thank staff members at the state museum and state law library in Augusta, Museum L-A in Lewiston, the Waterville Public Library, the Dyer Library in Saco, and the Sanford Historical Association.

Introduction

Most immigrants in the 19th century crossed the seas to reach America. But one ethnic group traveled south across the land, first by horse, then by train, and finally, by car and truck. These immigrants were from French Canada, later to be known as Franco-Americans.

Thousands came to Maine in the late 19th and early 20th centuries to work in the mills along the rivers. A smaller segment—the Acadians—arrived in the St. John Valley of Aroostook County beginning in the 18th century.

The proximity of the newcomers to their old country made them unique among immigrant groups and had lasting effects. Many Franco-Americans returned often to their native communities in Québec, and such trips encouraged them to keep their native culture alive. This was one ethnic group that seemed determined, initially at least, to maintain its old culture rather than discard it in favor of assimilation.

The migration of French Canadians to Maine grew out of a combination of necessity in the north and need to the south. A moribund economy in rural Québec made many French Canadians consider alternatives to farming. This lack of opportunity in eastern Canada coincided with labor shortage in Maine as new mills were being constructed. Relying on cheap river power, ready capital, and an intellectual climate that endorsed the growth of the business sector, industrialists pushed for major expansion in the late 19th century. Mammoth mills were built in Augusta-Hallowell, Bath-Brunswick, Biddeford-Saco, Lewiston-Auburn, Sanford-Springvale, and Waterville-Winslow, among other towns. Paper companies opened operations in communities including Rumford, Livermore Falls, Bangor, Old Town, and Millinocket.

New mills needed laborers, and lots of them. Owners looked to nearby Canada for more workers.

The first French Canadians to arrive were usually young men with a sense of adventure. They would spend winters in the mills, and then return to Québec for the summer harvest. The opportunity to earn cash and buy material goods was enticing. To own a gold watch or a new suit of clothes was unheard of for the sons of Canadian farmers, and young men returning from the United States were often the subjects of envy.

In 1860, Maine had 7,490 French Canadian residents. By 1900, the number had risen to 77,000, according to statistics cited in my first book, *Quiet Presence: Stories of Franco-Americans in New England*. And the word-of-mouth "endorsement" of migration was so good that the migration continued for the next three decades.

Migrants traveled by horse and buggy at first. Then the arrival of the Grand Trunk Railroad in 1853 accelerated immigration. It permitted thousands of French Canadians to reach Brunswick, Biddeford, and Sanford. As the railroad lines expanded, so did mill communities. Until the railroad reached Lewiston in the 1860s, the community had less than 100 French Canadians. By 1880, Lewiston had 4,714 Franco-Americans, and by 1900, a total of 13,300 French newcomers had arrived in that city, according to historian Ralph Vicero.

French Canadians traveled to mill cities in search of "streets paved with gold." By today's standards, the wages do not seem glittering. Payment ranging from $3.60 to $7 per week was common in the 1890s, a high point of the migration. And workers were prevailed upon to work for 60 to 70 hours per week. One New England observer of the day called Franco-Americans "the Chinese of the East." But this financial return was better than what they could generate in Québec, so they kept coming.

The French arrived at a time when New England was thriving. In the late 19th century, the United States produced 75 percent of the world's cotton. New England was at the forefront of textile production, and Franco-Americans accounted for more than half of the textile workers in Maine.

The relocation of the French Canadians brought immigrant families into a new English-speaking world, but the newcomers adapted lifestyles very similar to those in Québec. They established churches, parochial schools, and societies. The new residents spoke French as if they were in Québec; their warm family gatherings might have been in the living rooms of the old farmhouses they had left.

Their political assimilation was slower than other immigrant groups. Franco-Americans dominated city halls in mill communities, but they had a low profile on the state and federal level. One reason was that many newcomers, still connected to nearby Québec, did not always vote in general elections. That has all changed in the 21st century, of course, and there are Franco-American officials at every level of federal, state, and local office today.

In the old days, Anglo store owners, bankers, and professionals had few salespeople who spoke French, so motivated newcomers became entrepreneurs. Franco-Americans owned stores and offered services. F. X. Marcotte of Lewiston, for instance, is remembered as one of the first merchants in Maine to extend credit to the immigrants. In the late 19th century, he located his Lewiston store across from the railroad station and kept pots, pans, blankets, soap, and flour right out on the street. Those getting off the train could purchase immediately. Marcotte's faith in their willingness to repay was rewarded many times, and he became one of the leading merchants in the region. Today there are thousands of stores and businesses run by Franco-Americans.

The Franco-Americans developed the institutions that they valued: job, church, society, family, schools. Probably the most visible example of their efforts to retain their culture was their use of the French language. Some immigrants never learned English. Even in the late 20th century, it was not uncommon to meet older Franco-Americans in Maine who spoke very little English.

Perhaps because of their enduring ties with their native culture, Franco-Americans did not obtain a high public profile such as the Irish and the Italians. But that is changing. In 2002, for instance, Maine elected a congressman (Mike Michaud) with a Franco-American surname. And about the same time, the State of Maine declared an annual "Franco-American Day" to recognize the contributions of its largest minority.

In the overview of the French presence in Maine, there is a question of whether the Acadians were actually "immigrants." Many families fled the Acadian peninsula after the British expelled the French in 1755. Longfellow's famous poem "Evangeline" focused on this tragedy. Forced on to British warships, abducted family members were dropped off in Maryland or Georgia or Florida. Many landed in Louisiana and became known as Cajuns. But some stayed in New England, and some drifted west to the St. John Valley.

So while the French were populating Maine's industrial communities in the 19th and early 20th centuries, the Acadians already were living in rural isolation in northern Maine. They cut and drove timber; they planted crops and raised animals. Theirs was a rural, hard-won existence following the chaos their forefathers had endured in the 18th century. The French-speaking Acadians were, and still are, the dominant ethnic group in the region.

Though some historians say that (urban) Franco-Americans were kept poor by low wages and rank working conditions, most former workers I have talked with do not feel that they were exploited. They worked long hours for impersonal institutions, but what immigrant group didn't? It is difficult to advance the argument that they would have been better off laboring on the hard-scrabble farms of Québec.

This book focuses on the successful transition that Franco-Americans have made over the decades. It is designed to produce visual evidence of the happiness and prosperity that many families were able to achieve. Franco-Americans are proud that they were able to make a better life for themselves and their children.

One

WORK

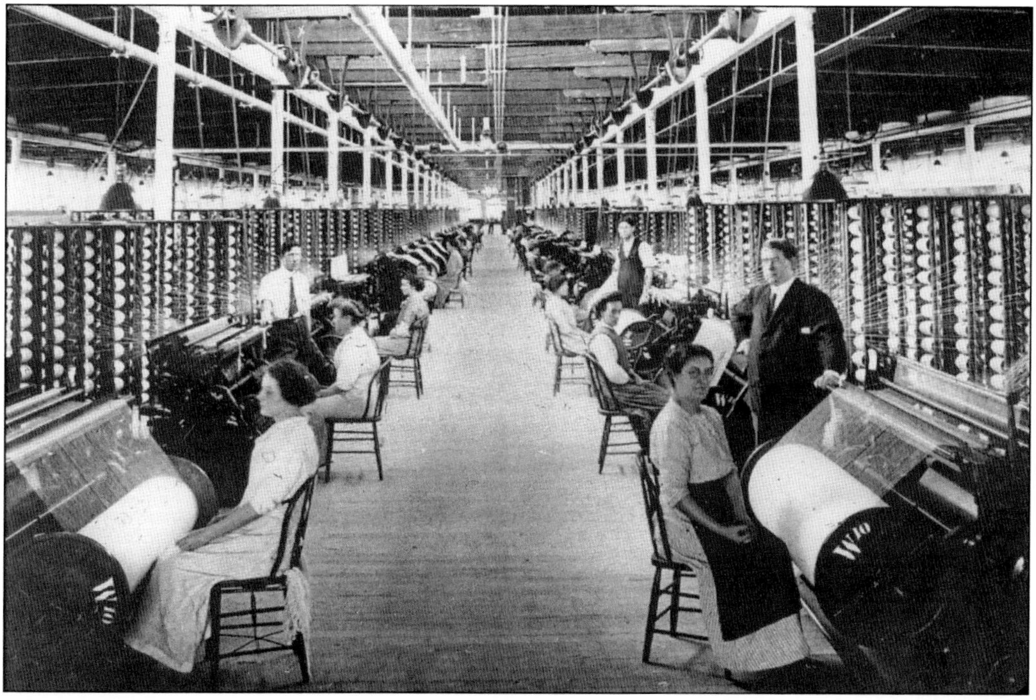

Many immigrants came from Québec to work in Maine's textile mills, which were mammoth and closely supervised, as this image shows. Mills recruited women for textile work, making them one of America's first industries to pay cash wages to females. (Courtesy of the Lewiston Public Library.)

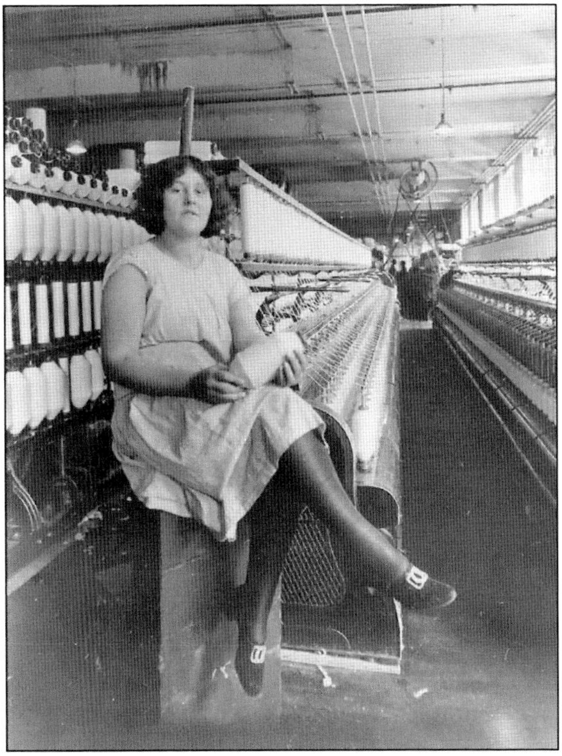

Youngsters of all ages worked in the mills. Here is a teenager in a photograph taken in Lewiston in 1905. (Courtesy of the University of Southern Maine, Lewiston-Auburn College Franco-American Collection.)

Agathe Morin was an employee at the Bates Manufacturing Company in Lewiston for 53 years. Franco-Americans took great pride in their work. (Courtesy of the University of Southern Maine, Lewiston-Auburn College Franco-American Collection.)

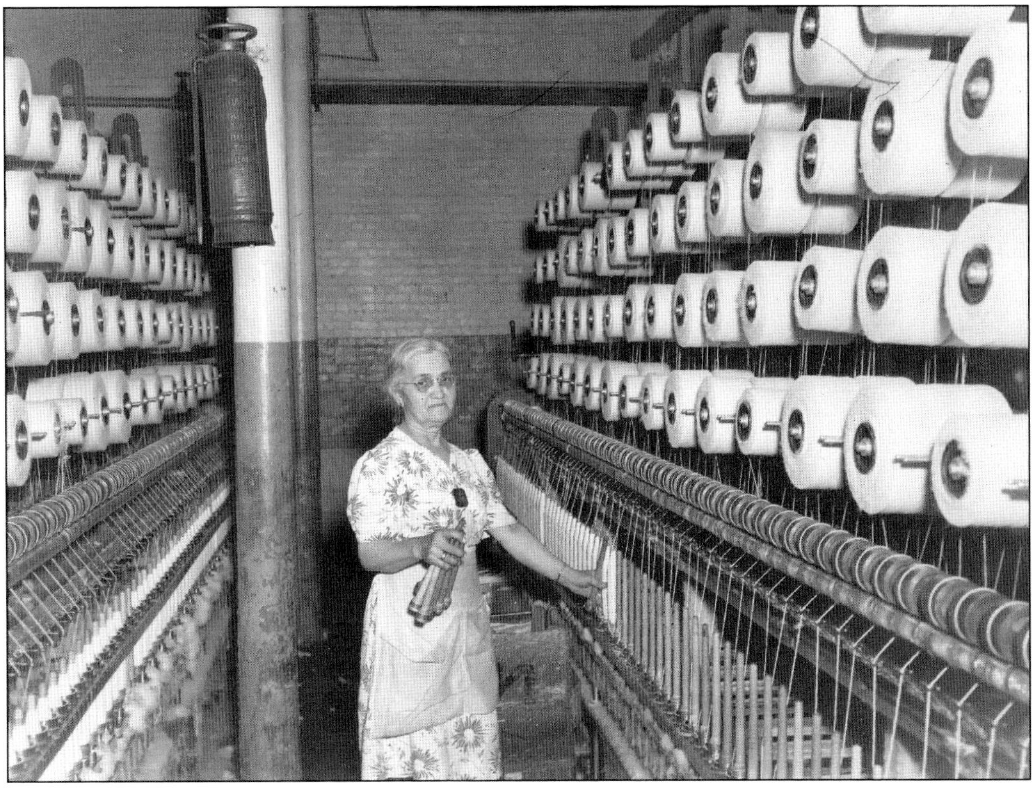

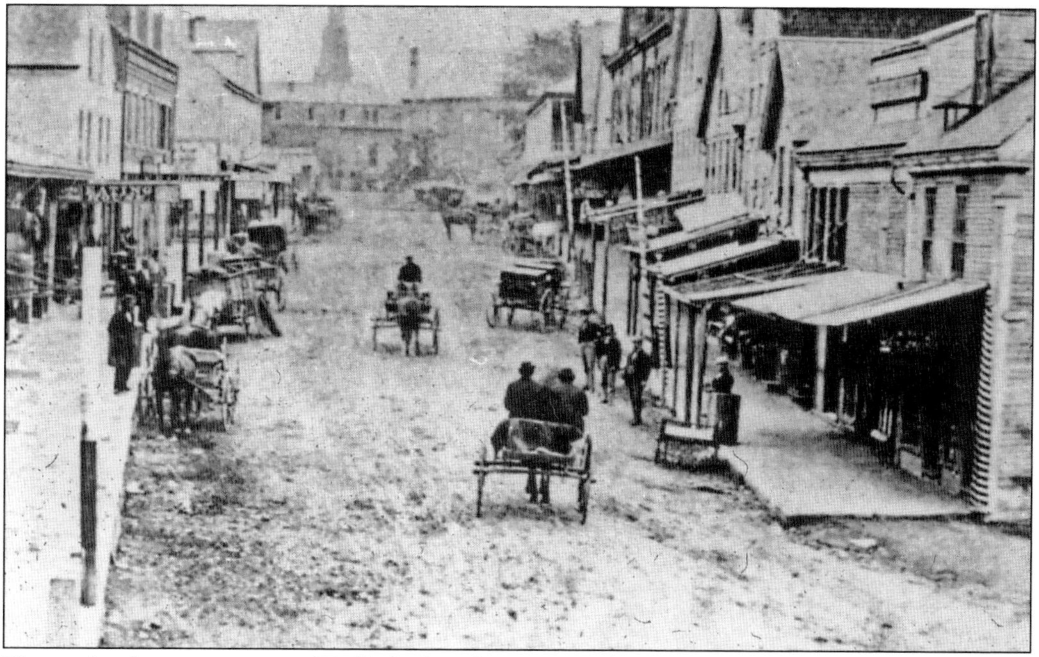

This is the downtown area of Biddeford in the 1870s and is the type of community that French-Canadian immigrants saw when they arrived in the late 19th century. (Courtesy of the McArthur Public Library.)

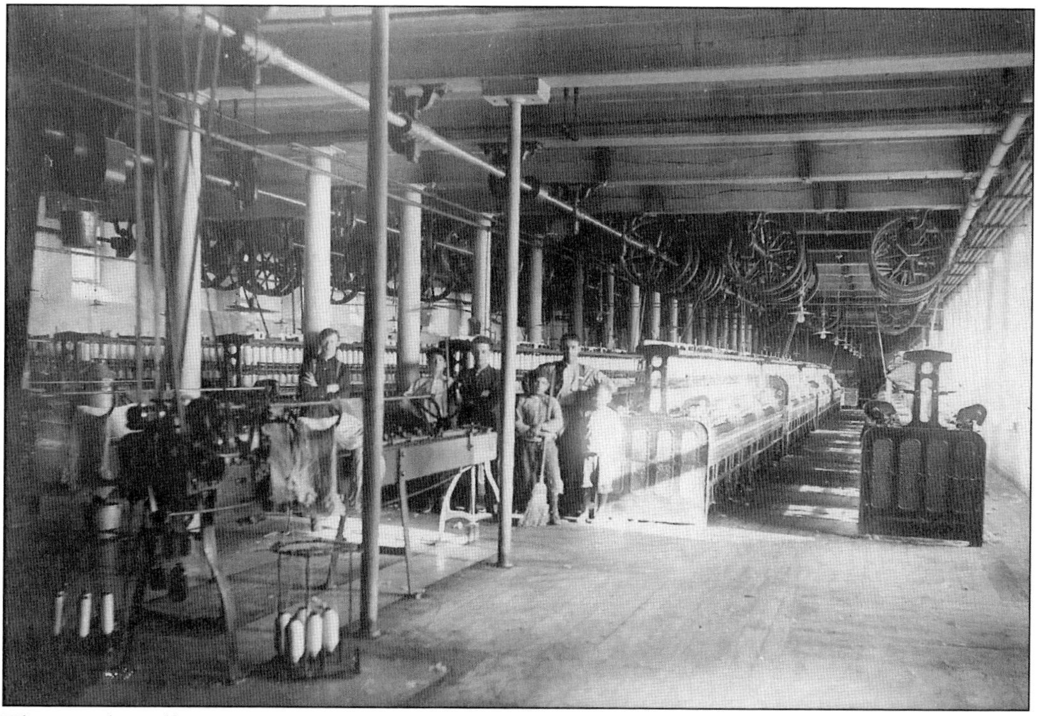

The textile mills were enormous and dwarfed the workers who toiled in them. Though some buildings were dark and unkempt, Franco-American workers were determined to develop useful lives within the brick confines. (Courtesy of Raymond Gaudette Sr.)

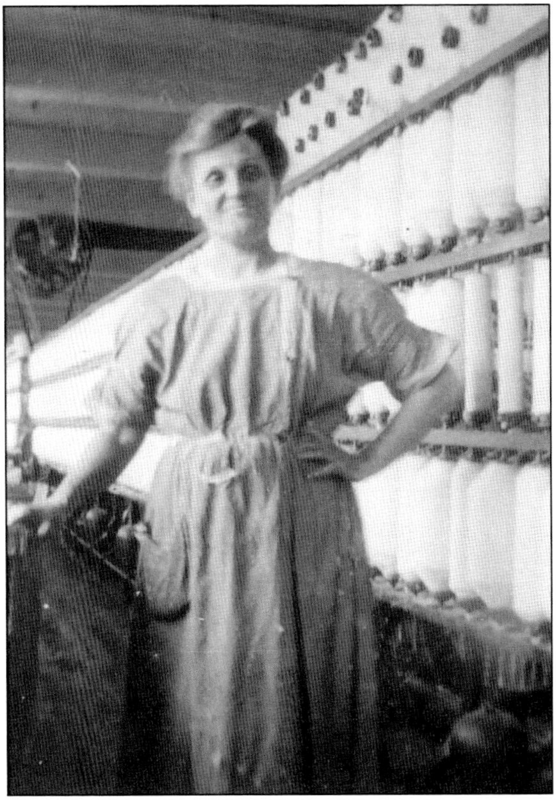

Aurelie Danis (née Bolduc) takes a break from her duties at the Pepperell Manufacturing Company in Biddeford in 1912. Workers would often write back to family in Québec to recommend that they come south to fill the many jobs that were available. (Courtesy of Raymond Gaudette Sr.)

In the late 19th century, New England was a world leader in the manufacture of textiles, and Maine mills hired thousands of workers to meet their quotas. Managers went to Québec to recruit workers. (Courtesy of Raymond Gaudette Sr.)

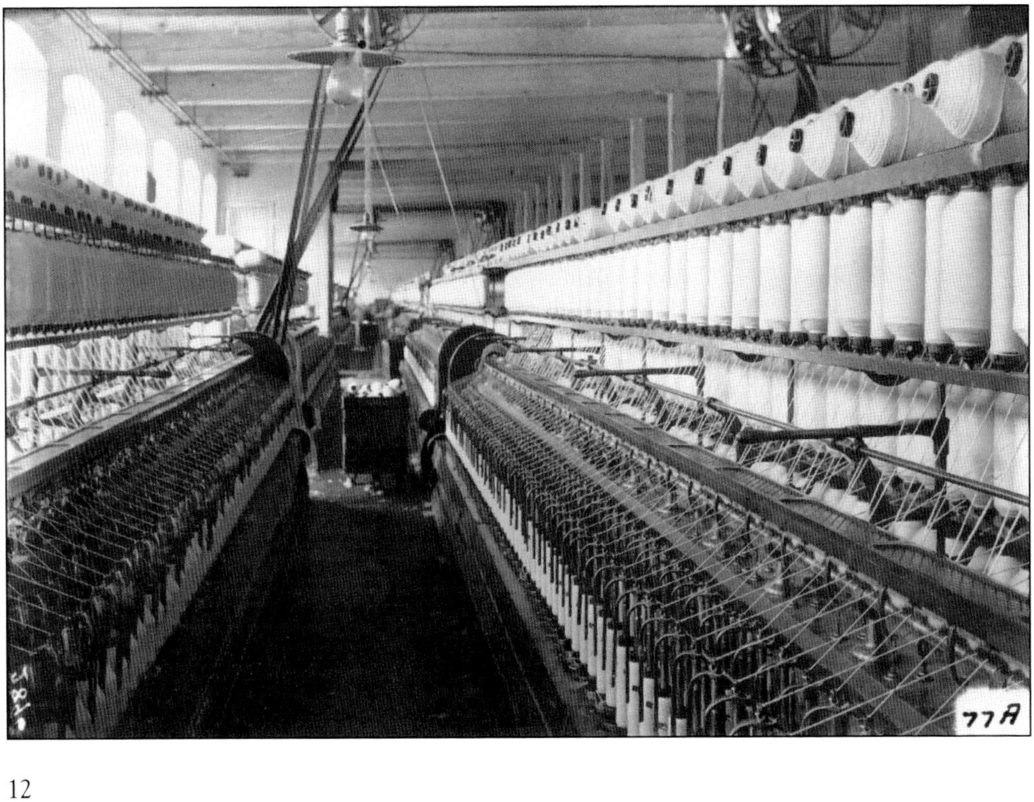

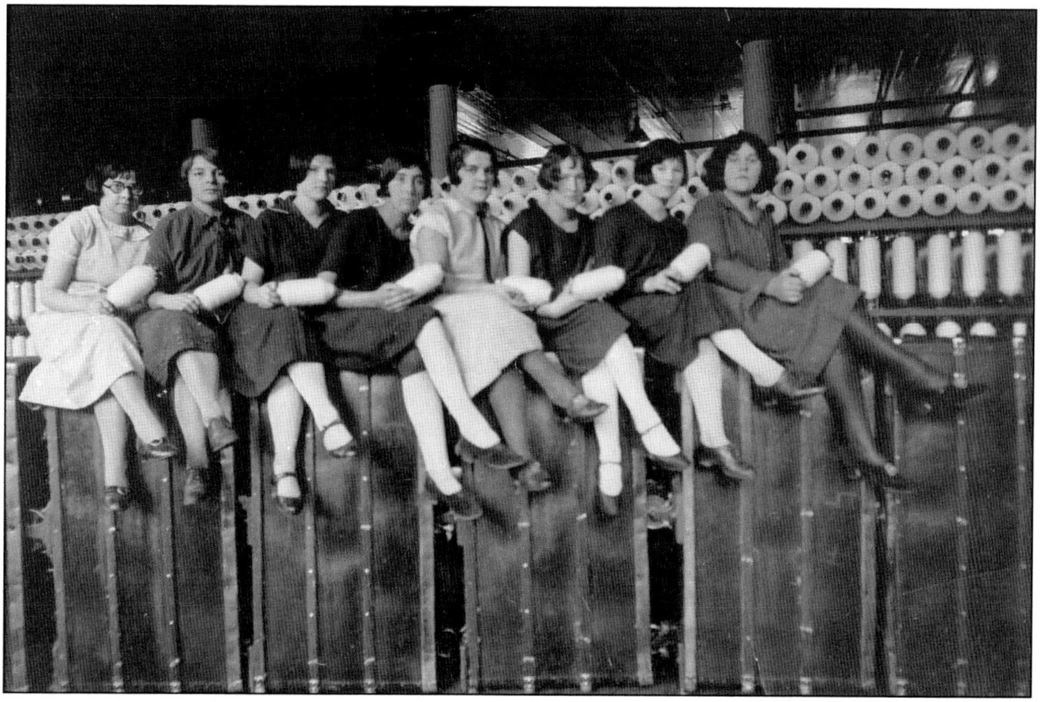

Young workers in Lewiston posed for an informal photograph in the early 1900s. Many girls and young women spent their formative years in the mills. (Courtesy of the University of Southern Maine, Lewiston-Auburn College Franco-American Collection.)

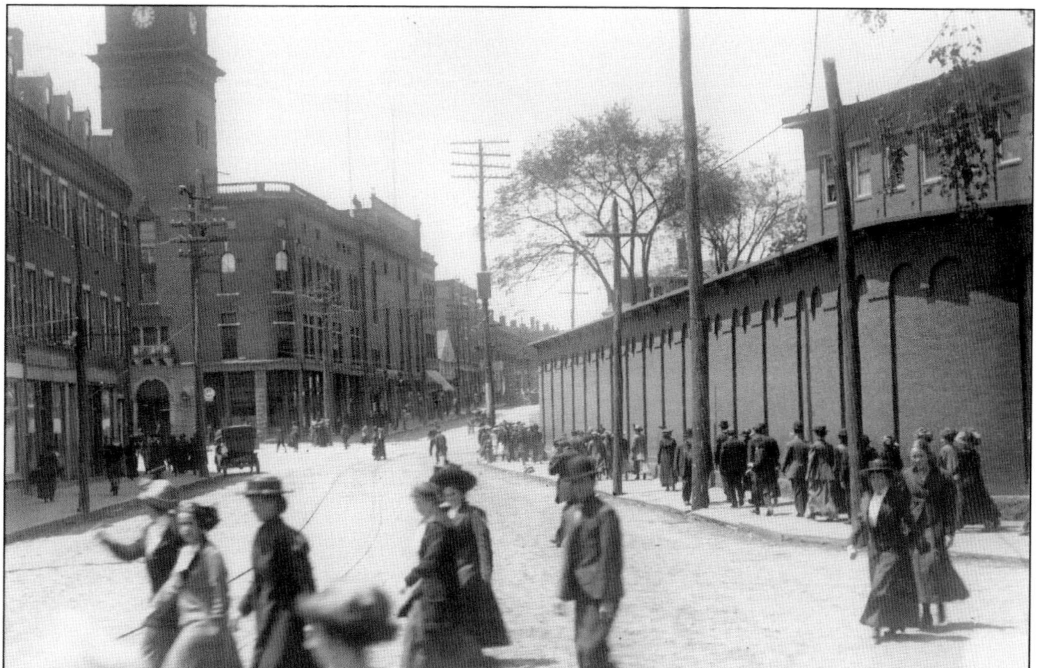

The downtown business districts of mill cities were lively places during shopping hours or shift changes. Here is a scene from Biddeford in the 1920s. (Courtesy of the McArthur Public Library.)

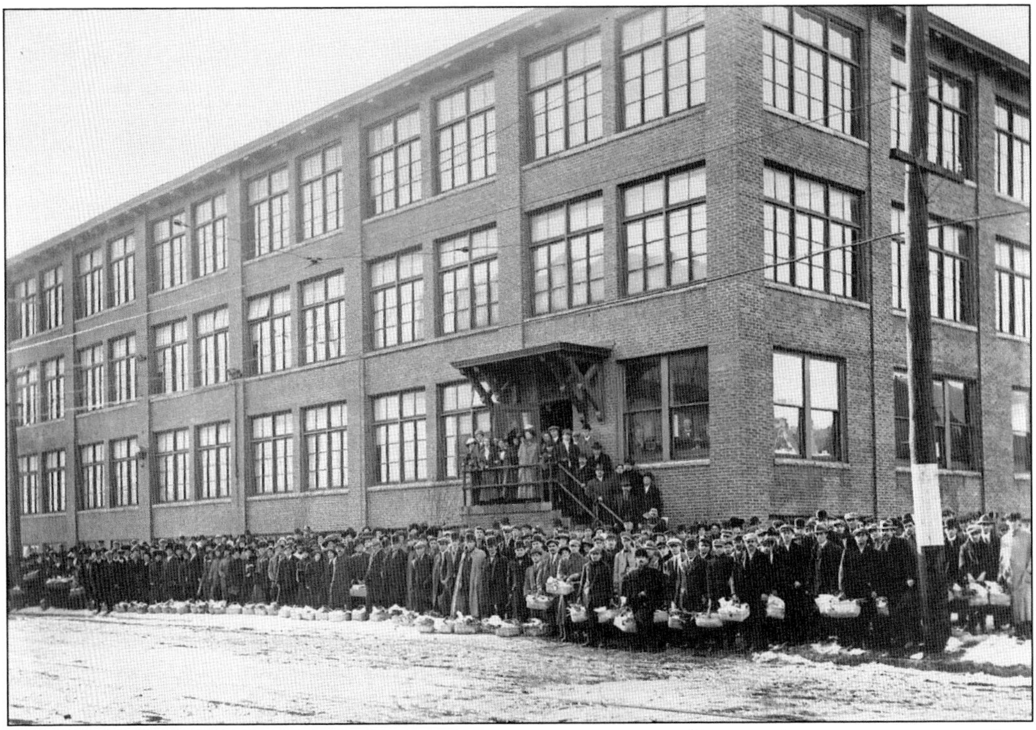

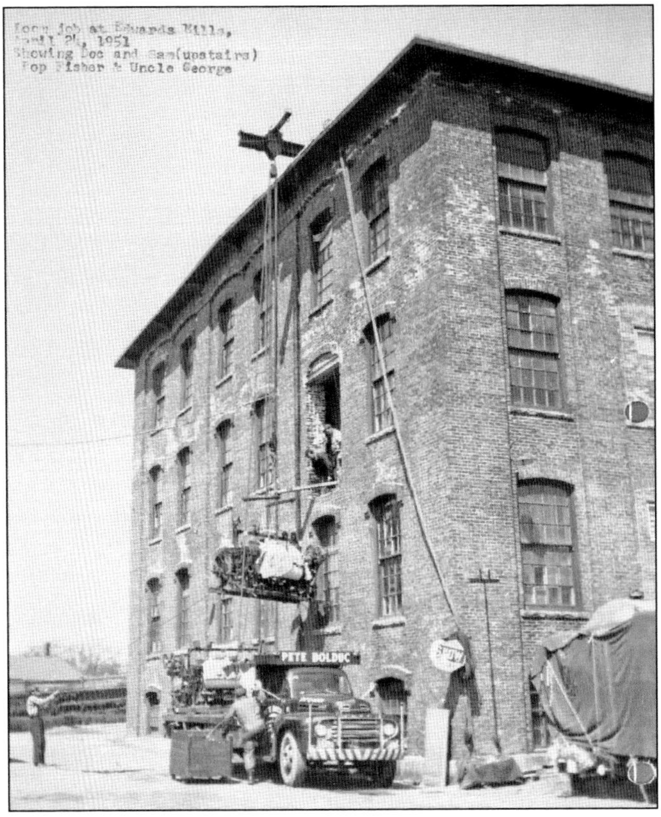

Franco-Americans possessed a strong work ethic and a commitment to quality and were sometimes rewarded for good work. Here employees receive annual Christmas food packages from the Lunn and Sweet Shoe Shop in Auburn. (Courtesy of the University of Southern Maine, Lewiston-Auburn College Franco-American Collection.)

Heavy equipment had to be installed on the upper floors of mill buildings. This team of workers from the Bolduc trucking operation is moving a loom into the Edwards Mill in 1951. (Courtesy of the University of Southern Maine, Lewiston-Auburn College Franco-American Collection.)

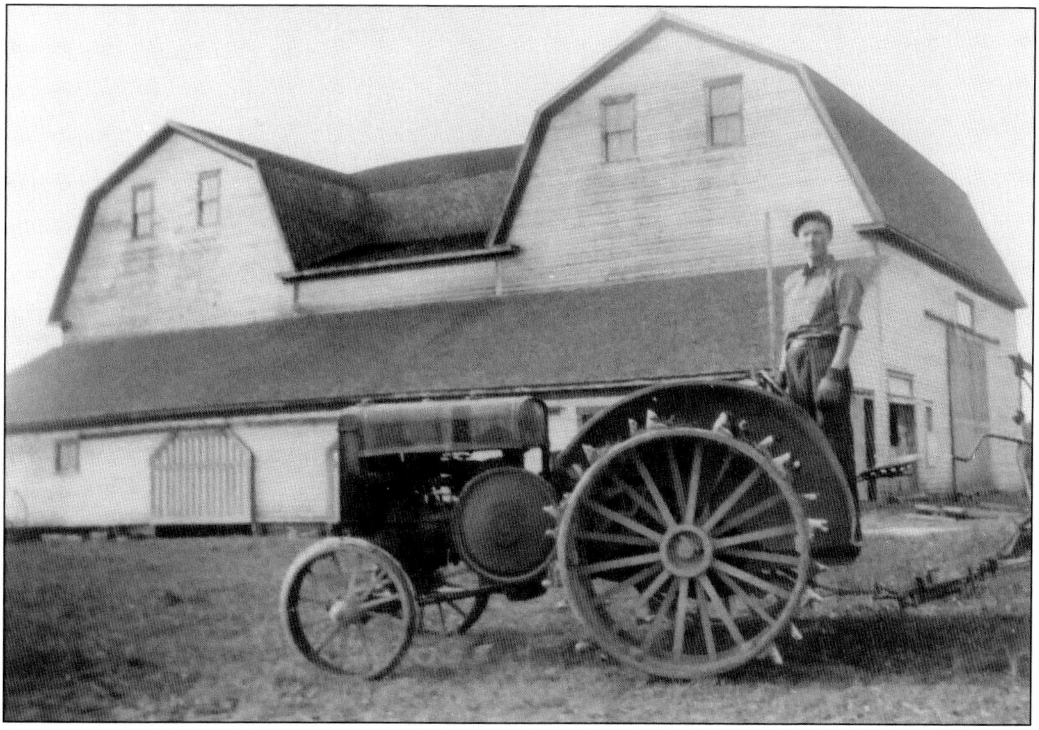

Franco-Americans worked on farms as well as in mills. Here is Alphie Levesque on a tractor in 1931 in the St. John Valley, in front of what was known as a French double barn. (Courtesy of the Madawaska Historical Society.)

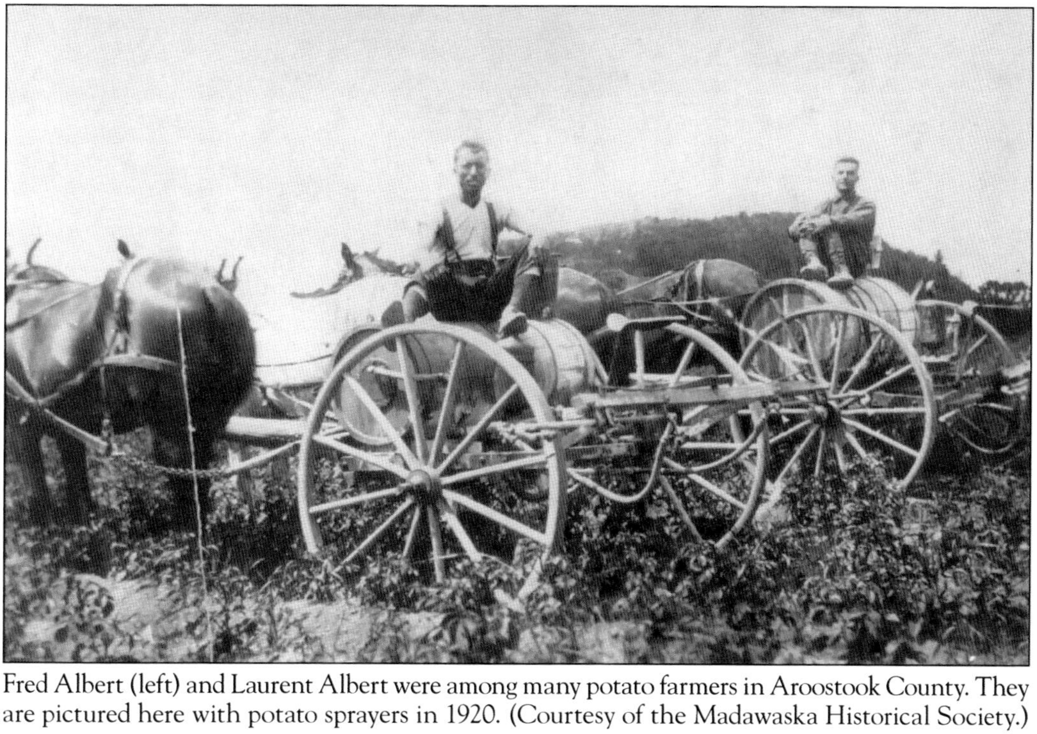

Fred Albert (left) and Laurent Albert were among many potato farmers in Aroostook County. They are pictured here with potato sprayers in 1920. (Courtesy of the Madawaska Historical Society.)

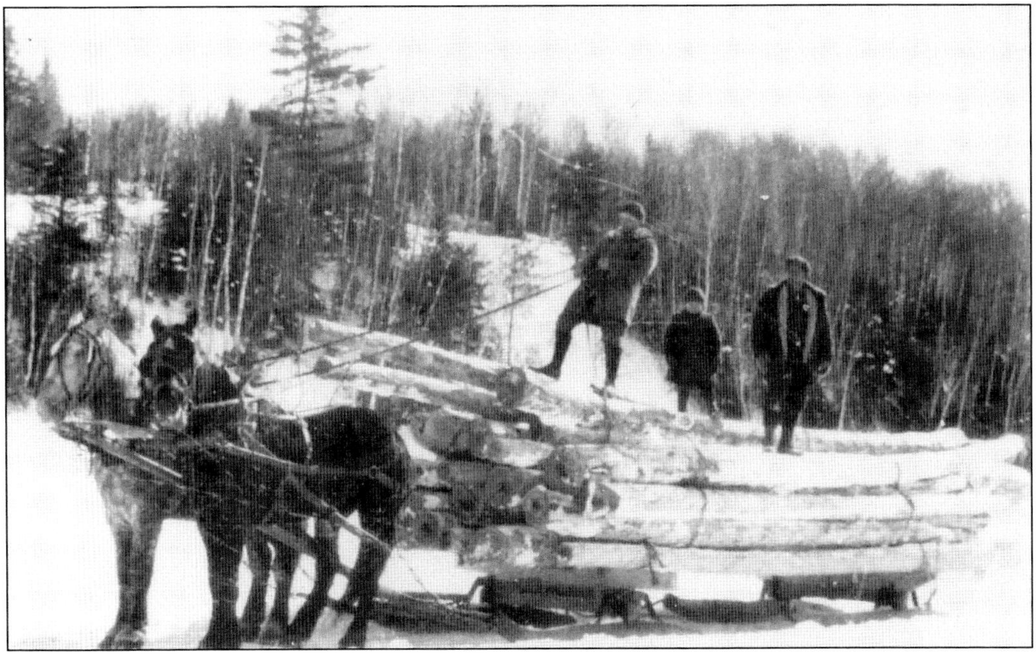

Working in the lumber industry was a way of life for many Franco-Americans a century ago. Arthur Daigle, shown here holding the reins, managed logging operations in the Madawaska area during the first decade of the 20th century. (Courtesy of the Madawaska Historical Society.)

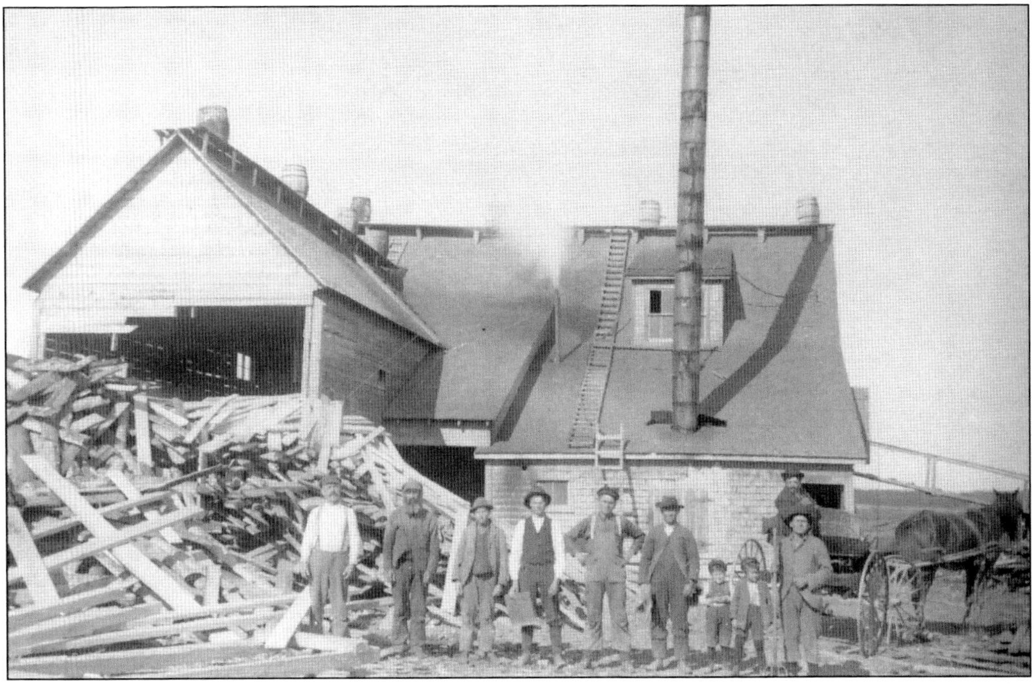

Workers gather in front of the Alexis Morneault sawmill in Grand Isle in 1906. (Courtesy of the Madawaska Historical Society.)

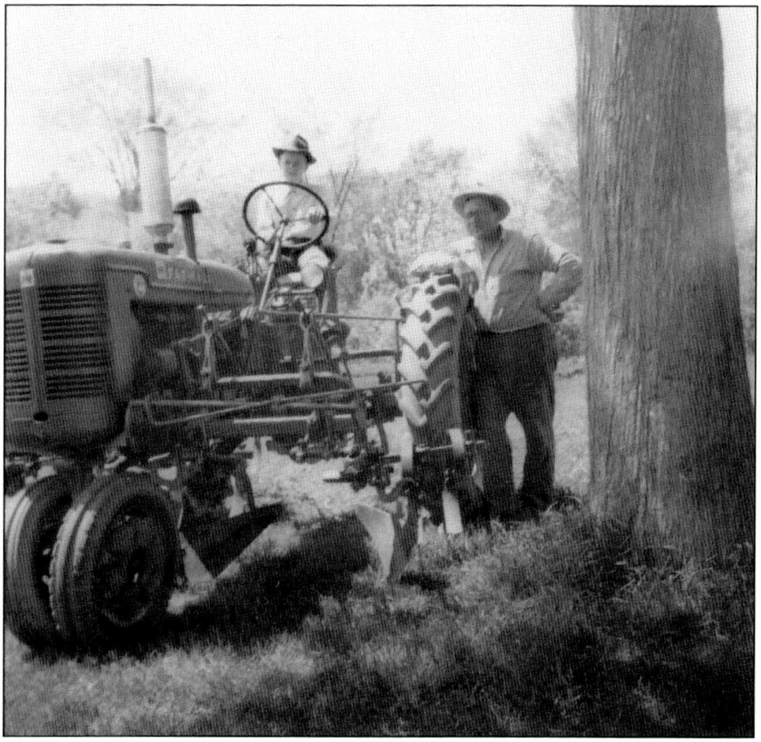

Farms thrived near urban areas as well as in the wide-open spaces, as this 1951 photograph at the Mathieu farm in Lewiston reflects. Their farm covered 40 acres, and the family grew corn, tomatoes, cucumbers, and potatoes. Here Nöel Mathieu stands with his son, nine-year-old André Mathieu. (Courtesy of the University of Southern Maine, Lewiston-Auburn College Franco-American Collection.)

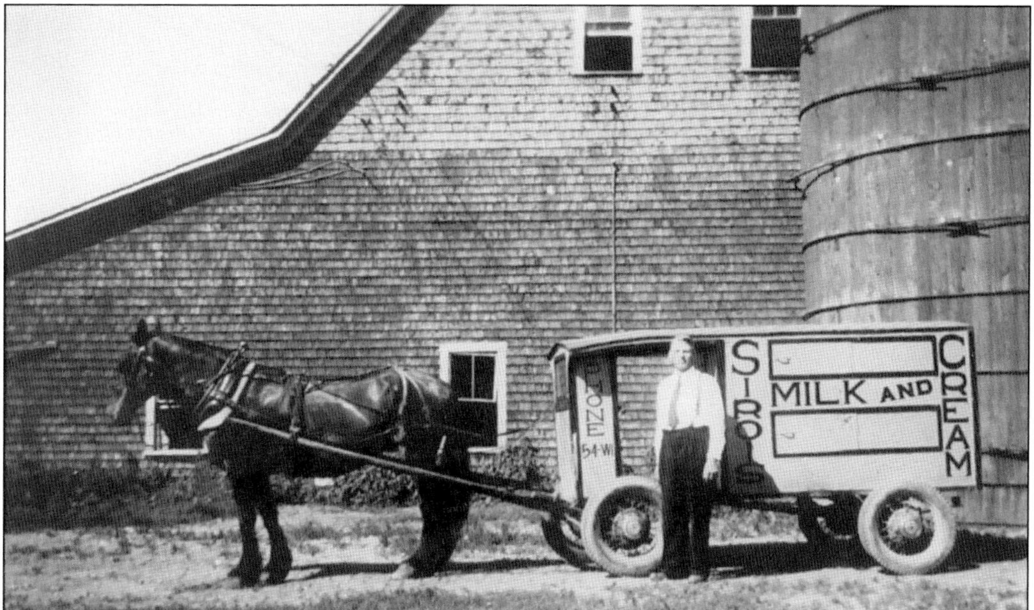

When farms succeeded, their proprietors often started related businesses. Charles Sirois of the Sirois dairy farm is pictured here preparing to start his milk-delivery route in the St. John Valley. (Courtesy of the Madawaska Historical Society.)

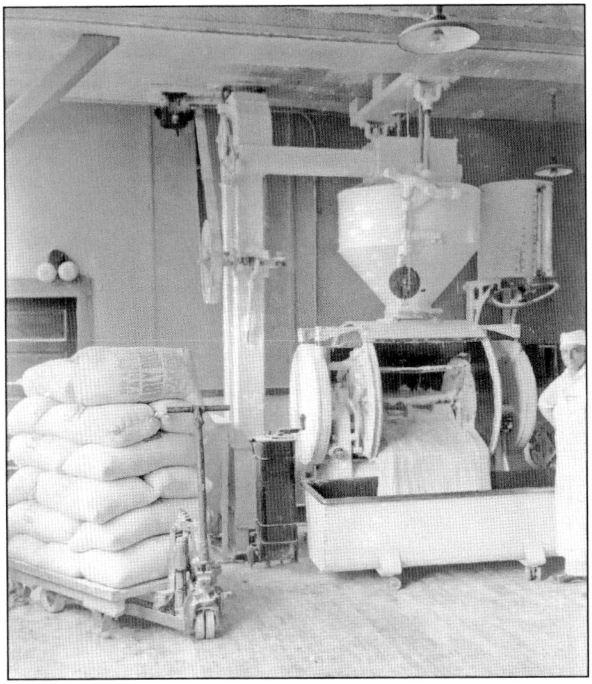

Franco-Americans entered every trade and business in their new cities. This photograph shows dough preparation at the Maine Baking Company in Auburn in the 1930s. The proprietor was Philippe J. Couture. (Courtesy of the University of Southern Maine, Lewiston-Auburn College Franco-American Collection.)

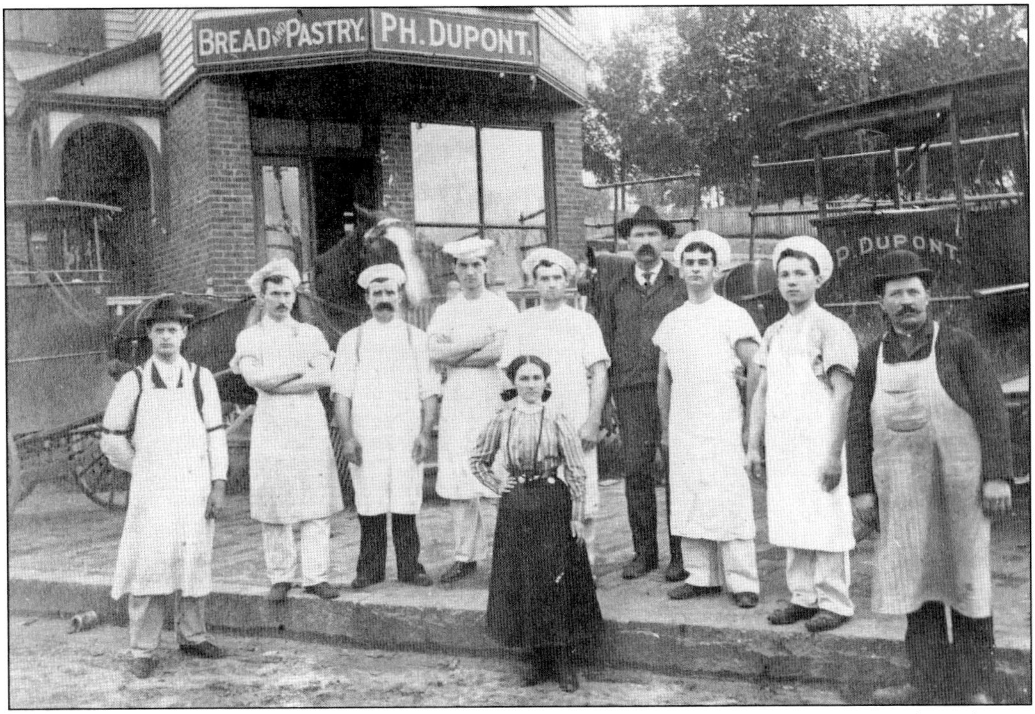

Dupont Bakery employees identified here in 1901 are owner Philippe Dupont (center), with two workers who would develop their own companies: E. W. Mailhot (second from right), who founded Mailhot Sausage Company, and F. R. Lepage (third from right), founder of Lepage Bakeries. Dupont started the business in 1893 in New Auburn, and it was later sold to Lepage Bakeries. (Courtesy of the University of Southern Maine, Lewiston-Auburn College Franco-American Collection.)

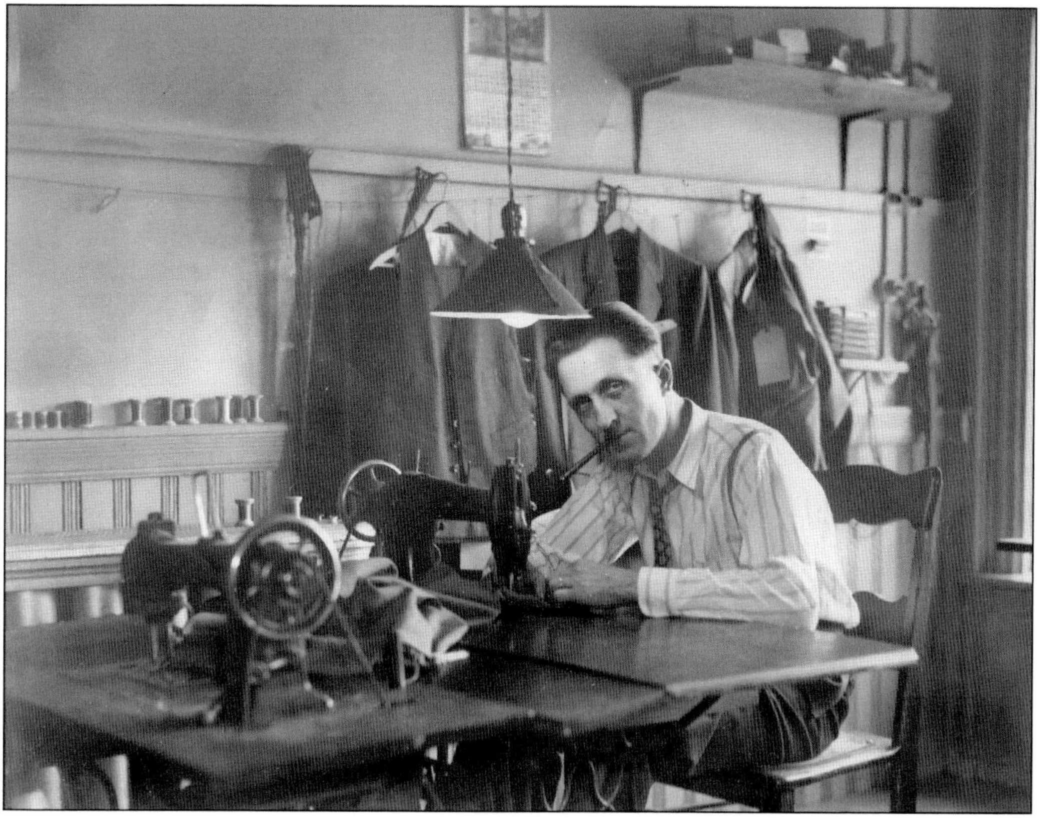

Franco-Americans were excellent craftsmen, and one of the best tailors who came to Lewiston was Charles Beaulieu, shown here in his shop. He was born in Québec in 1903 and, in 1931, arrived in Lewiston, where he started a successful business on Lisbon Street. (Courtesy of the University of Southern Maine, Lewiston-Auburn College Franco-American Collection.)

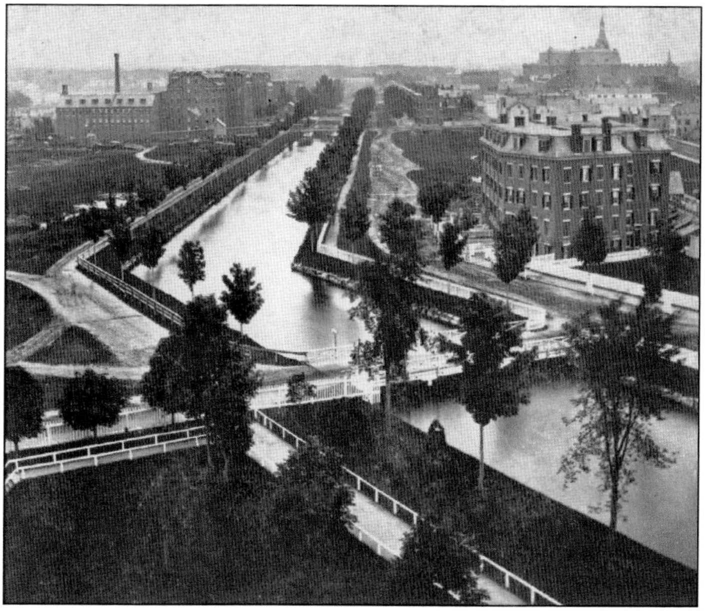

Most mills in Maine were powered by rivers and canals. This is the Lewiston Canal seen from the Androscoggin Mill in 1877. (Courtesy of the University of Southern Maine, Lewiston-Auburn College Franco-American Collection.)

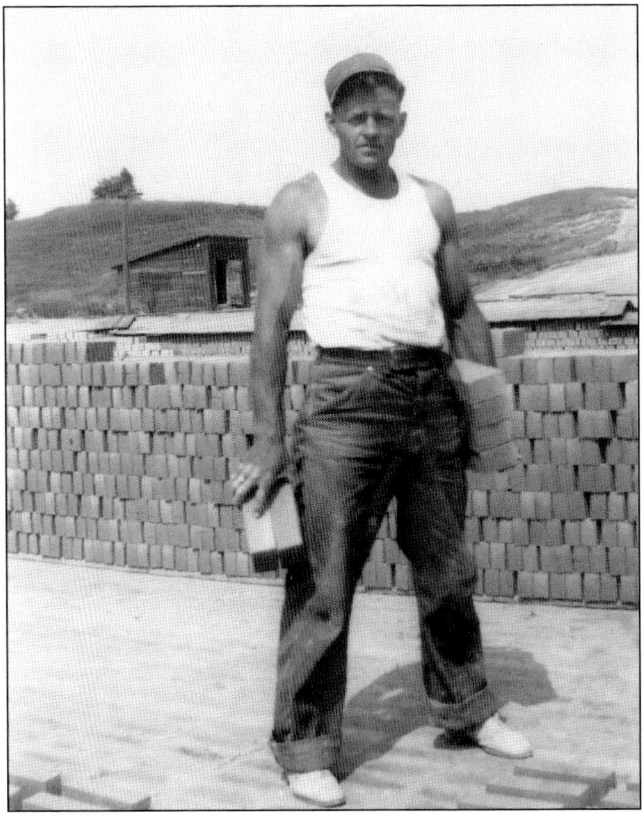

The making of bricks took energy—and muscle. Alphee Grenier poses at the Bergeron Brickyard of Lewiston in 1940. He was born in Lac Megantic, Québec, in 1907 and spent much of his life making bricks. But each fall he went into the woods to work in the lumber industry, as did many Franco-American men. (Courtesy of the University of Southern Maine, Lewiston-Auburn College Franco-American Collection.)

Franco-Americans cut wood, either for sale or home use, in every season. Here a team lays into some timber in Fort Kent. (Courtesy of the Acadian Archives, University of Maine at Fort Kent.)

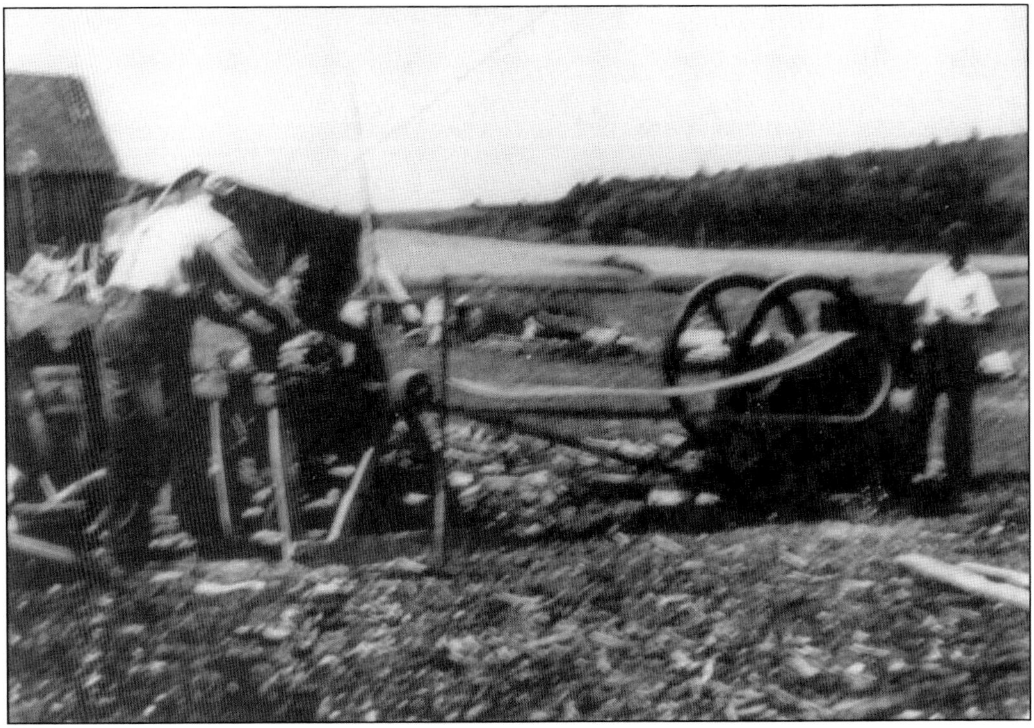

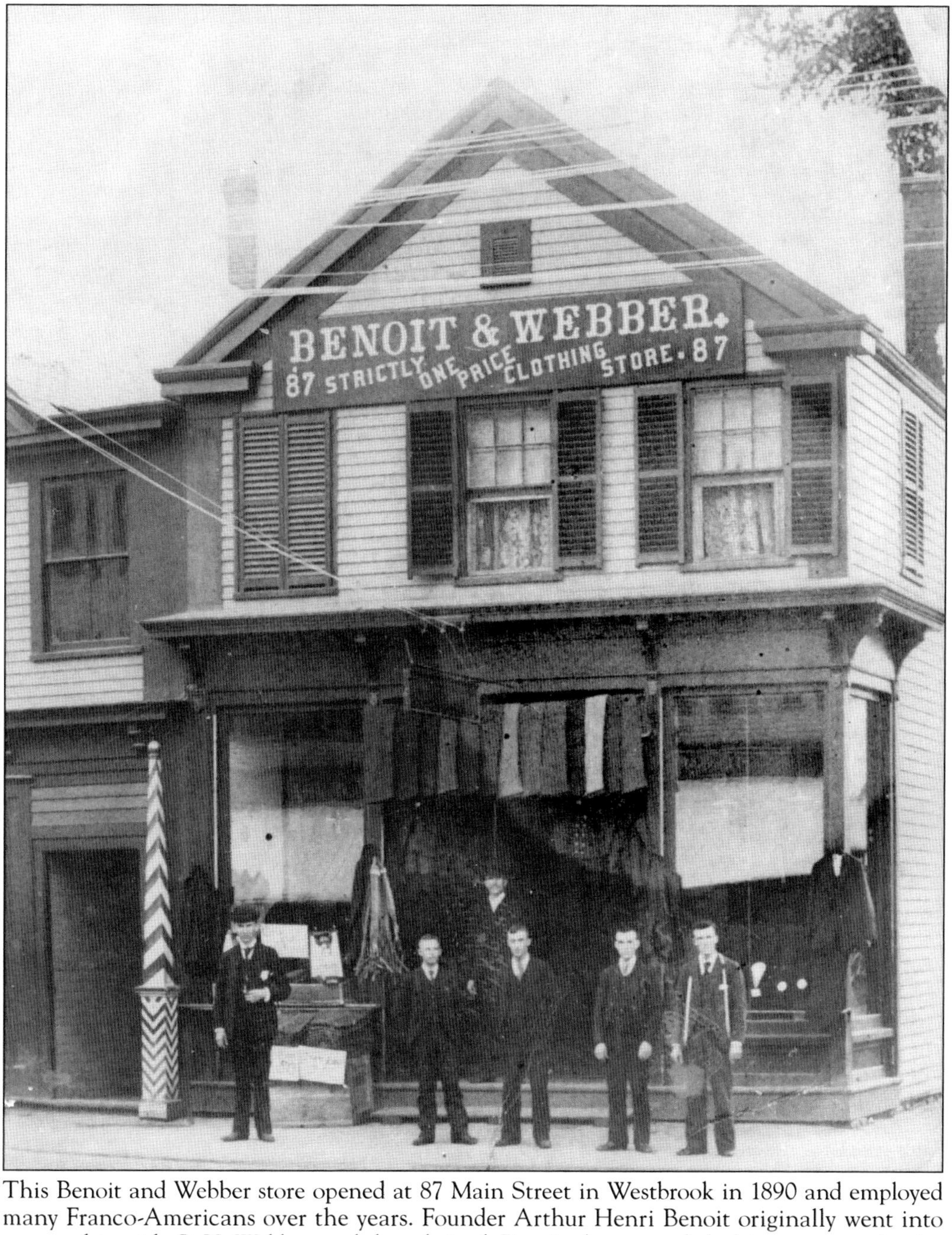

This Benoit and Webber store opened at 87 Main Street in Westbrook in 1890 and employed many Franco-Americans over the years. Founder Arthur Henri Benoit originally went into partnership with C. H. Webber, and they thrived. Benoit also opened clothing stores under the names A. H. Benoit Company and Benoit's in Portland, Lewiston, Brunswick, Biddeford, and Ogunquit. (Courtesy of the Maine Historical Society.)

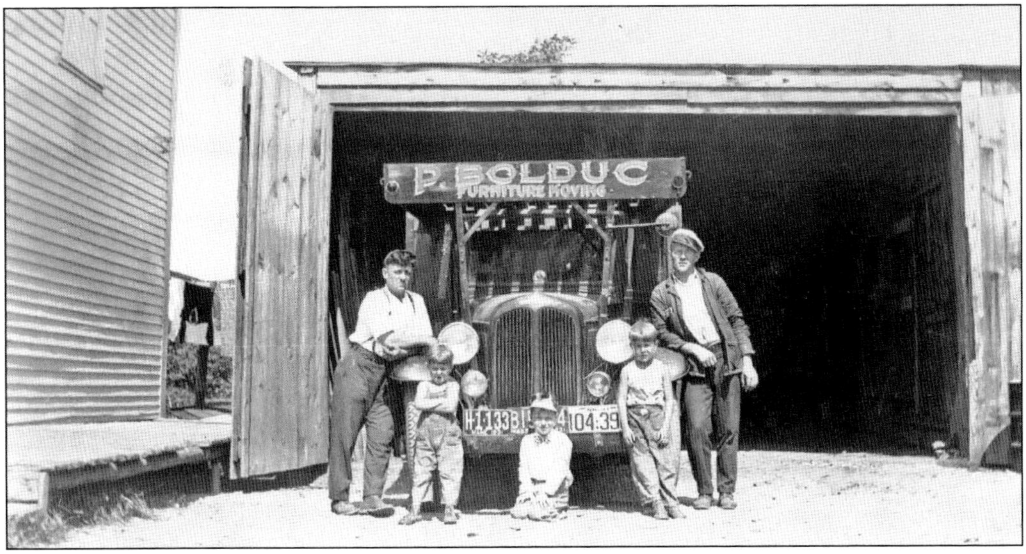

Moving vans helped Franco-Americans get established in new residences, and by 1931, the date of this photograph, many transportation businesses were thriving. The Pete Bolduc Trucking and Moving Company was prominent in central Maine, and Pete's three sons—Lionel, Roger, and Doc—all worked for the company. It was purchased in 1974 by Cote Crane and Rigging, and today Cote is one of the largest such companies in the state. (Courtesy of the University of Southern Maine, Lewiston-Auburn College Franco-American Collection.)

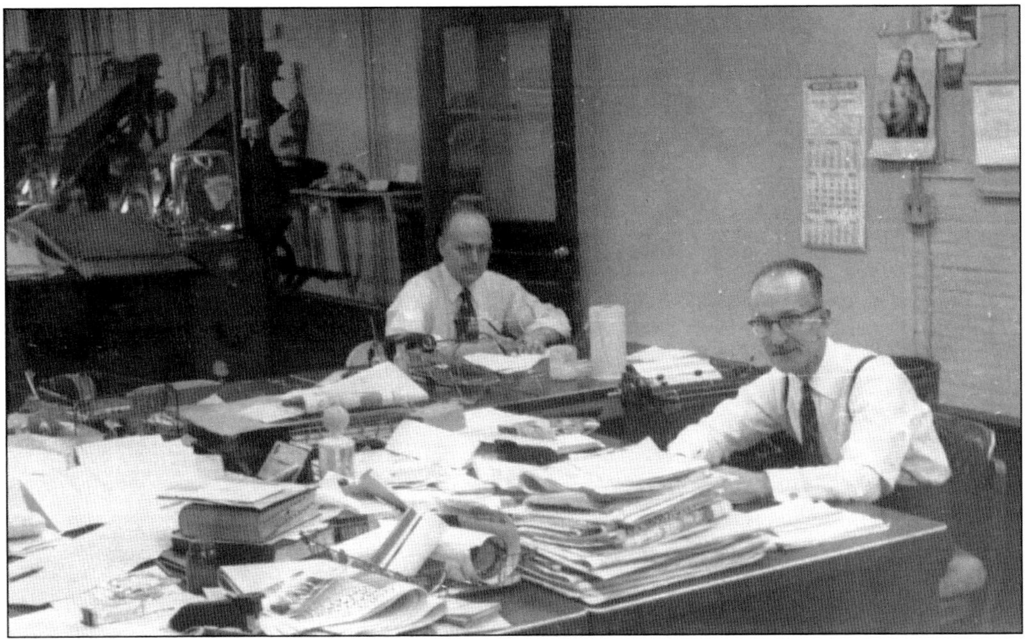

Newspapers offered employment as well as information. This photograph shows the editor of *Le Messager*, Louis Phillipe Gagné (right), with coworker Vincent Bernier in the paper's offices at 223–225 Lisbon Street, Lewiston. Gagné was born in Québec in 1900 and migrated to Lewiston in 1922. He was mayor of Lewiston (1947–1949), founder of Le Club Montagnard, and a leader in the snowshoe movement throughout the region. (Courtesy of the University of Southern Maine, Lewiston-Auburn College Franco-American Collection.)

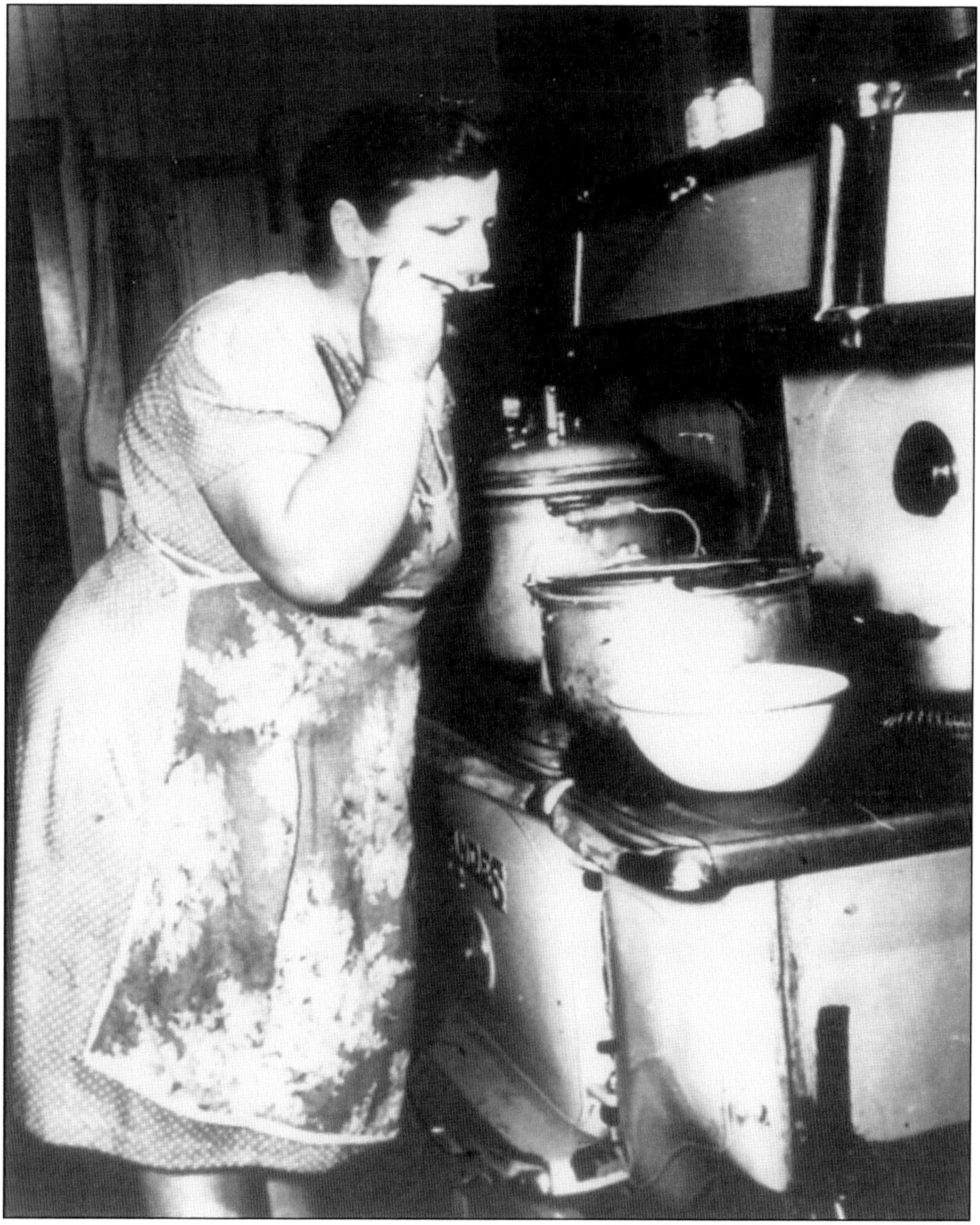

One of the most challenging "jobs" in Franco-American life was that of being mother and home supervisor, especially in large families. Here Emma Gagnon is making soup at the Gagnon farm in Frenchville in 1942. Next to the soup on the wood stove is a pressure cooker, used for canning and meal preparation. (Courtesy of the Acadian Archives, University of Maine at Fort Kent.)

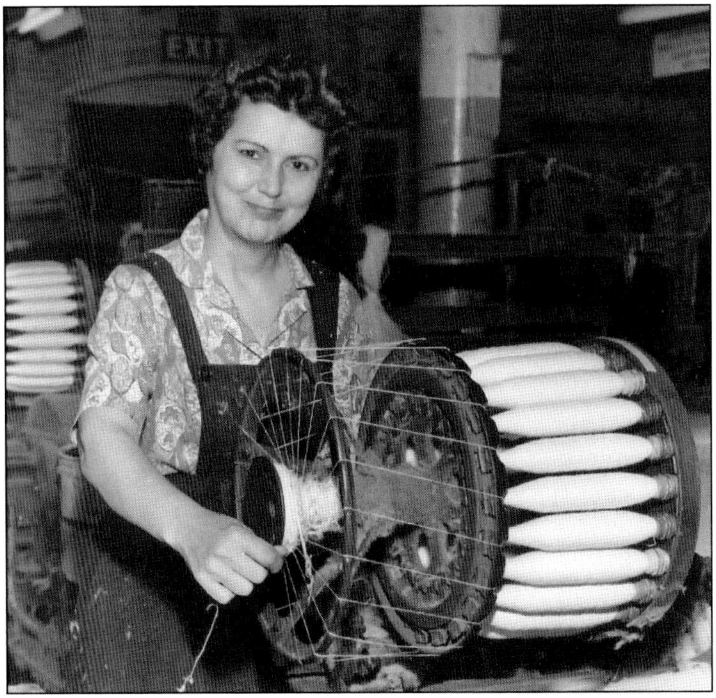

Delia Lambert tended the circular holder of bobbins in the 1950s. When a bobbin was almost empty, it was automatically ejected into a box, and a full one was inserted so the thread was not broken. Franco-Americans helped make Maine one of the nation's top producers of textiles. (Courtesy of the Lewiston Historical Commission.)

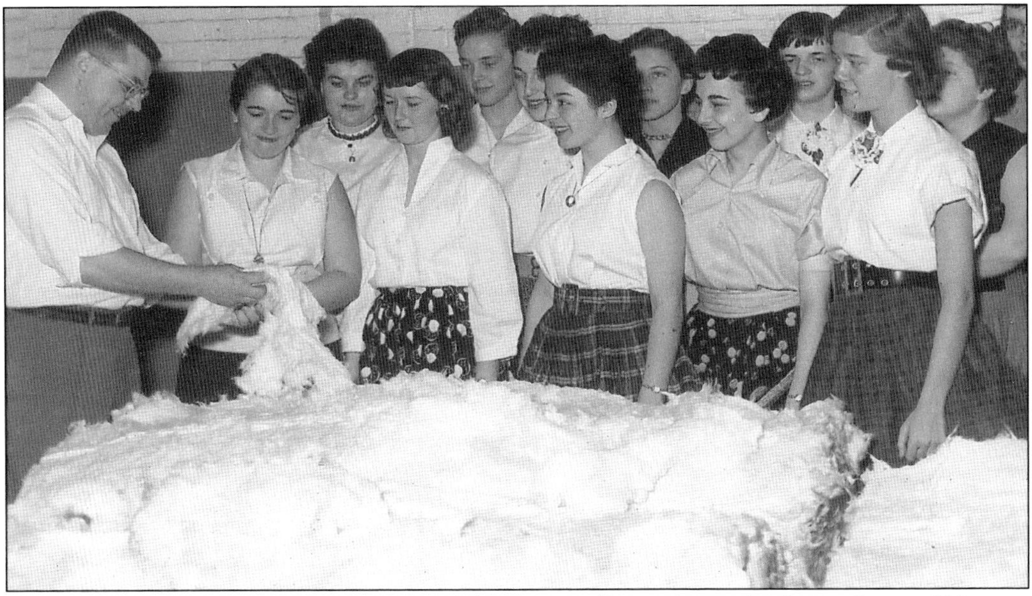

Lewiston High School students often toured the Bates Mill complex under the guidance of Maurice Hemond, shift supervisor for the Bates Manufacturing Company. Many high school students took jobs in the mills following graduation. (Courtesy of the Lewiston Historical Commission.)

Two

FAMILY

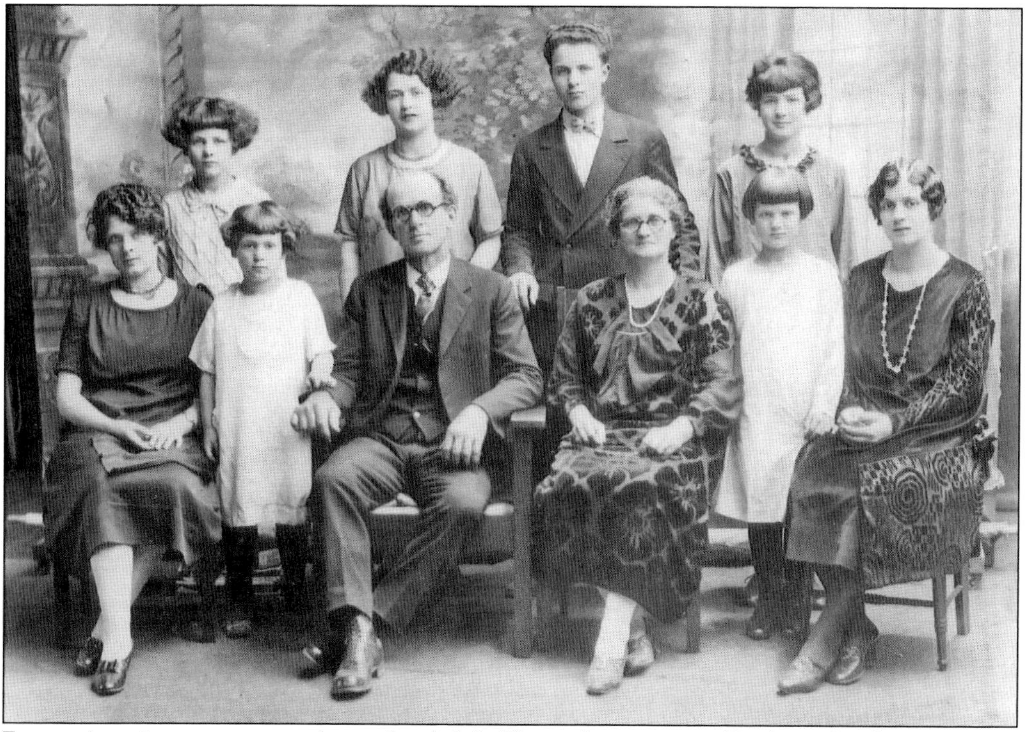

Franco-Americans put great value on family life. This is the prosperous Desfosses family in a portrait taken in 1925 in Lewiston. In 1900, Joseph Desfosses married Delia Paradis in Québec, and they moved to Lewiston. From left to right, they are (first row) Donalda, Florianne (Robitaille), Joseph, Delia Paradis Desfosses, Patricia (Robitaille), and Yvonne (Robitaille); (second row) Marie-Oglore (Grigorian), Laurette (Labrie), François, and Dolorèse (Mathieu). (Courtesy of the University of Southern Maine, Lewiston-Auburn College Franco-American Collection.)

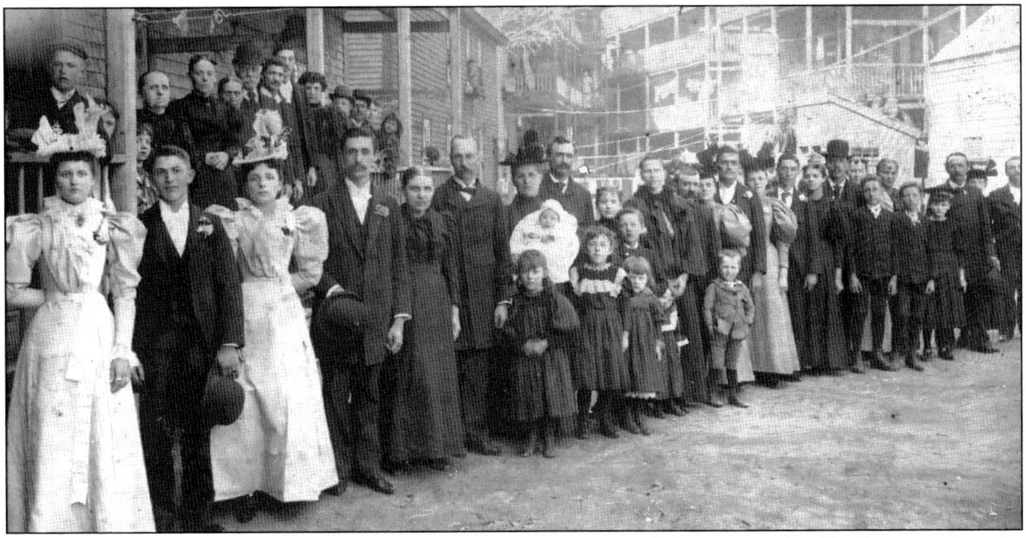

Here is the wedding party of the 1897 marriage of Marie Philippon and Alfred Tancrel at 24 River Street in Lewiston. Celebrants included, from left to right, Marie Philippon; Alfred Tancrel; attendants Emilie Philippon and an unidentified man; Zenaide Tancrel, mother of the groom; Ozios Tancrel, father of the groom; and Emilie Philippon, mother of the bride with a baby in her arms. (Courtesy of the University of Southern Maine, Lewiston-Auburn College Franco-American Collection.)

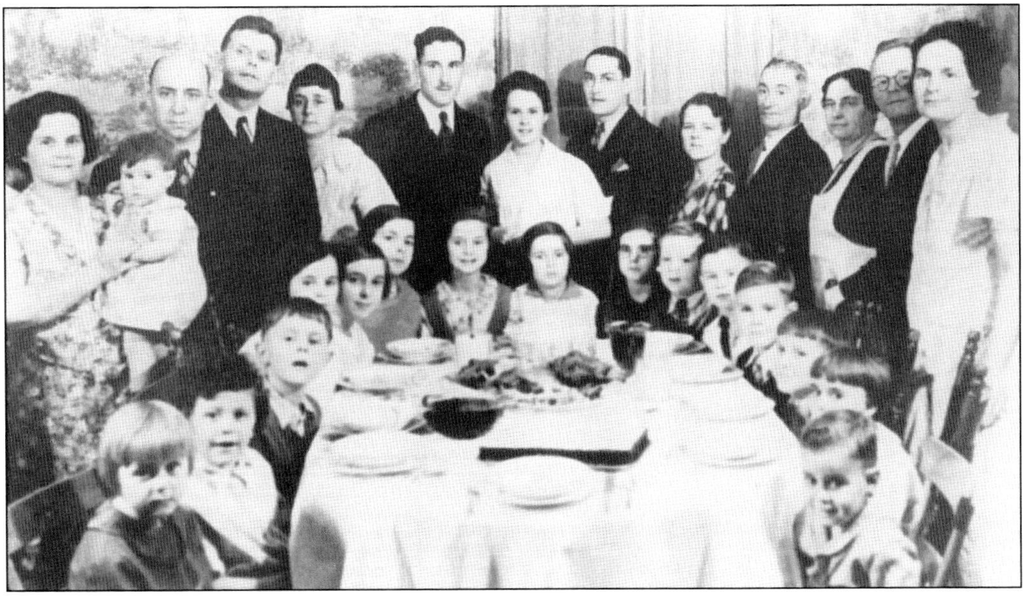

This is the Trottier home in Sanford on Thanksgiving 1935, when the family hosted 16 children and 12 adults. The children, from left to right, are Bertha Cantin, Arthur Cantin, Josephat Cantin, Alma Trottier, Lucille Cantin, Rita Cantin, Marie Ange Cantin, Annette Cantin, Eva Proulx, Leo Cantin, Louis Trottier, Hervey Proulx, Andree Proulx, Agnes Proulx, and Amedee Proulx, who grew up to became a bishop. Standing from left to right are Rose Proulx, Therese Proulx (baby), Francis Proulx, Odias Cantin, Laura Cantin, Albert Gauvreau, Cecille Trottier, Gerard Gauvreau, Clara Gauvreau, Jimmy Gauvreau, Alma Gauvreau, Willie Trottier, and Louisa Trottier. (Courtesy of Solange Thibodeau Lamontagne and Gerald Lamontagne.)

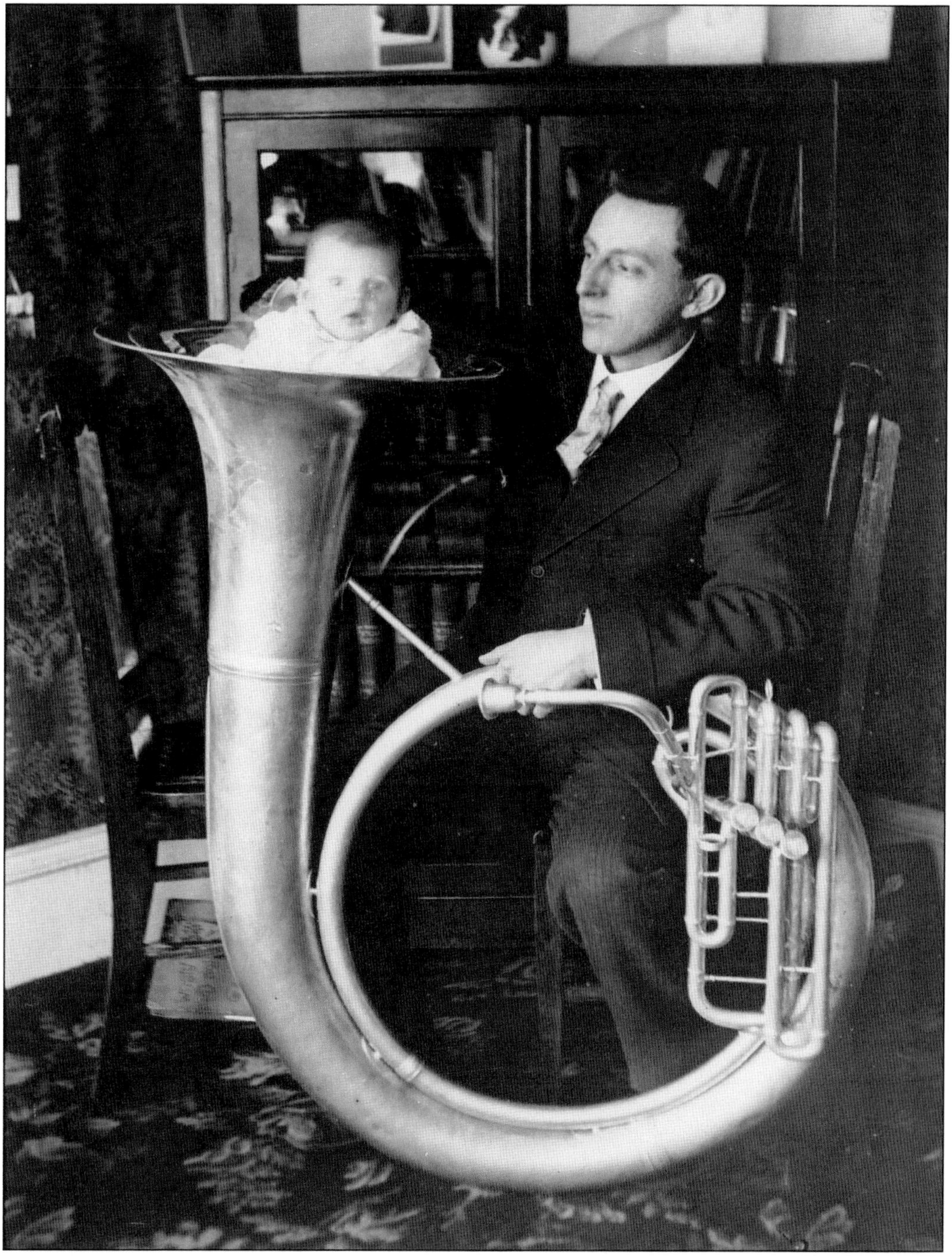

Parental ties with their children started early. Here is a unique father-son photograph from 1916 featuring Joseph Poulin, a violinist with the Portland Symphony and director of St. Peter's Choir, with his three-month-old son, Carroll. Carroll Poulin eventually founded Carroll's School and Music Center in Lewiston and established it as one of the city's leading music stores for decades. His son, Carroll Jr., later took over the store. (Courtesy of the University of Southern Maine, Lewiston-Auburn College Franco-American Collection.)

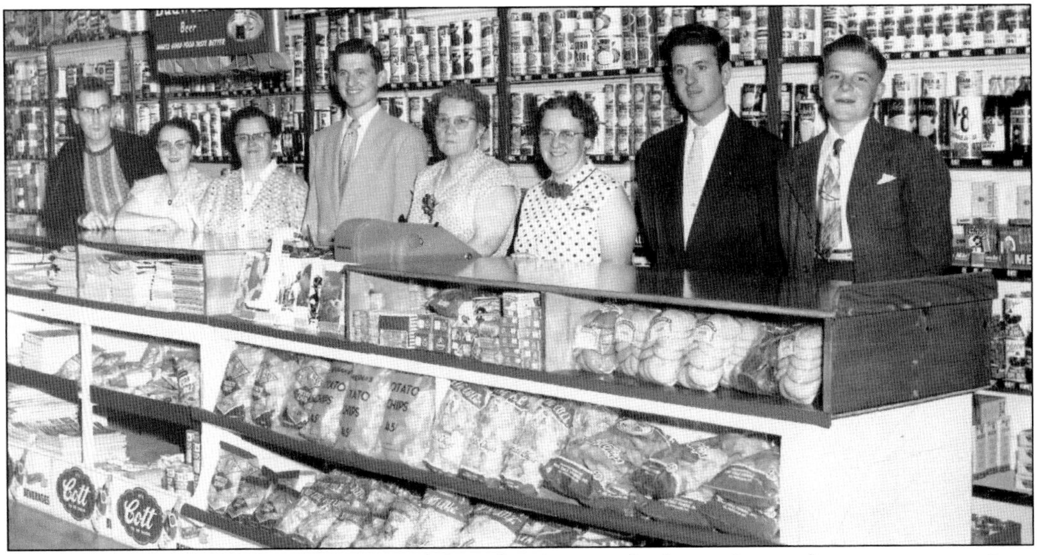

Franco-American family members and friends often worked together in business enterprises. The team from the Laurendeau Market in Lewiston, shown here from left to right, is Anatole Roy, Marie Jeanne Laurendeau, Liliane Laurendeau, Norman Lacasse, Marie Laura Deschênes Laurendeau, Thérèse Laurendeau, Paul Lacasse, and Richard Mathieu. (Courtesy of the University of Southern Maine, Lewiston-Auburn College Franco-American Collection.)

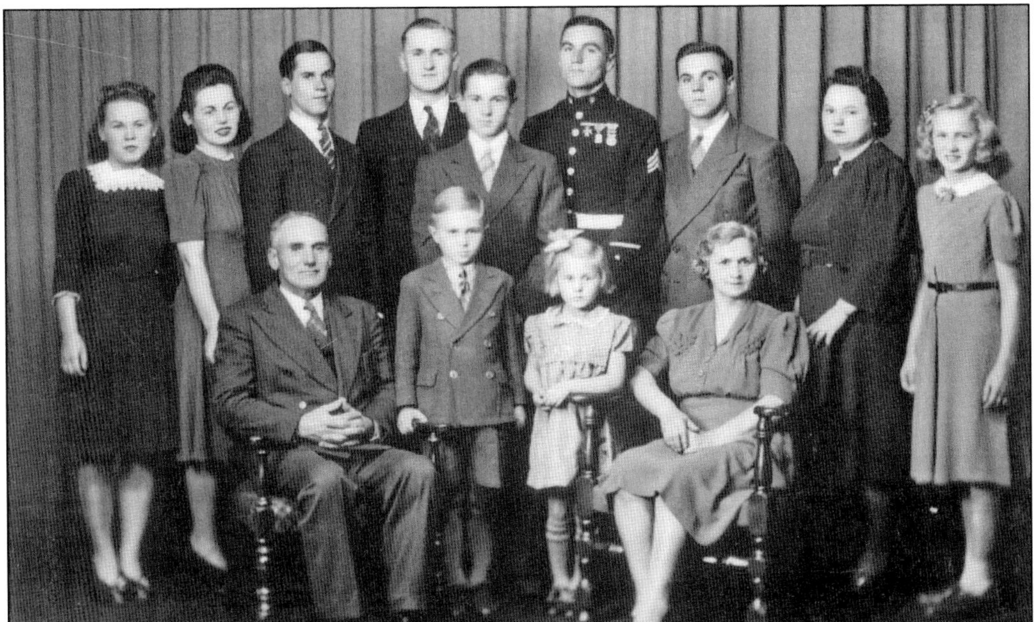

Many Franco-American families thrived and became prosperous, which belies the grim photographs taken in some mills. This is the family of Pierre Fournier of Lewiston, a prosperous, well-dressed group with roots in Québec. From left to right are (first row) Pierre Fournier, Joseph, Juliette, and Celestine Castonguay Fournier; (second row) Therese, Priscille, Aime, Gilbert, Henri, Adelard, Romeo, Laurianne, and Germaine. (Courtesy of the Franco-American Heritage Center at St. Mary's.)

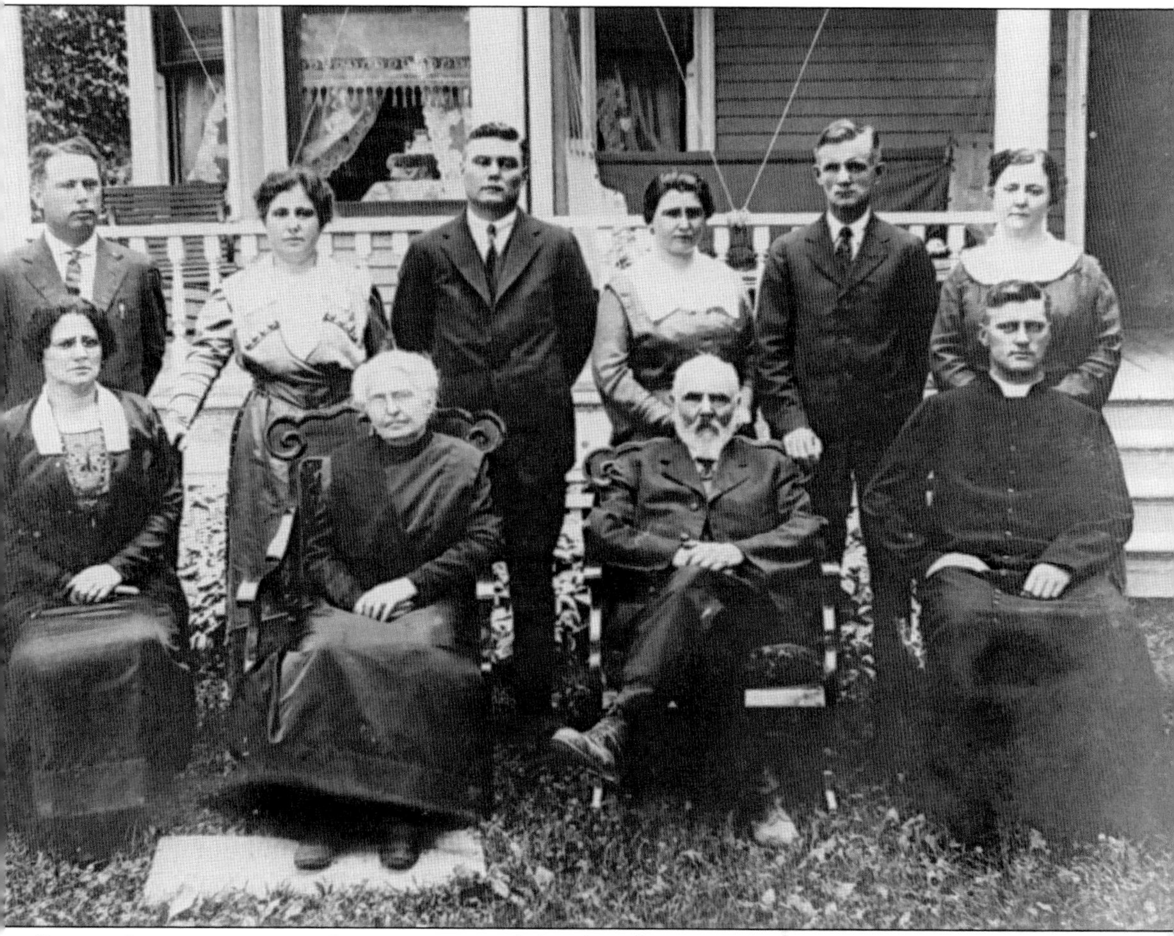

Franco-Americans arranged portraits to mark family milestones, though smiles were rare in this era of portraiture. Here is a wedding anniversary photograph of Dr. Thomas and Malvina Pelletier in Van Buren in July 1919, when the family gathered to mark the day. From left to right are (first row) Leola Pelletier, Malvina Pelletier, Dr. Thomas Pelletier, and the Reverend Louis Pelletier; (second row) Dr. Ludget Pelletier, Alma Thibodeau, Joseph Pelletier, Rosalie Daicole, Alphonse Pelletier, and Helene Pelletier. (Courtesy of the Madawaska Historical Society.)

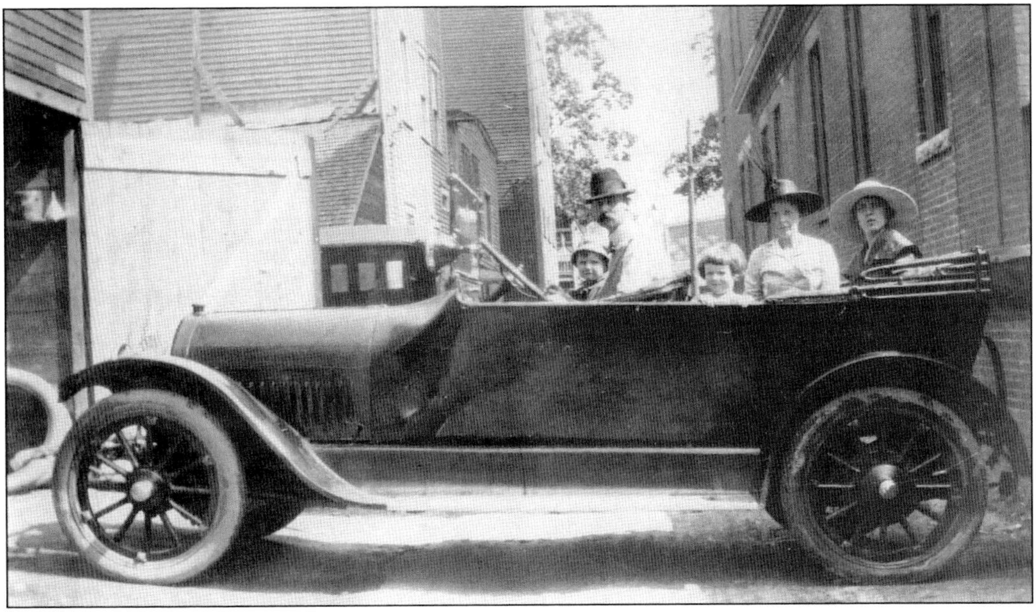

Prosperous families were quick to buy stylish automobiles, and this photograph from 1917 shows the Levesque family in their Marion near their fish market on Lincoln Street in Lewiston. From left to right are son Charlie Levesque, father Paul, daughter Bernadette, wife Corinne (Dumais), and Lucienne, a relative. (Courtesy of the Maine Historical Society.)

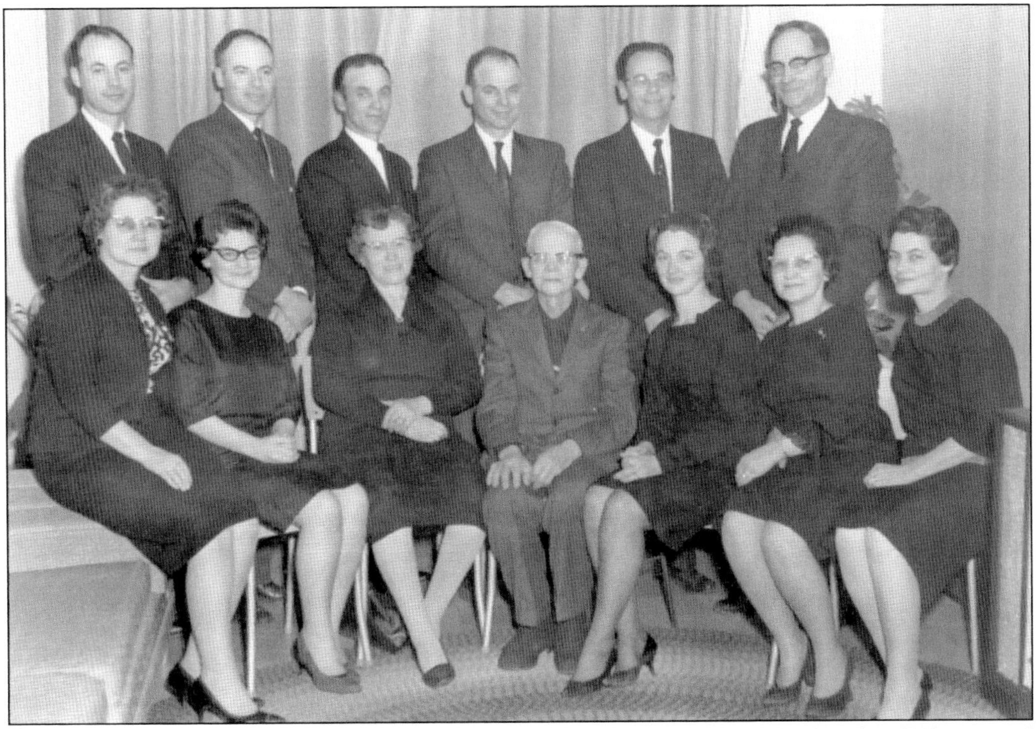

Large families were common in Franco-American communities. Here is the family of Ulysses and Caroline Theriault, who grew up on a farm in the St. John Valley. (Courtesy of the Madawaska Historical Society.)

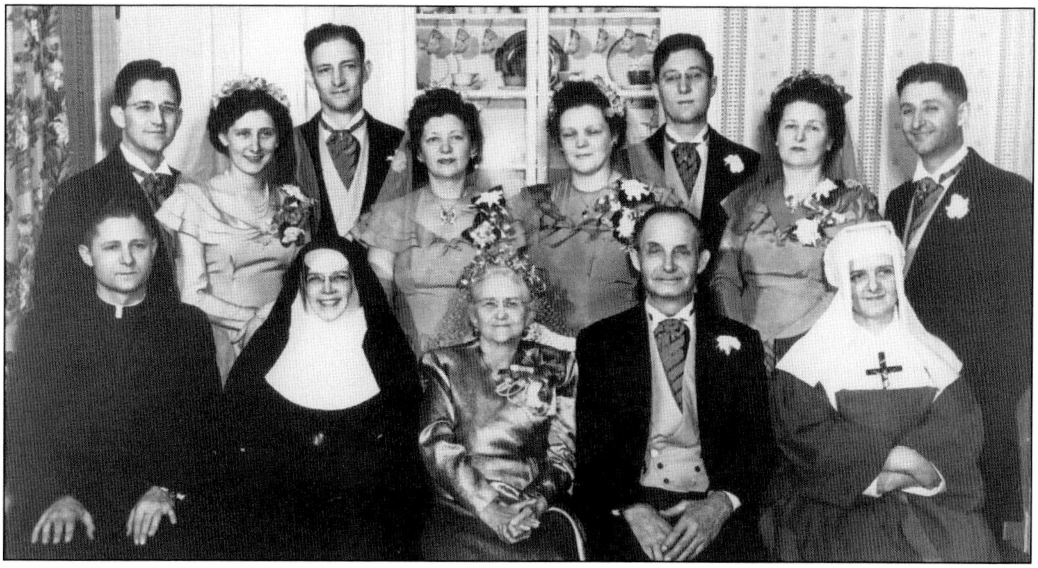

Here is the golden anniversary of Mr. and Mrs. Pierre Cyr in 1949 in Lille, a small town between Van Buren and Madawaska. From left to right are (first row) Msgr. Armand Cyr, Sister Alien, Mrs. Cyr, Pierre Cyr, and Sister Gertrude; (second row) Dr. Donate Cyr, Simone Cyr, J. Wilfred Cyr, Rose Cyr Levesque, Alice Violante, Edward Cyr, Josephine Cyr, and Patrick Cyr. (Courtesy of the Madawaska Historical Society.)

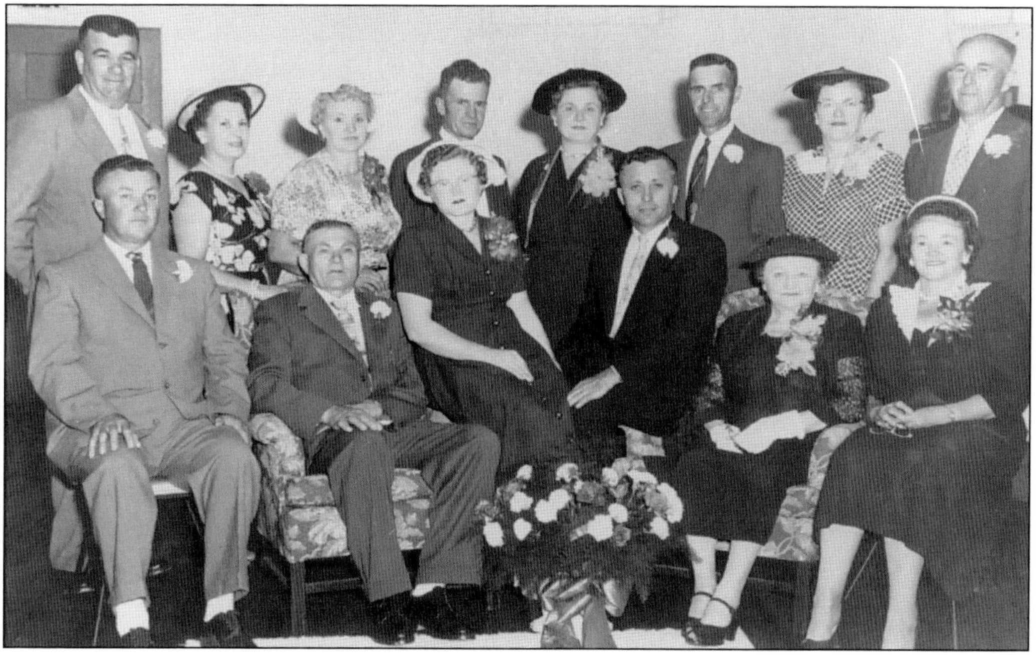

Major anniversaries were special events that helped bring families together. Here is the golden anniversary of Alex and Dorine Levesque in 1956 in Madawaska. From left to right are (first row) Alphie Levesque, Alex Levesque, Blanche Levesque Pelletier, Arthie Pelletier, Dorine Pelletier, and Azelie Levesque LaCroix; (second row) Eddie Dionne, Bertha Levesque, unidentified, Henrie Cyr, Jeanne Levesque Cyr, Eric Ouellette, Alma Cyr, and Levite Cyr. (Courtesy of the Madawaska Historical Society.)

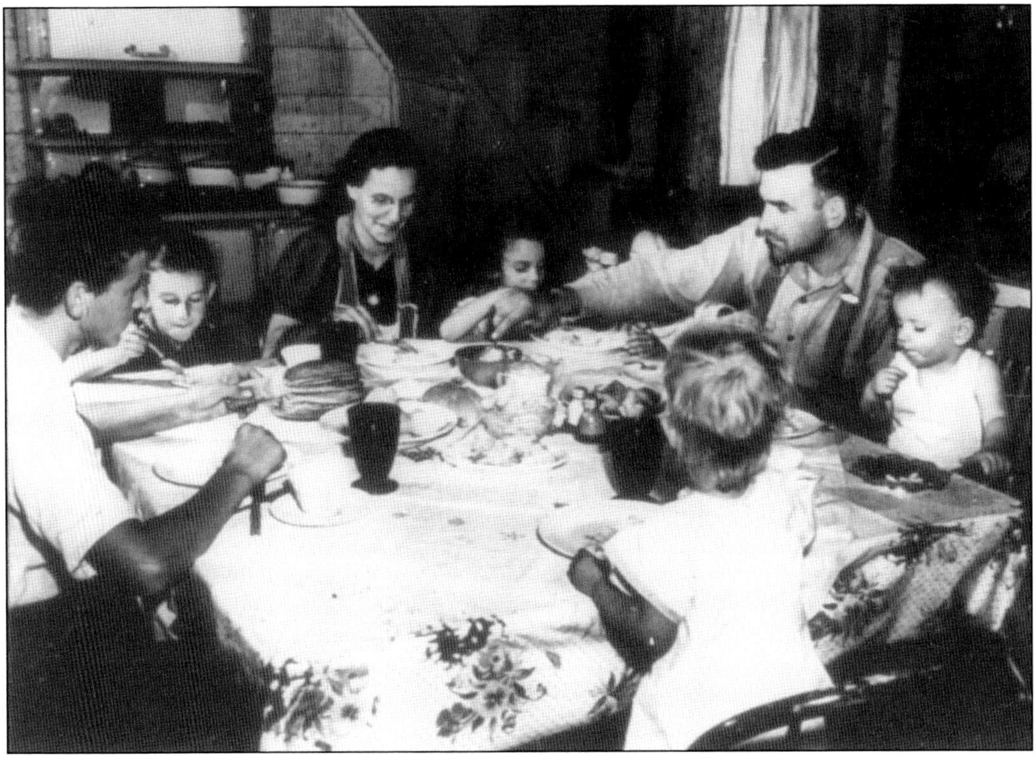

Franco-American families ate meals together, especially when youngsters needed assistance. This photograph and the next few were taken in 1942 by photographers from the Farm Security Administration, which was studying the hard times that had arrived in the St. John Valley following the Depression. This is the Daigle family of Fort Kent. Clockwise from left are an unidentified farm worker, Berenice, Irene Daigle, Joan, Doris (partially hidden), Oneil Daigle, Richard, and Jacqueline. (Courtesy of the Acadian Archives, University of Maine at Fort Kent.)

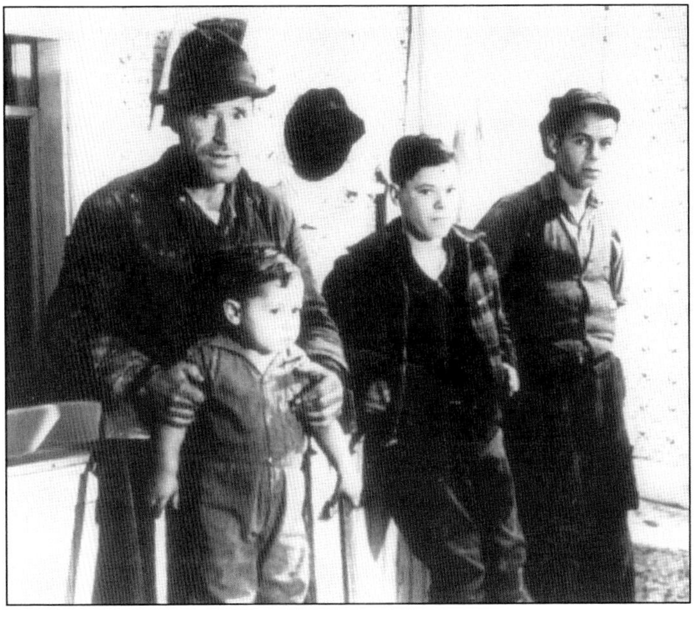

Baptiste Gendreau stands at the sink at his home in St. David with sons, from left to right, Real, Hervey, and Edwin. Having sturdy children to help with the chores was an asset when running a potato farm in northern Maine. (Courtesy of the Acadian Archives, University of Maine at Fort Kent.)

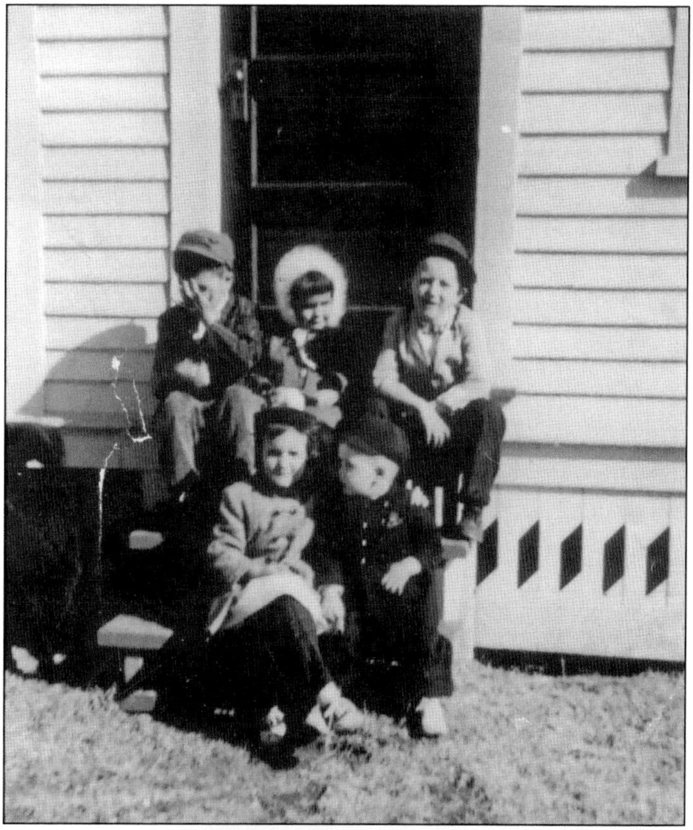

Siblings often played together during the formative years. Here the young Cloutiers of Lewiston socialize on the family steps. From left to right are (first row) Rita and Marc; (second row) Maurice, Vivian, and Michael. (Courtesy of the Franco-American Heritage Center at St. Mary's.)

Franco-American families in Maine spent many hours indoors, often with a grandparent. The Dumond family lived in Lille, and here some youngsters gather around a large stove used for both cooking and heating. Melvina Dumond is at right, and her grandchildren, from left to right, are Annette (rear), Flora Mae, Jacqueline, Gloria, and Jeannine. (Courtesy of the Acadian Archives, University of Maine at Fort Kent.)

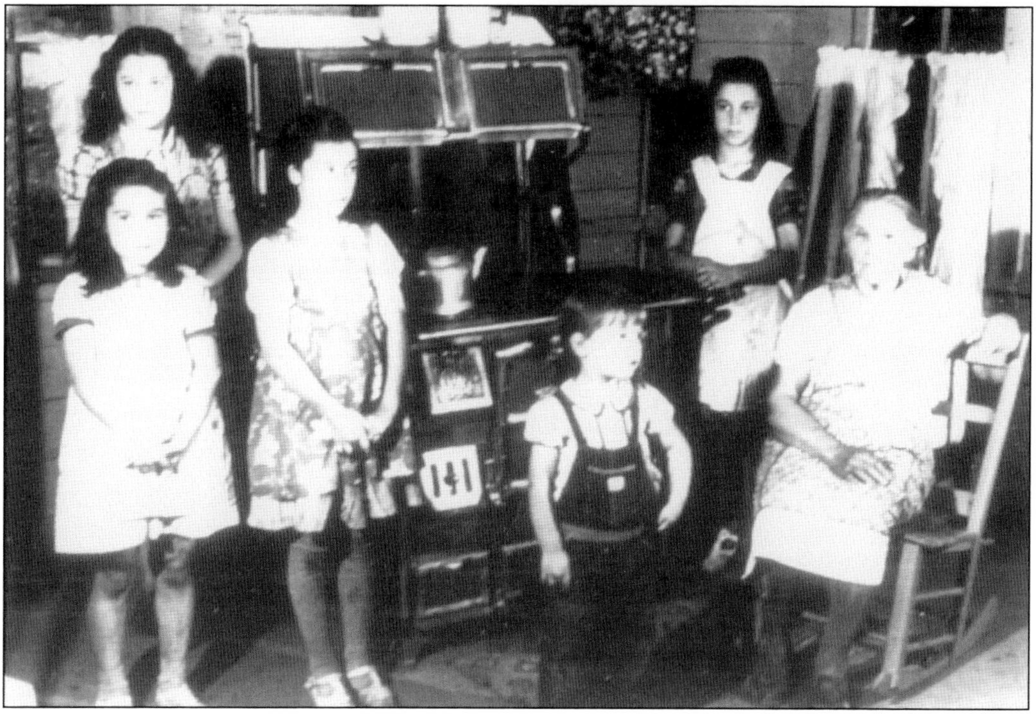

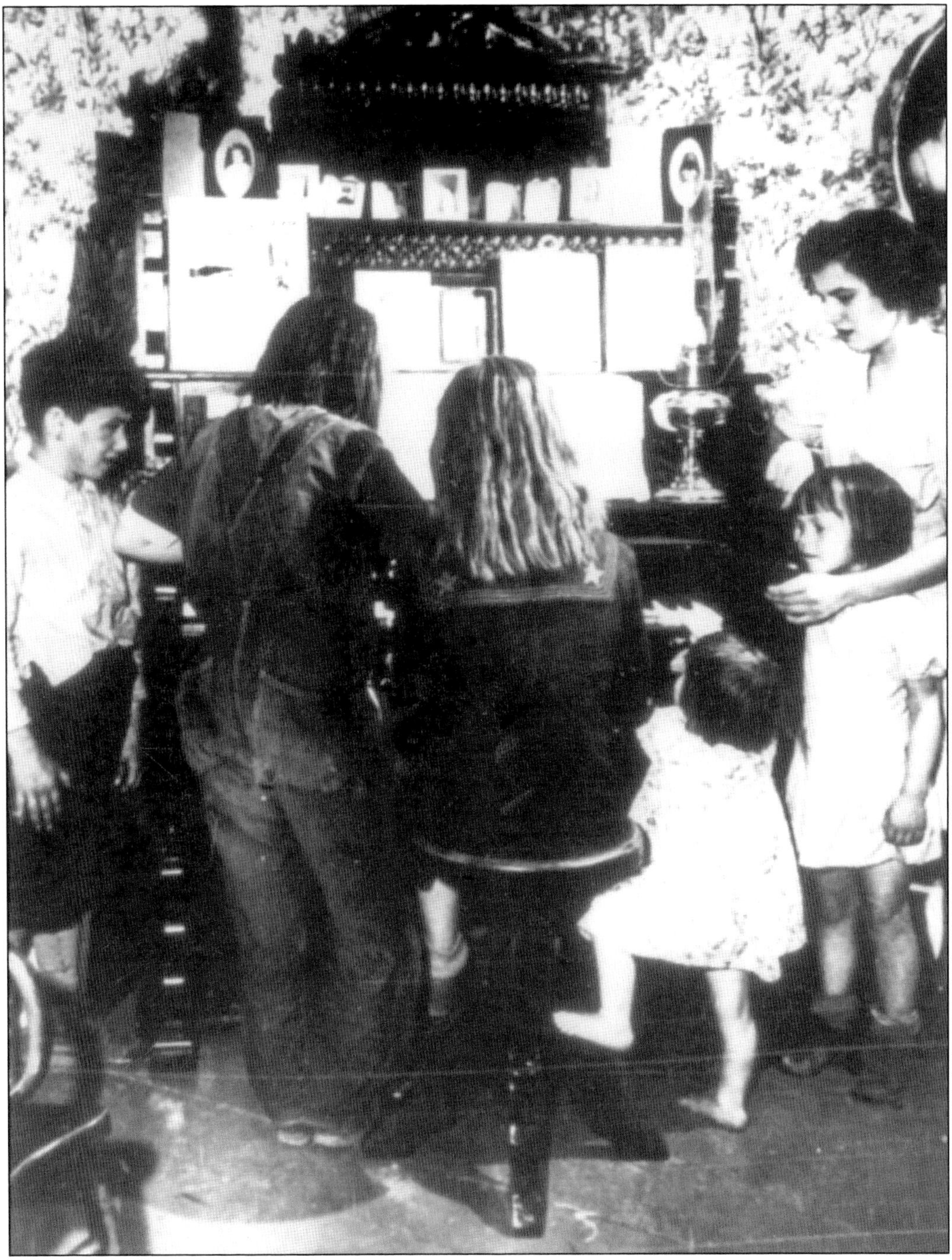

Before the era of television, entertaining at home was common. At the organ, which in this 1942 image held many family photographs, are children of the Gagnon household in Frenchville: (from left to right) Tony, Marie Anne, Therese, Alien, Rita, and Lillian. (Courtesy of the Acadian Archives, University of Maine at Fort Kent.)

Three

Religious Life

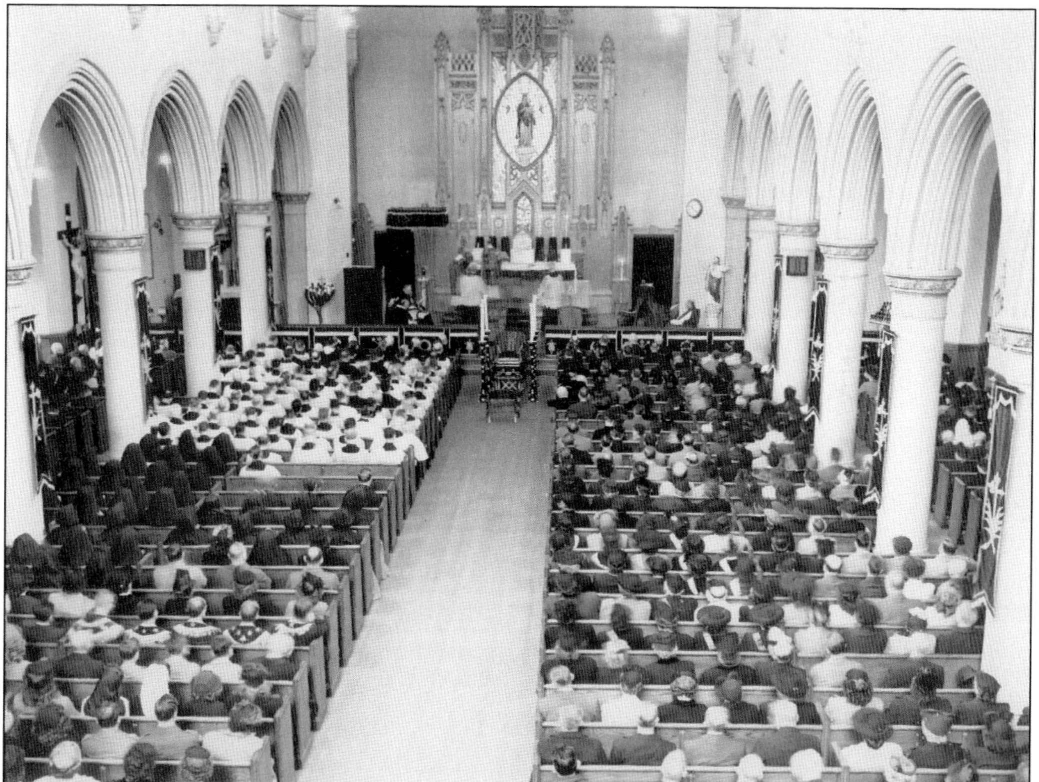

The Catholic Church has been a powerful institution in almost every community in which Franco-Americans lived. Here is St. Mary's Church in Lewiston, which is now a heritage center and entertainment venue. This photograph was taken during a funeral service, perhaps of a priest or nun, and many members of the clergy can be seen at the front of the church. (Courtesy of the Maine Historical Society.)

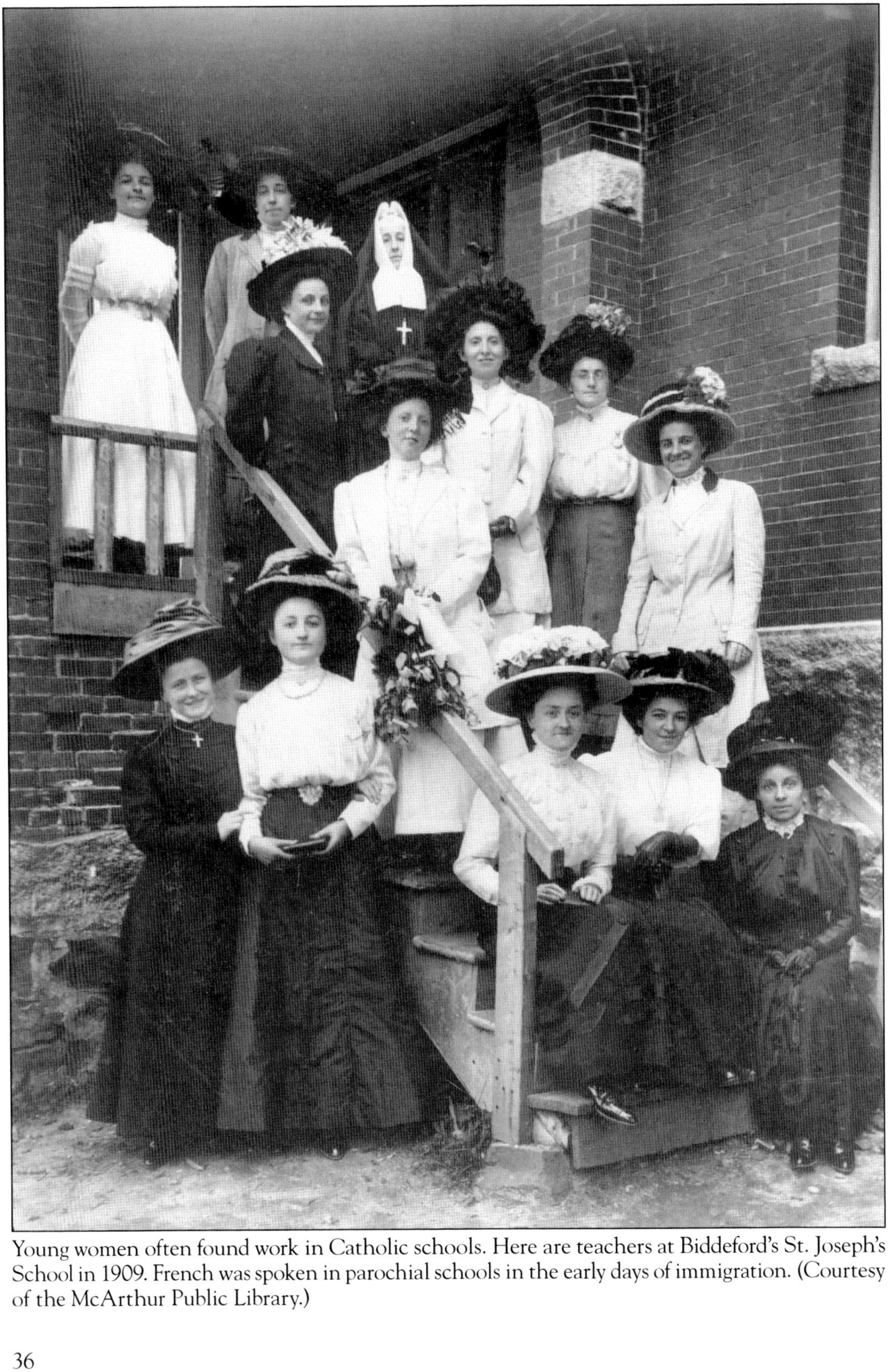

Young women often found work in Catholic schools. Here are teachers at Biddeford's St. Joseph's School in 1909. French was spoken in parochial schools in the early days of immigration. (Courtesy of the McArthur Public Library.)

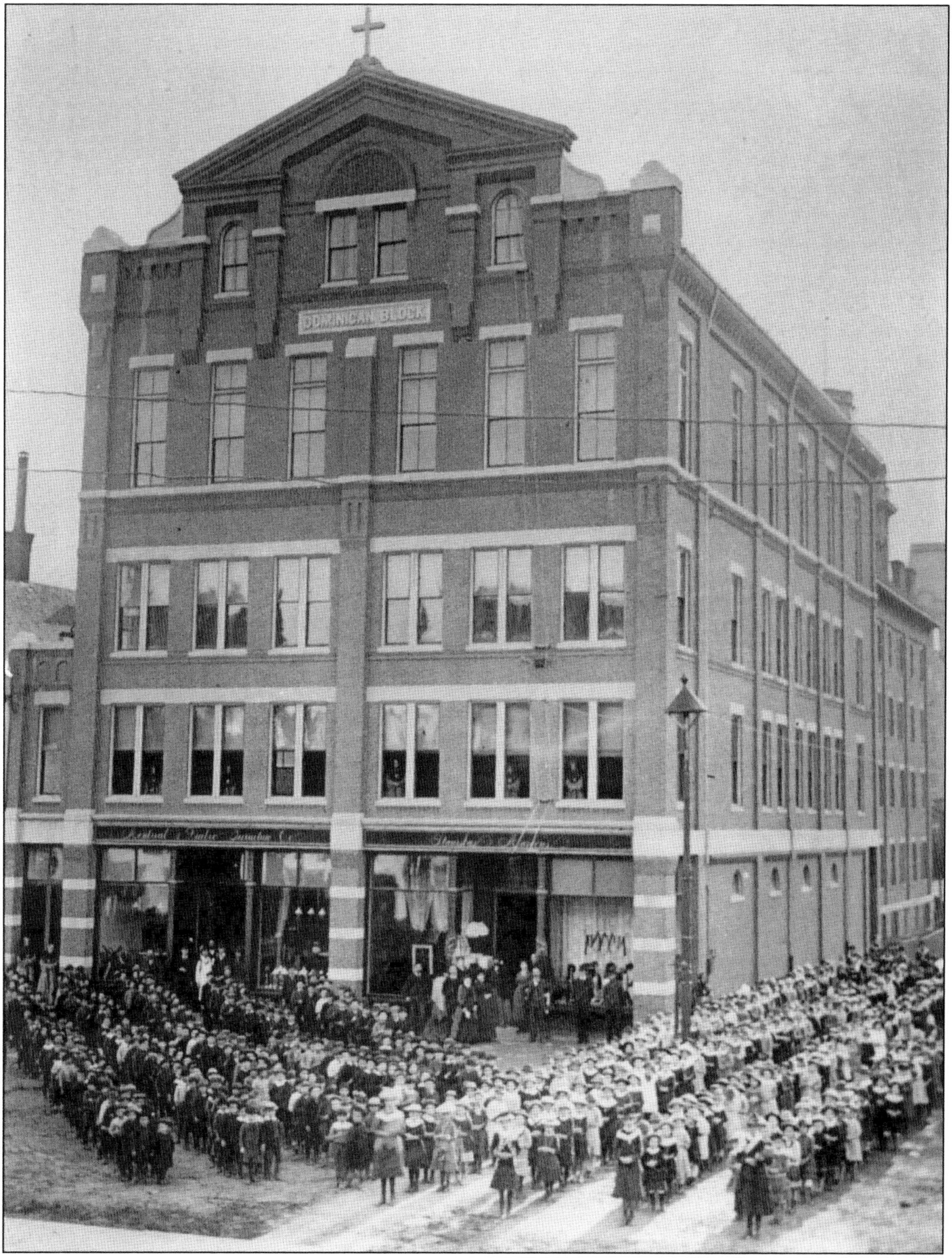

The Dominican Block at the corner of Lincoln and Chestnut Streets in Lewiston was established in 1883 and served as a social and religious center of Franco-American life in that community. As a school, it opened its doors to 650 students in the 1880s and later served as a house of worship and a social center. Because of its role in local Franco-American culture, the building became the social and political center of the French Catholic community. (Courtesy of the University of Southern Maine, Lewiston-Auburn College Franco-American Collection.)

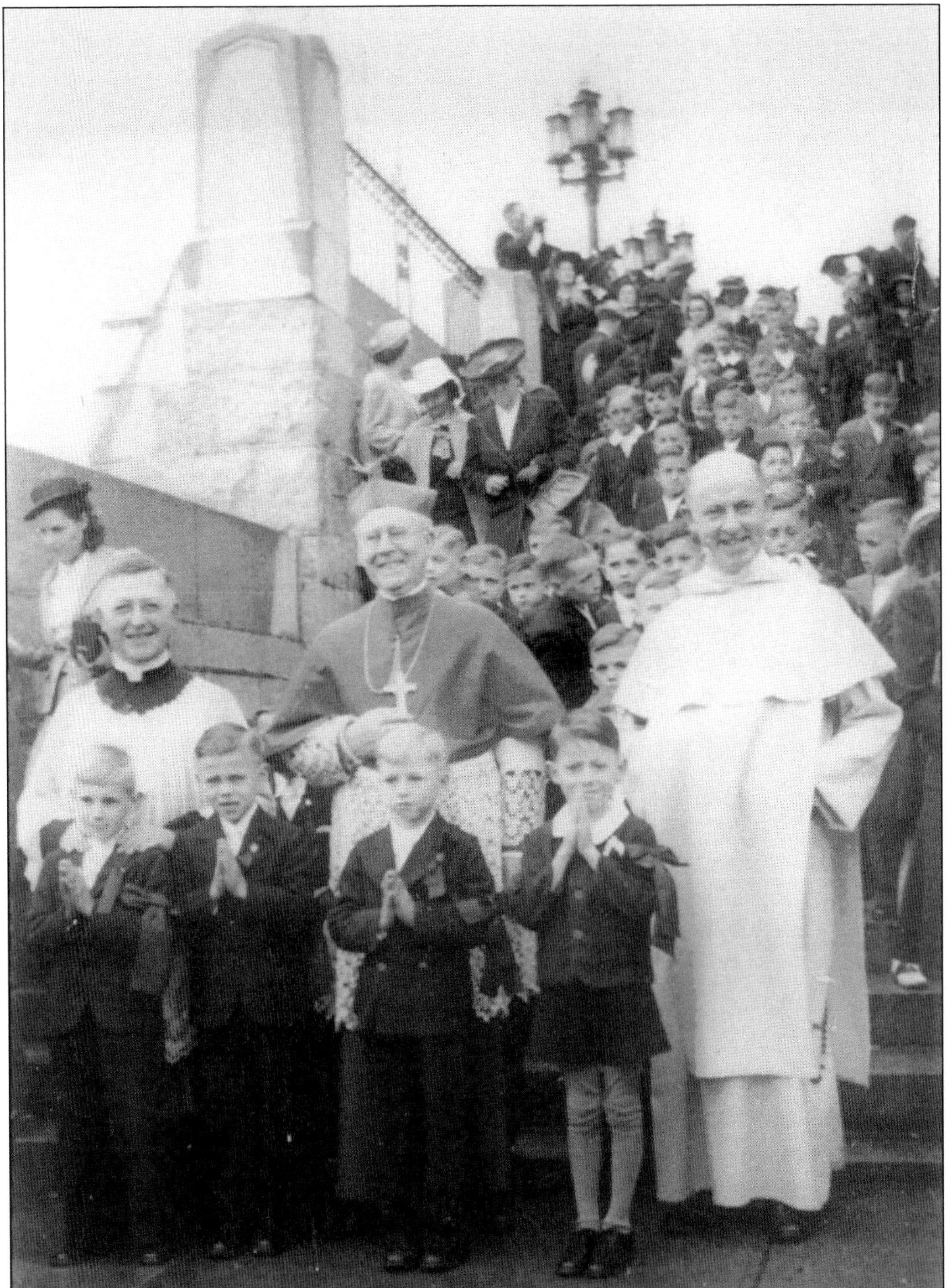

Religious leaders provided instruction to generations of Franco-Americans. Here youngsters leave mass in Lewiston, celebrated by the Most Reverend Joseph E. McCarthy (center). He was bishop of the Diocese of Portland from 1932 to 1955. (Courtesy of the Franco-American Heritage Center at St. Mary's.)

Many Franco-Americans were deeply religious. Here Melvina Dumont sits in the home of her son, Patrick, a potato farmer in Lille, beneath a depiction of the crucifixion. The year was 1940. (Courtesy of the Acadian Archives, University of Maine at Fort Kent.)

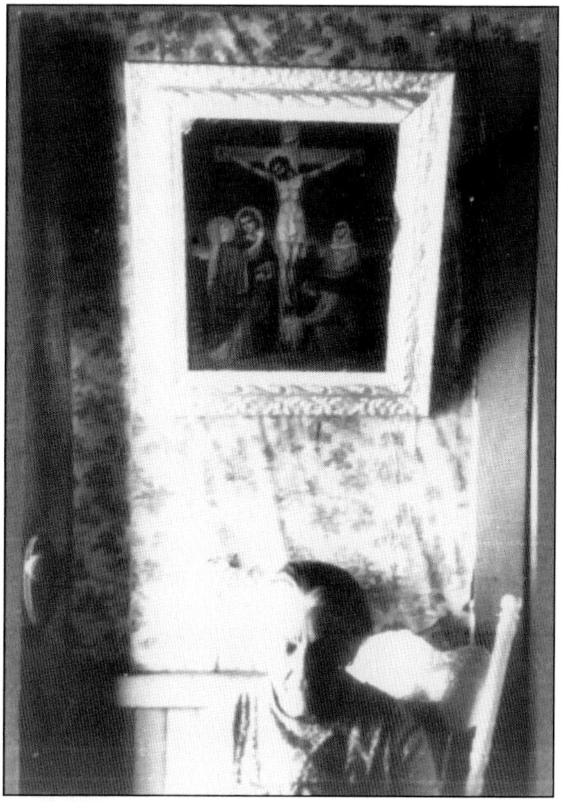

The Reverend Francois Drouin was pastor of the SS. Peter and Paul Church in Lewiston from 1940 to 1952. (Courtesy of the University of Southern Maine, Lewiston-Auburn College Franco-American Collection.)

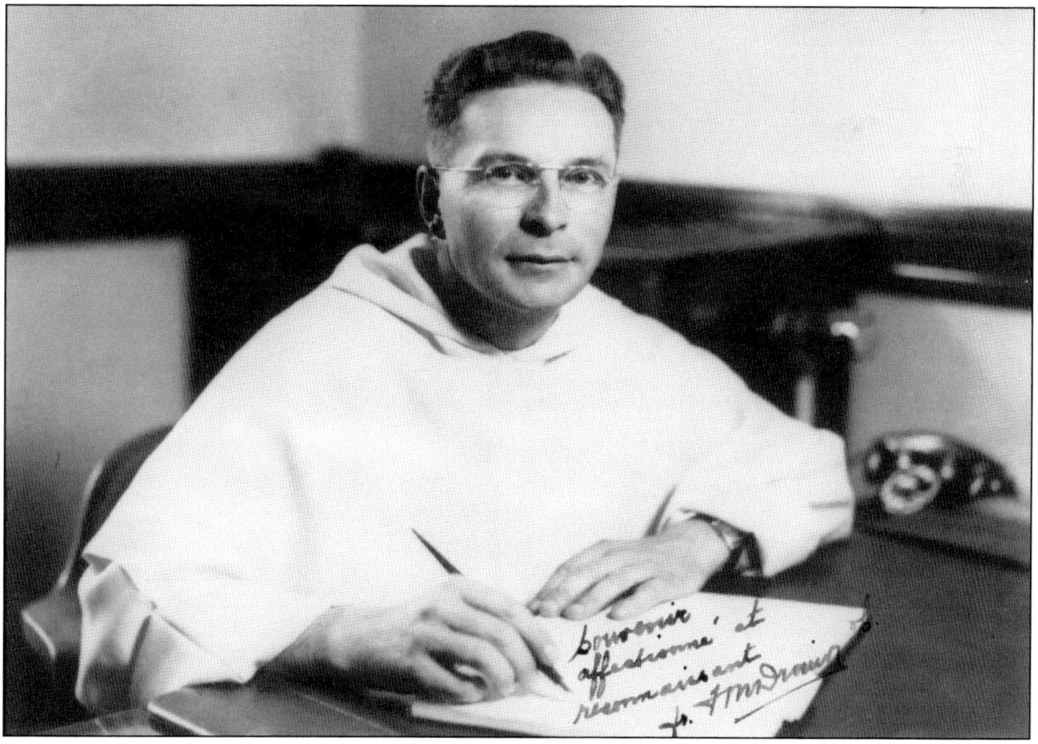

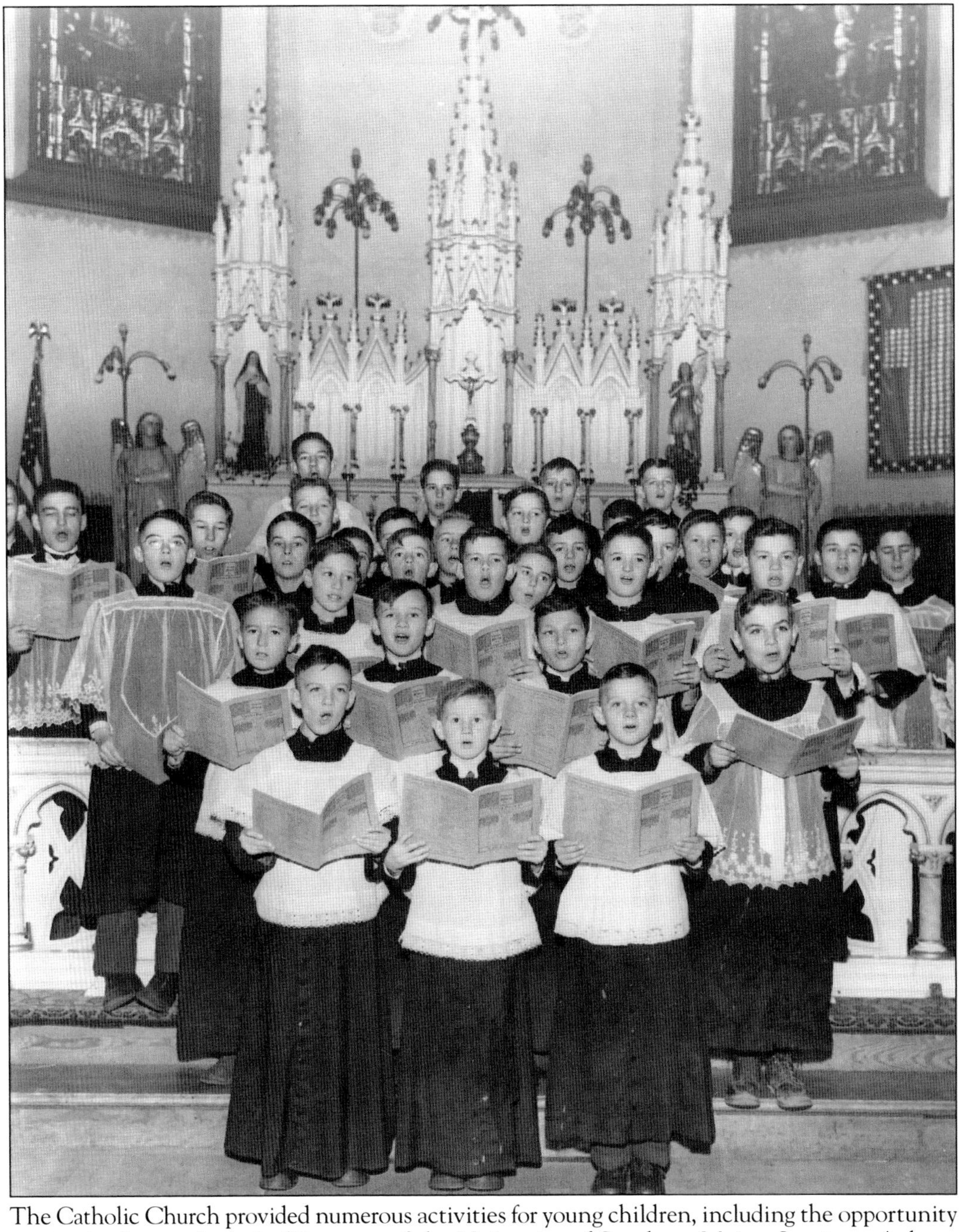

The Catholic Church provided numerous activities for young children, including the opportunity to sing in the youth choir. (Courtesy of the University of Southern Maine, Lewiston-Auburn College Franco-American Collection.)

Nuns cheerfully climb church stairs on their way to services in Lewiston. Many Franco-American families were pleased if at least one daughter joined the church. (Courtesy of the University of Southern Maine, Lewiston-Auburn College Franco-American Collection.)

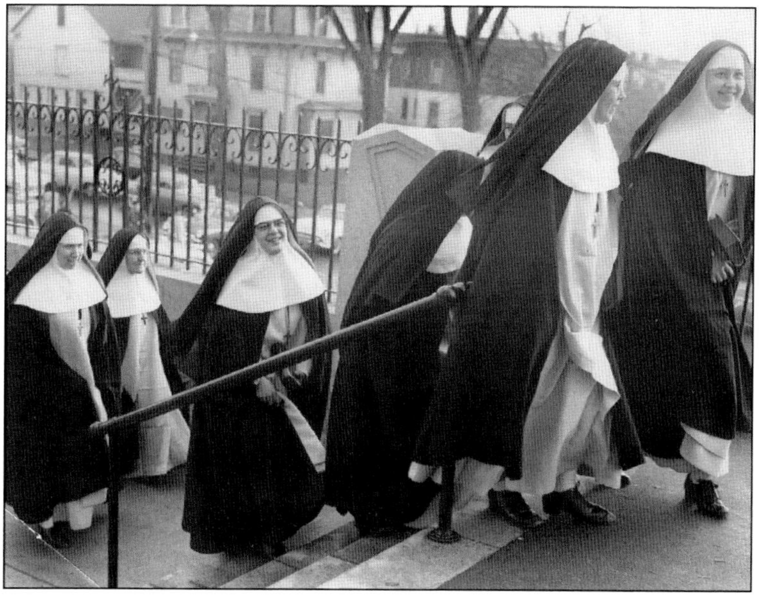

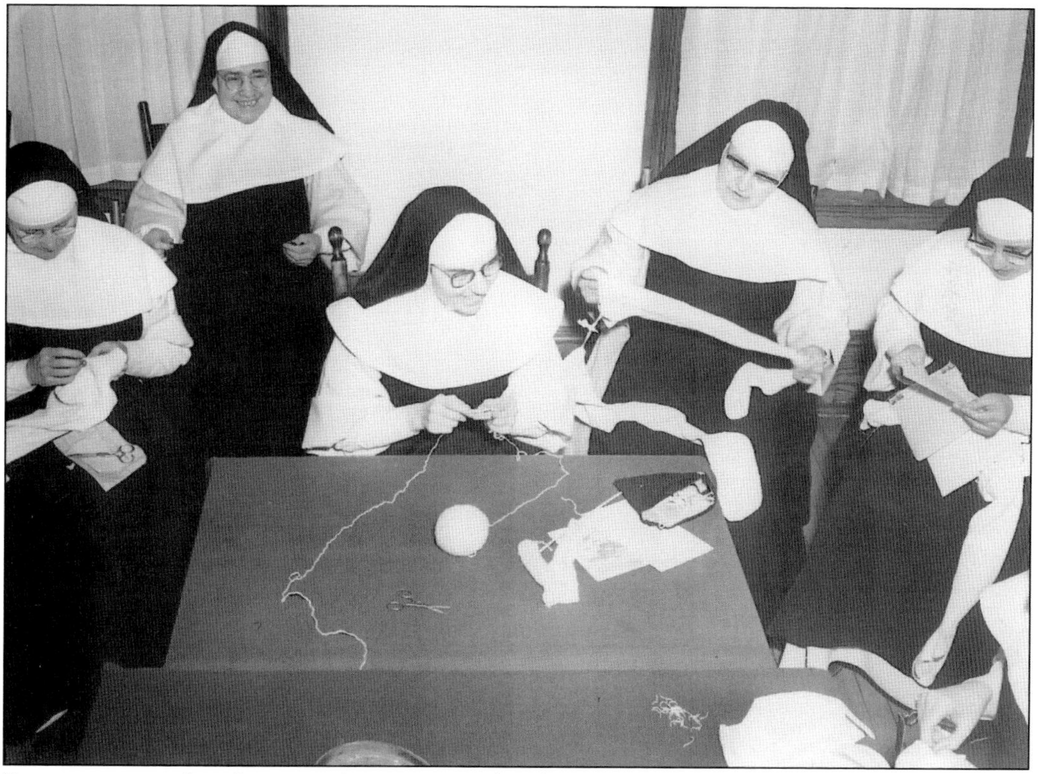

Becoming part of a religious order was a popular choice in years past, and this photograph from the mid-1950s indicates nuns enjoyed community activities such as knitting. (Courtesy of the University of Southern Maine, Lewiston-Auburn College Franco-American Collection.)

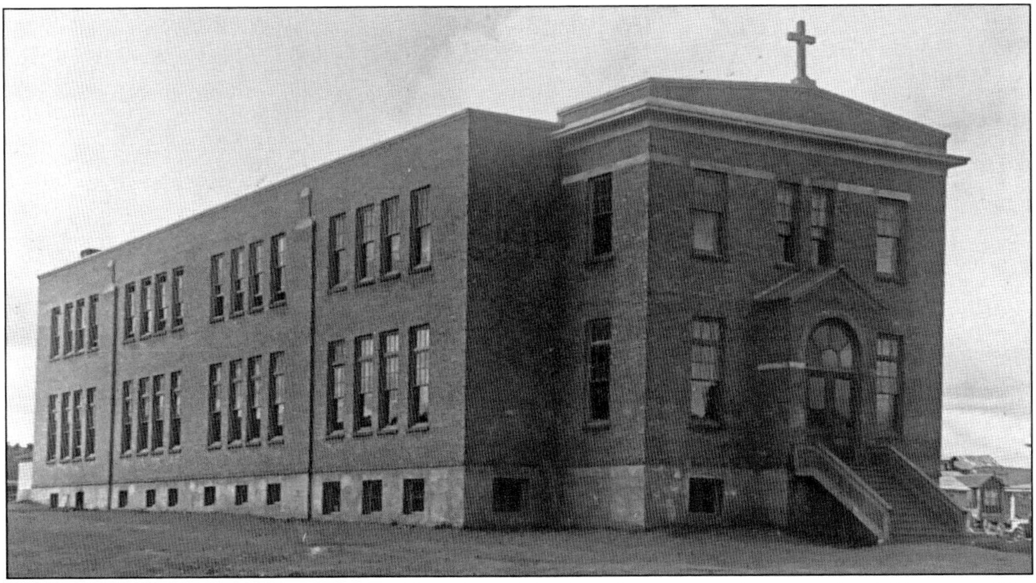

The St. Thomas Aquinas Catholic Church in Madawaska, shown here in the 1930s, was like many churches in that it offered both religious services and school lessons. Mass was on the first floor, and classes were on the second. (Courtesy of the Madawaska Historical Society.)

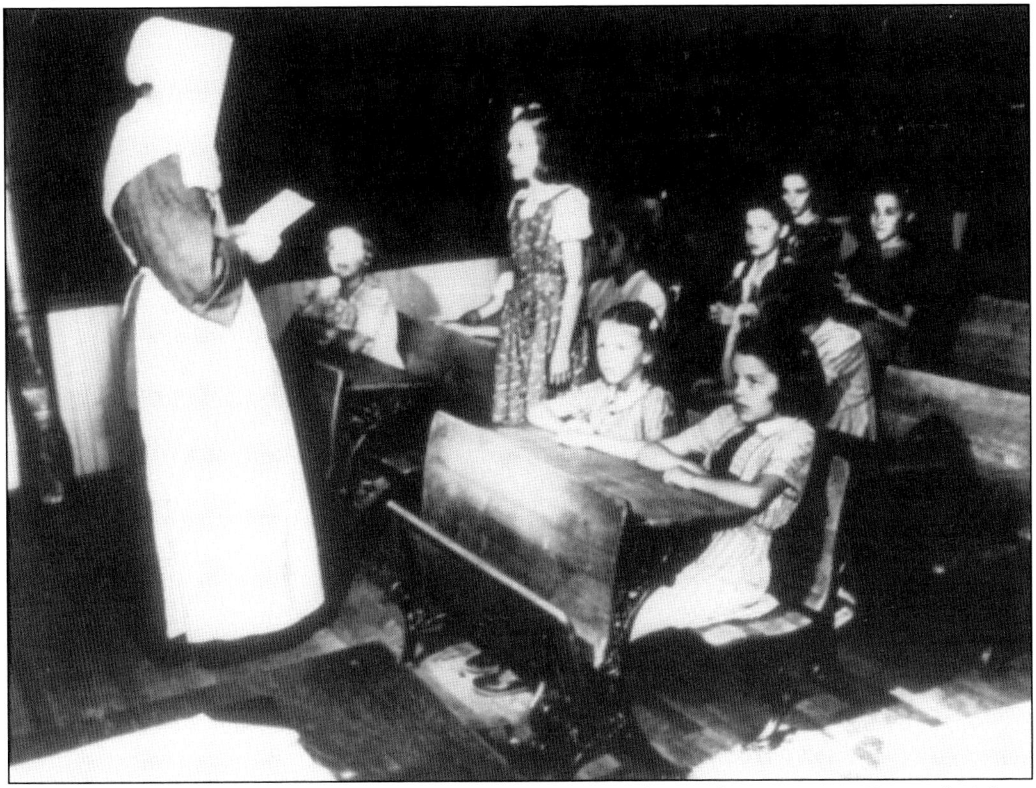

Sister Simeon of the Daughters of Wisdom teaches a catechism class at Notre Dame du Mont Carmel Roman Catholic School in Lille in August 1942. She was also the cook at the convent. (Courtesy of the Acadian Archives, University of Maine at Fort Kent.)

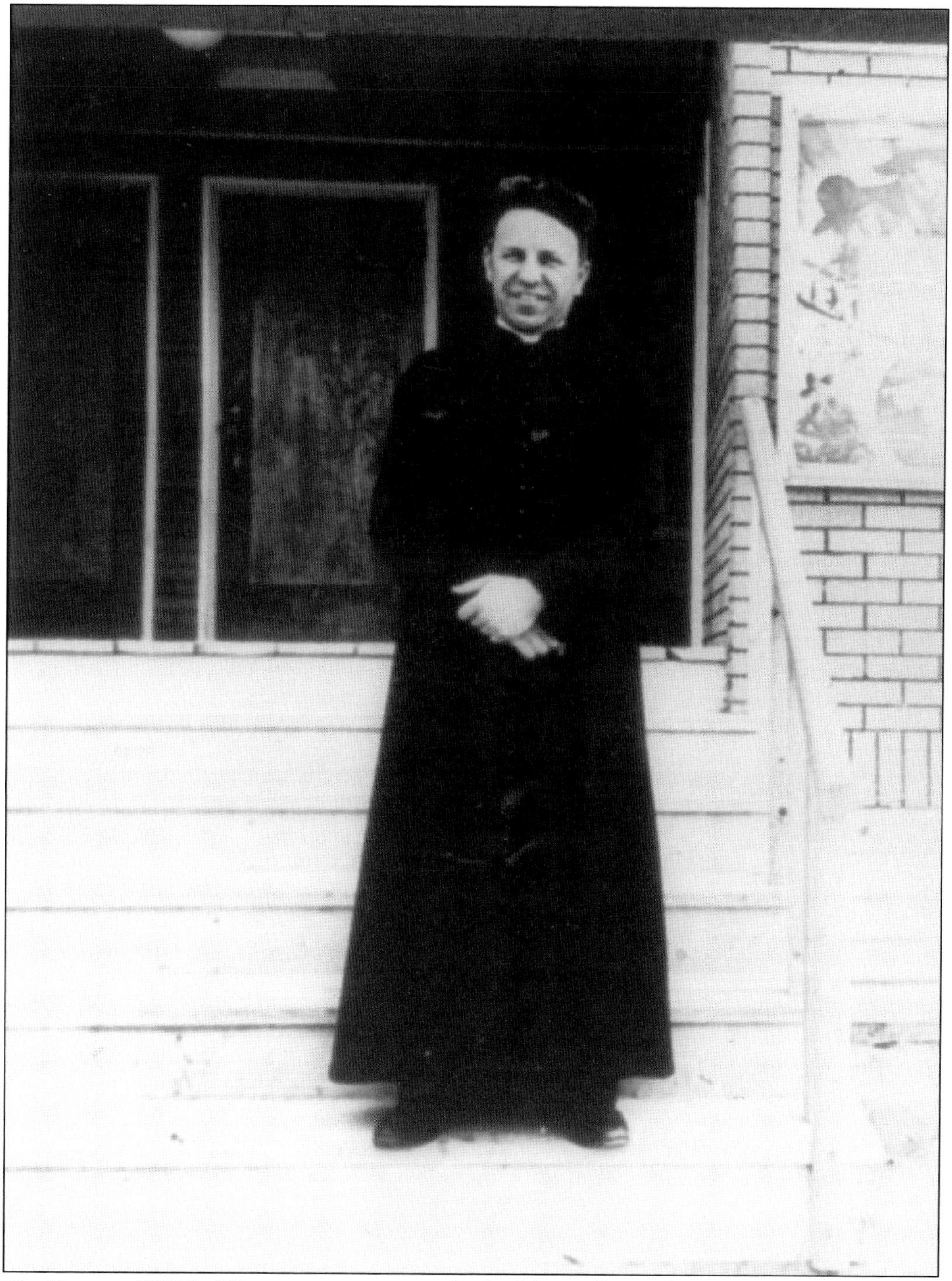

The Reverend Wilfred Soucy was a priest in the St. John Valley and an advocate of community theater. Here he stands outside his church in Sinclair in 1942, which also hosted cinematic events. At right is a poster advertising a film starring Tex Ritter. (Courtesy of the Acadian Archives, University of Maine at Fort Kent.)

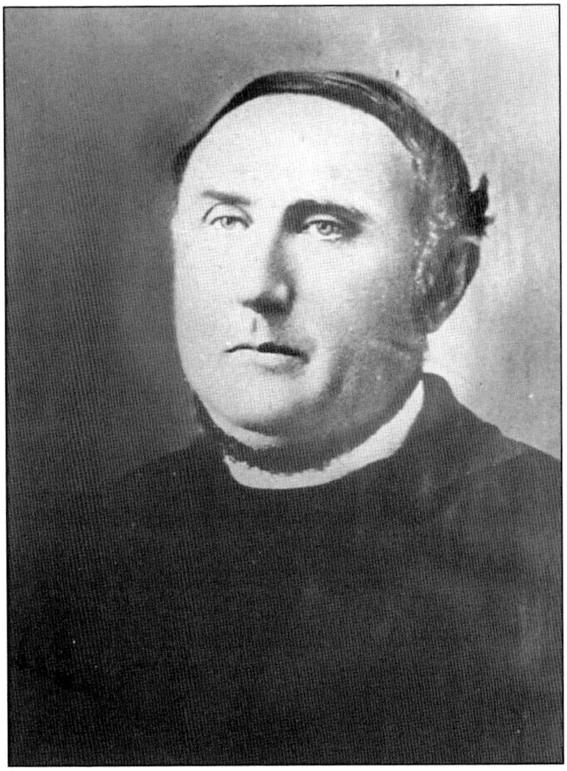

The Reverend Charles Swearon of the St. David Church and Rectory is shown here in 1871. The life of priests in rural Maine was often a solitary existence, and yet they were leaders in their tight-knit communities. (Courtesy of the Madawaska Historical Society.)

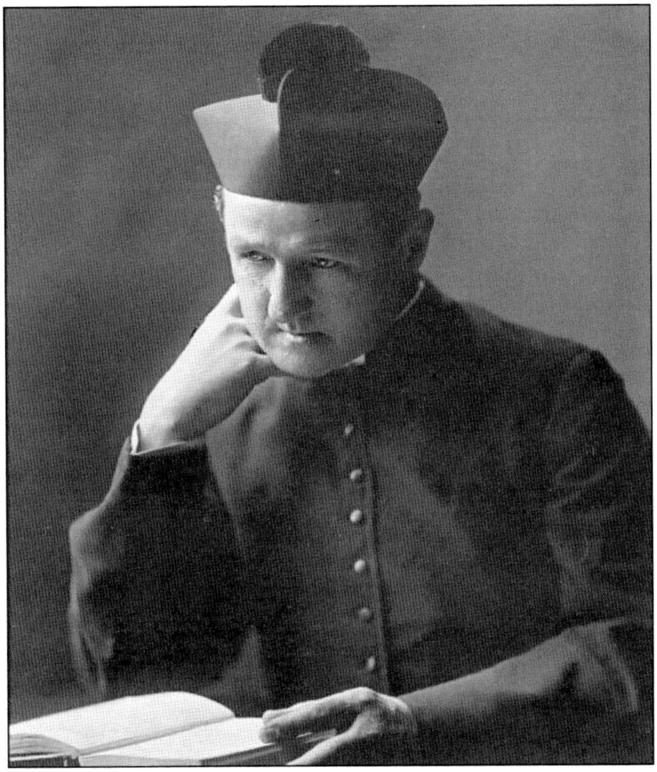

The Reverend Louis Huot served as pastor in St. David from 1907 to 1916 and led efforts to build a church there. (Courtesy of the Madawaska Historical Society.)

Thousands of Franco-Americans attended St. Joseph's Church in Biddeford over the years. (Courtesy of the McArthur Public Library.)

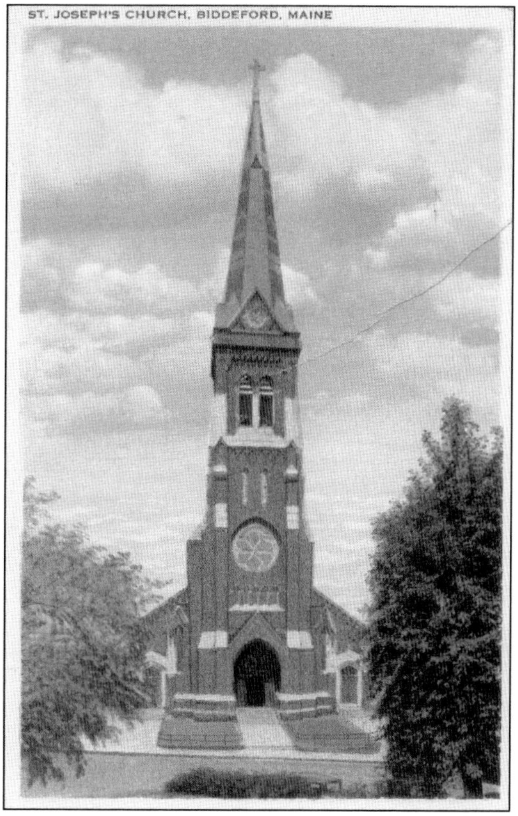

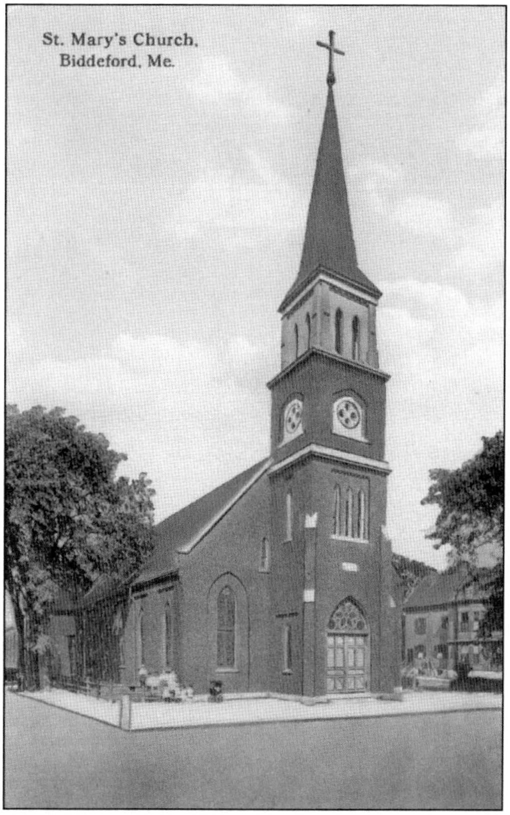

Most mill communities had more than one Catholic church. Here is a photograph of St. Mary's Church in Biddeford. (Courtesy of the McArthur Public Library.)

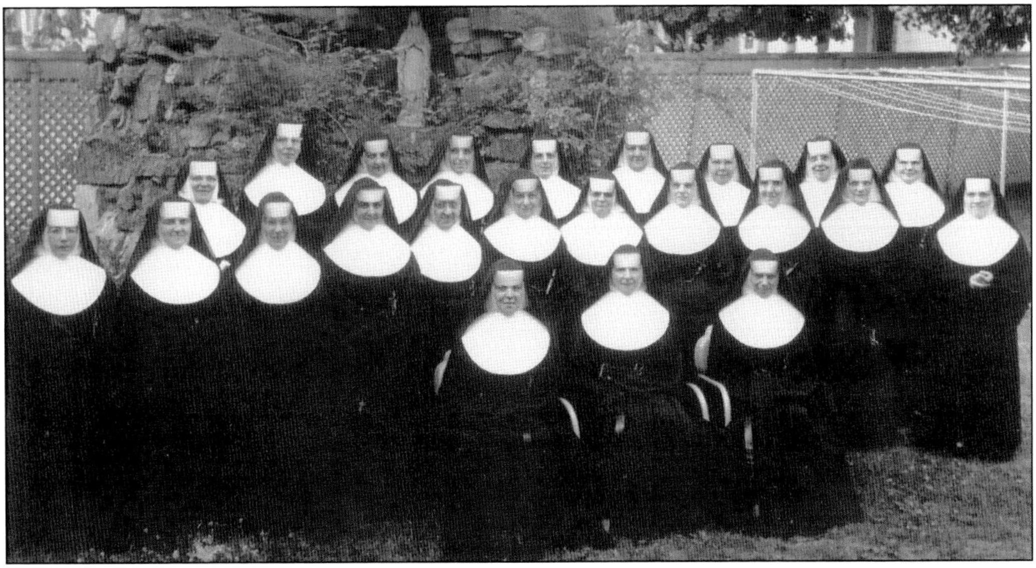

St. Ignatius Church in Sanford opened in 1927 to accommodate the growing number of French Canadian immigrants, and for years, it ran an elementary school and high school in that community. Both schools are closed now. In this photograph from the early 1960s, former teachers are (first row) Aimee de Jesus Bouffard, Alfreda Morrissette, and Delphina Bernier; (second row) M. Marc Cantin, Beatrice Vallee, Cecile Albert, Priscilla Boucher, Camille Lizzotte, Jeanne de Marie Dufresne, M. du Bon Pasteur Laforce, Benoit Plante, Angelique Leclerc, Adele Lavoie, and Eva Marie Rancourt; (third row) Emile Ouellette, Calveria Laflamme, Eva Marie Laffely, M. du Sacre Coeur St. Onge, Aurelie Tertreau, Yvonne Maynard, Isidore Albert, M. des Anges Normand, and Leonie Tetreault. (Courtesy of Solange Thibodeau Lamontagne and Gerald Lamontagne.)

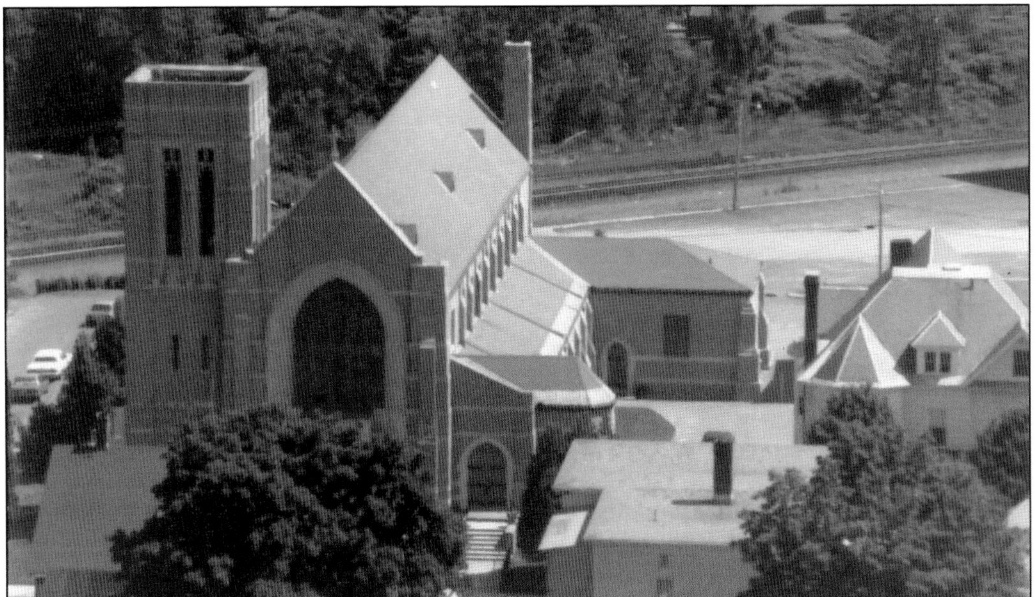

Religious complexes grew within residential neighborhoods so that priests could be within walking distance of the people. Complexes included church, school, rectory, and living quarters, as this photograph from Biddeford portrays. (Courtesy of the McArthur Public Library.)

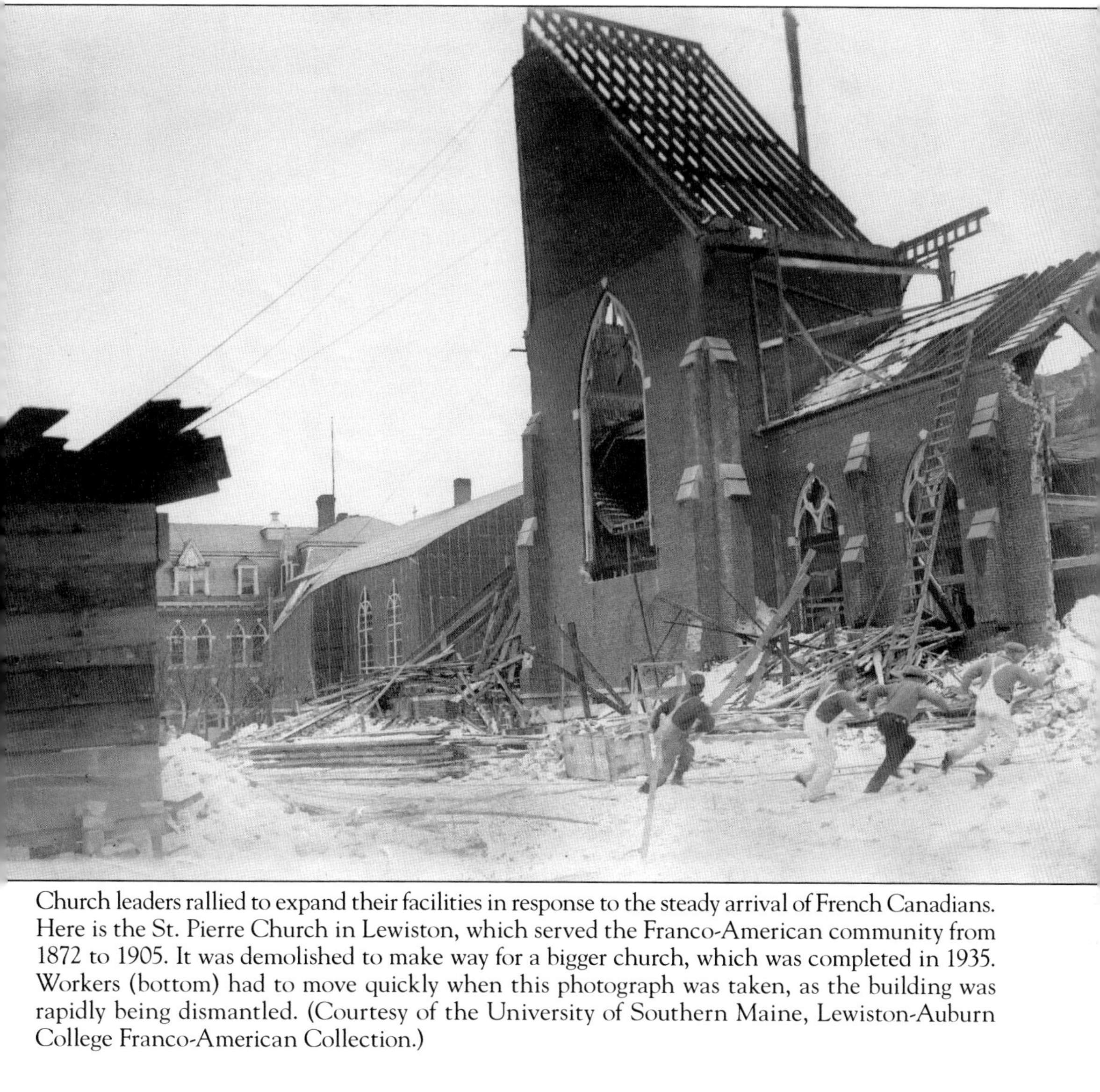

Church leaders rallied to expand their facilities in response to the steady arrival of French Canadians. Here is the St. Pierre Church in Lewiston, which served the Franco-American community from 1872 to 1905. It was demolished to make way for a bigger church, which was completed in 1935. Workers (bottom) had to move quickly when this photograph was taken, as the building was rapidly being dismantled. (Courtesy of the University of Southern Maine, Lewiston-Auburn College Franco-American Collection.)

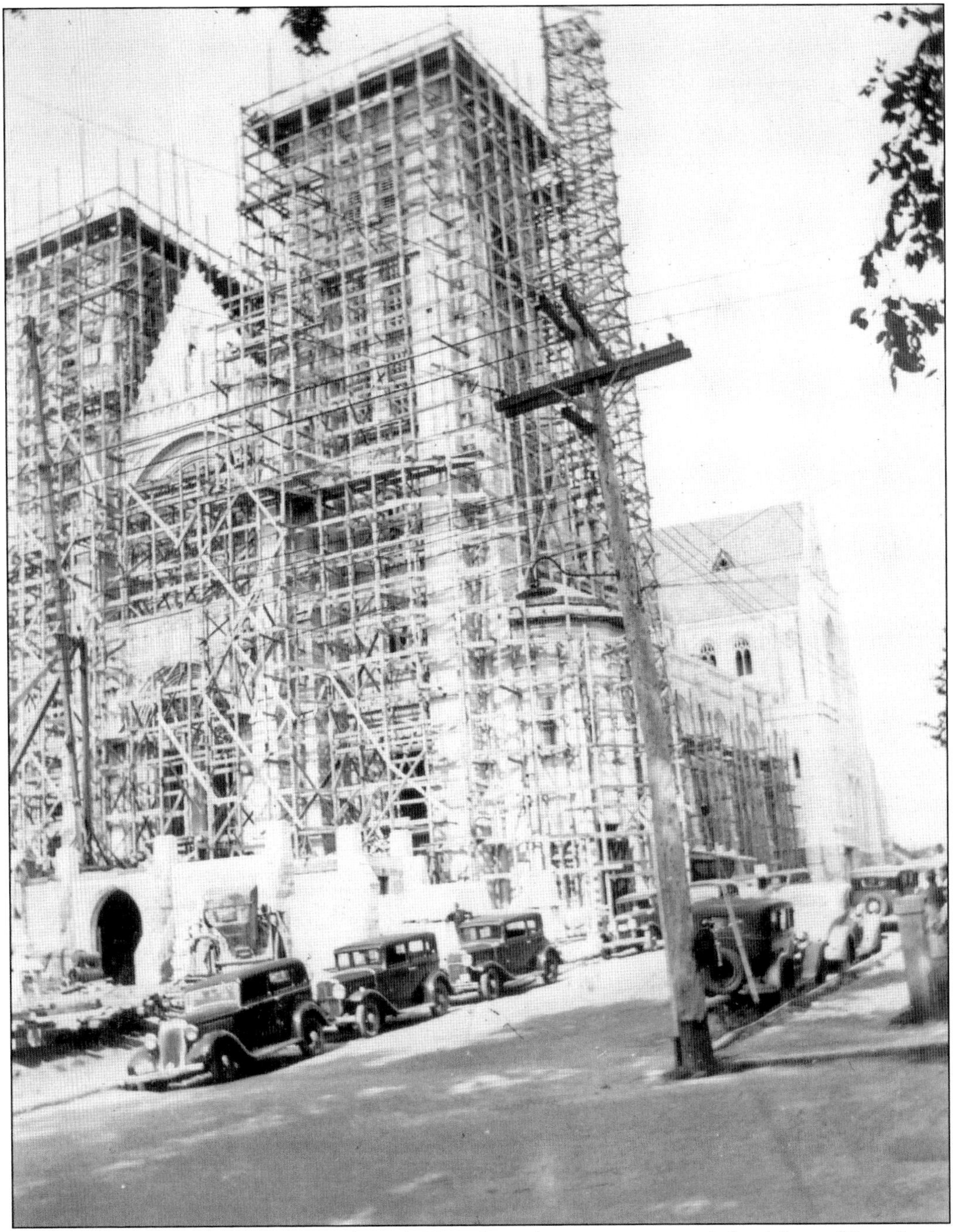

Construction of the SS. Peter and Paul Church took many years and the labor of hundreds. Here is a photograph of the structure in its final stages in 1935 with cars of the day parked near the building. (Courtesy of the University of Southern Maine, Lewiston-Auburn College Franco-American Collection.)

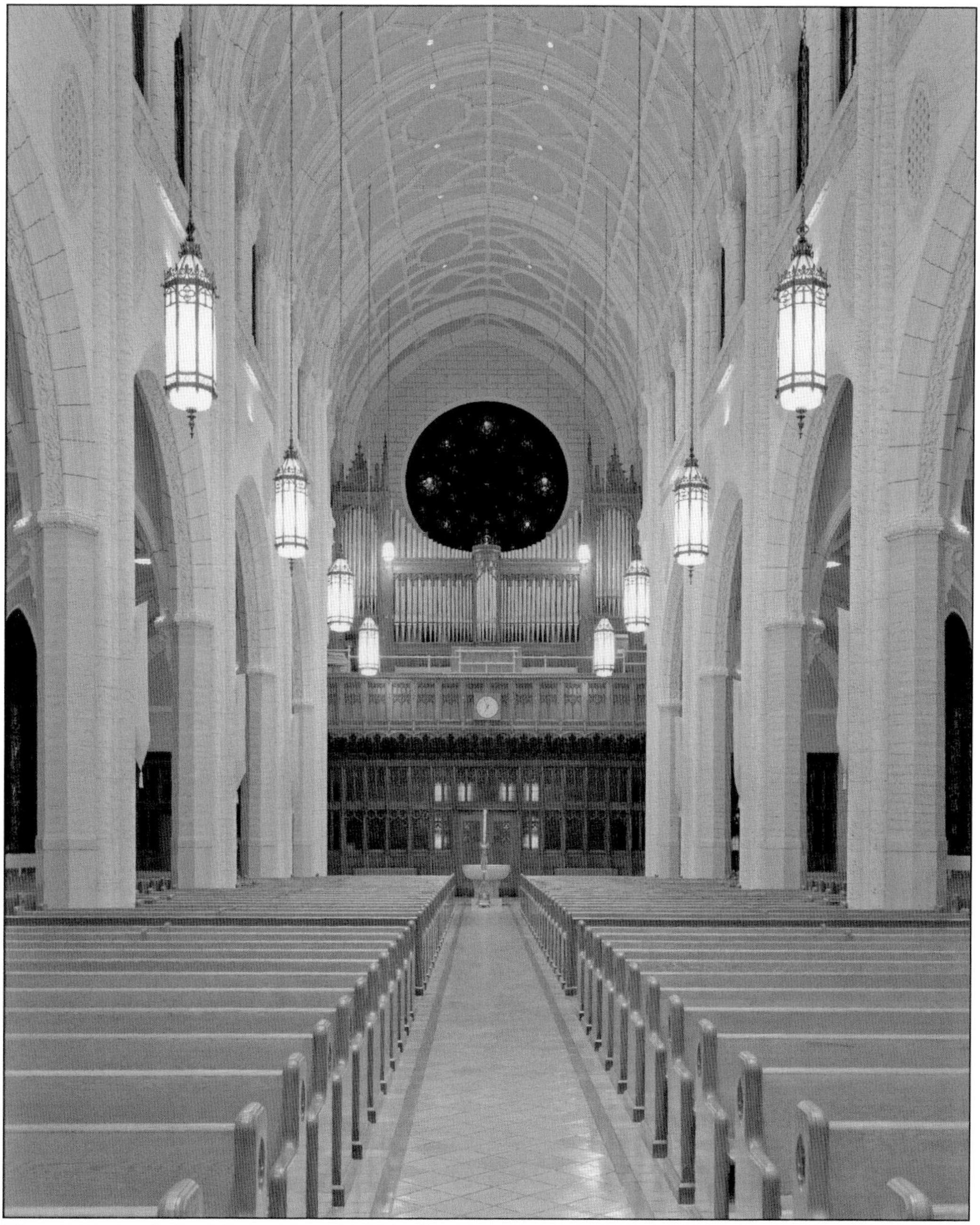

The interior of the SS. Peter and Paul Church is a tribute to the Catholic community, as this photograph taken in 2004 shows. Because of its grandeur and significance to the community's spiritual life, it was designated a basilica. (Courtesy of the University of Southern Maine, Lewiston-Auburn College Franco-American Collection.)

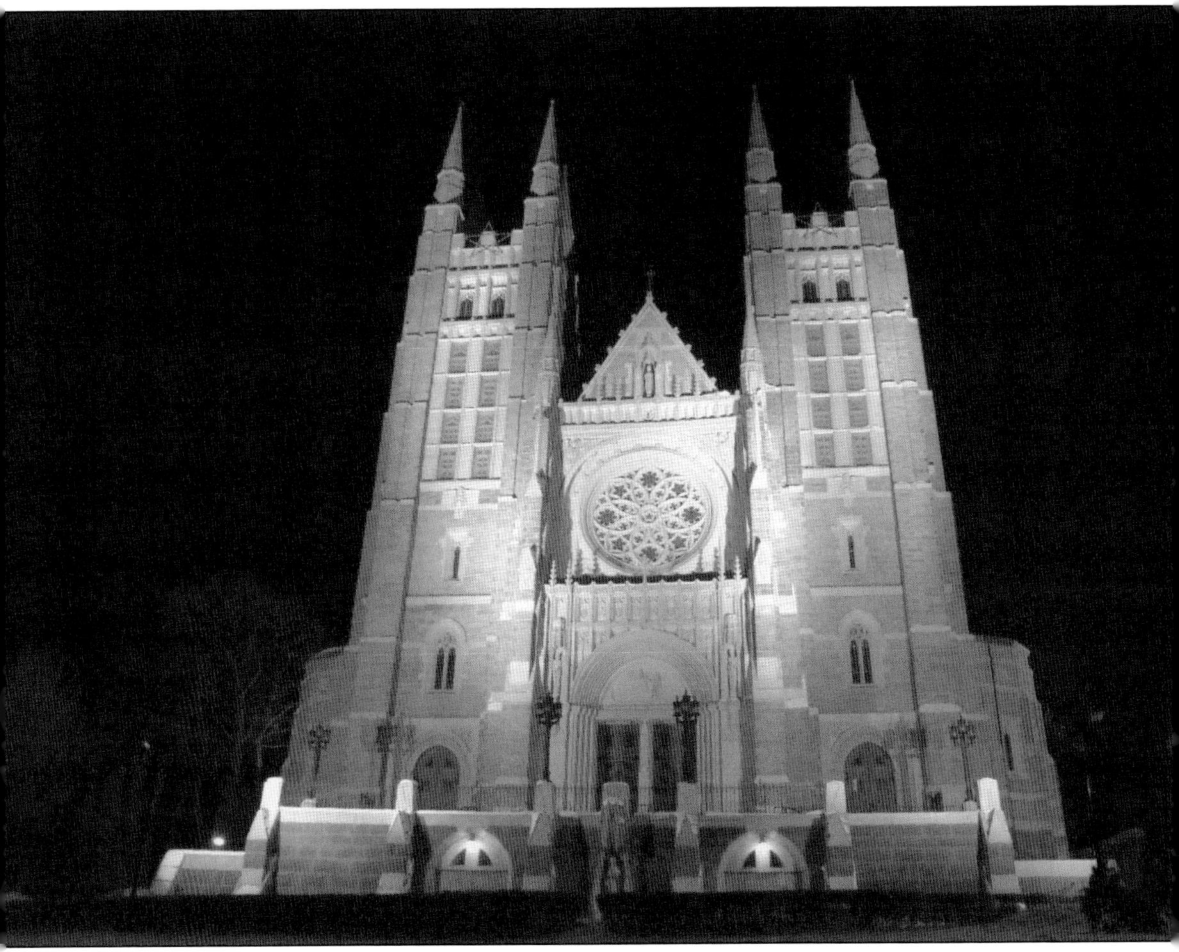

The current SS. Peter and Paul Basilica glows at night, as this 2005 photograph demonstrates. It hosts one of the largest parishes in the state. (Photograph by Dan Philbrick.)

Four

COMMUNITY

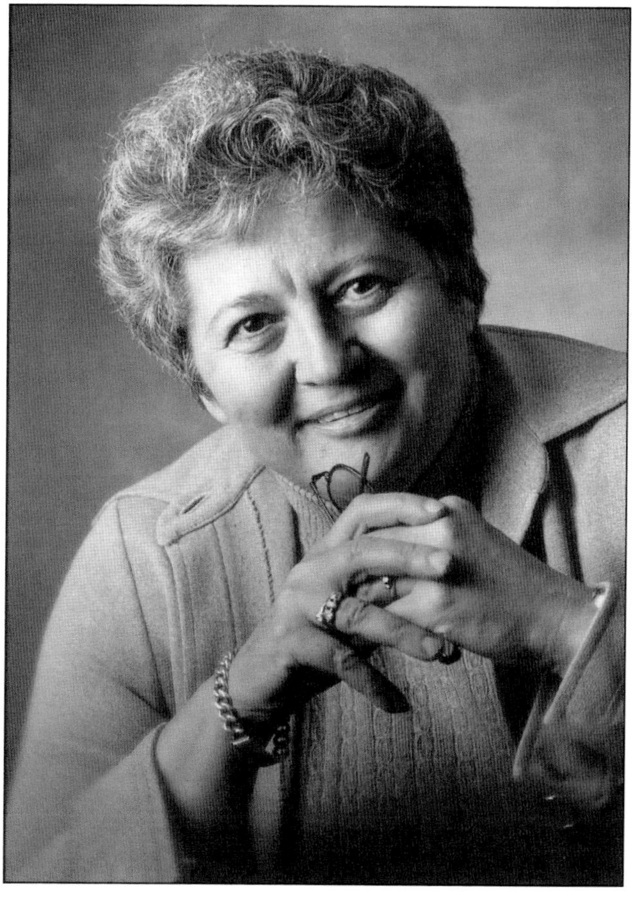

A belief in the achievements of the Franco-American community was embodied in the work of the late Dr. Madeleine Giguère, a native of Lewiston, a professor at the University of Southern Maine, and an intellectual leader in the late 20th century. In her writing and lectures, she stressed the strong family and religious values of those who had come from French Canada. (Courtesy of the University of Southern Maine, Lewiston-Auburn College Franco-American Collection.)

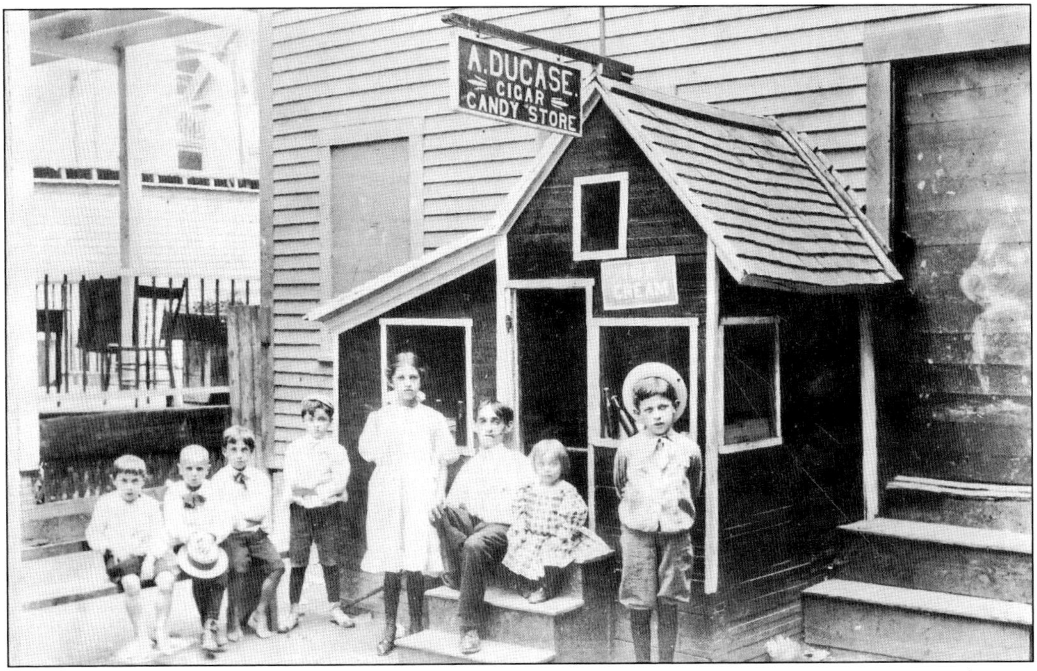

Youngsters often gathered near neighborhood stores to play, socialize, or even earn some change doing chores. These children stand in front of the Ducase store in Lewiston. (Courtesy of the University of Southern Maine, Lewiston-Auburn College Franco-American Collection.)

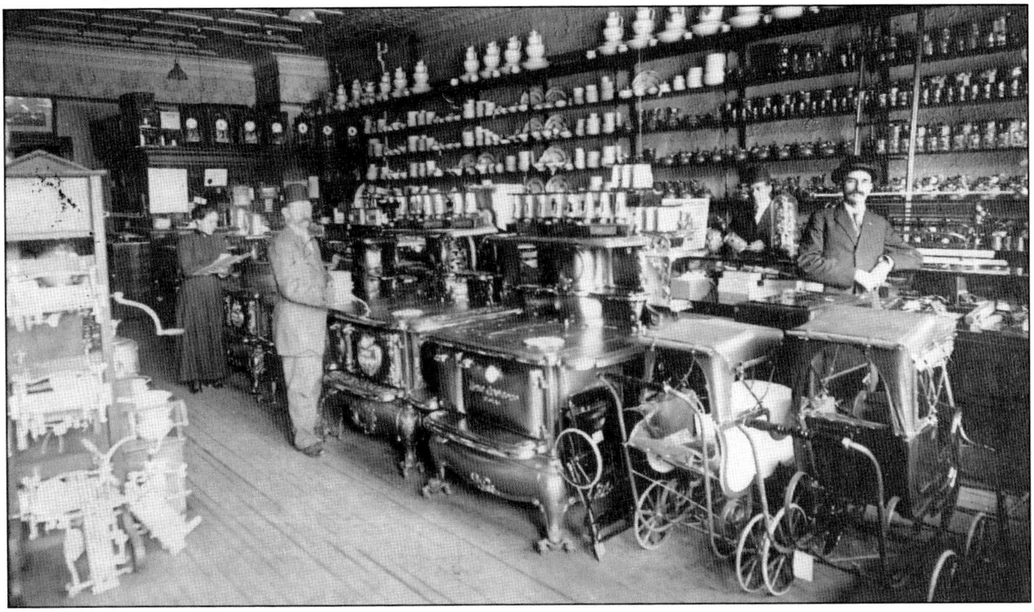

Before families had cars, the local store was central to shopping and social needs. Here in 1902 is the F. X. Marcotte Furniture Store, a business that is still prominent today. Marcotte was from Wotton, Québec, and moved to Lewiston in 1878. In 1888, he took his life savings of $350 to start the store, which was first known as F. X. Marcotte, Undertaker and Dealer in Furniture and Stoves. (Courtesy of the University of Southern Maine, Lewiston-Auburn College Franco-American Collection.)

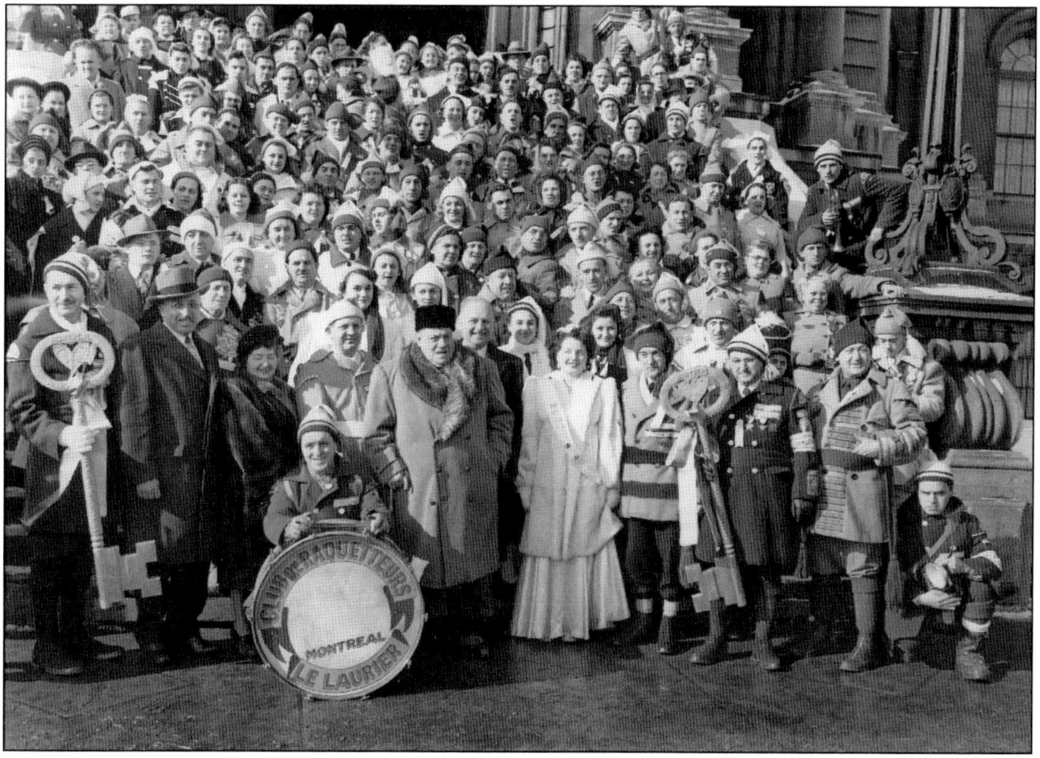

This photograph shows the good cheer of men and women who would gather for a mid-winter event such as a snowshoeing convention. (Courtesy of the University of Southern Maine, Lewiston-Auburn College Franco-American Collection.)

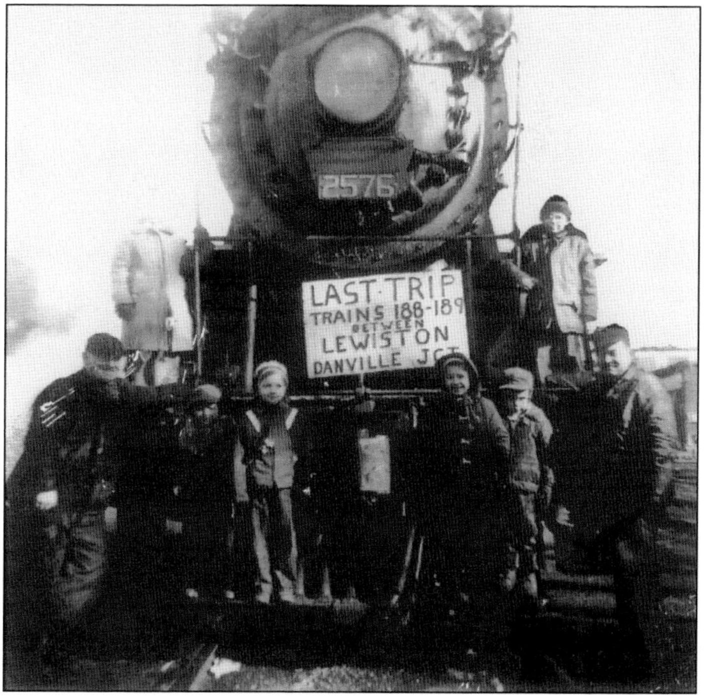

Children and a few adult supervisors have a light moment in front of a train that appears to be heading from Lewiston to Danville Junction, a section of neighboring Auburn. Trains were a major means of transportation between Maine and Québec and kept extended families in close contact. (Courtesy of the University of Southern Maine, Lewiston-Auburn College Franco-American Collection.)

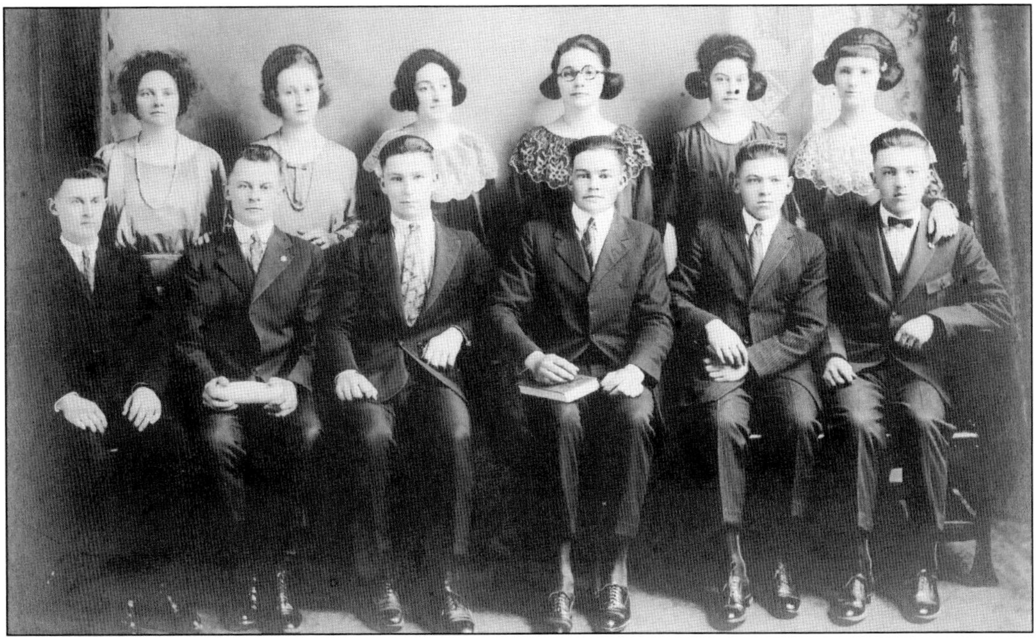

Many young Canadians worked in Maine in the winter and returned to Québec in the summer. These young French Canadians from the St. Felix de Kinsey area were boarding in the home of Yvonne Comeau (née Frechette) of Sanford in 1922. From left to right are (first row) Lorenzo Thibodeau, Maurice Thibodeau, Arthur Comeau, Victor Herbert, Eugene Comeau, and Ernest Comeau; (second row) Marie Perreault, Olina Comeau, Florida Hebert, Rosa Comeau, Georgette Hebert, and Yvonne Comeau. Only Lorenzo Thibodeau settled in Maine. (Courtesy of Solange Thibodeau Lamontagne and Gerard Lamontagne.)

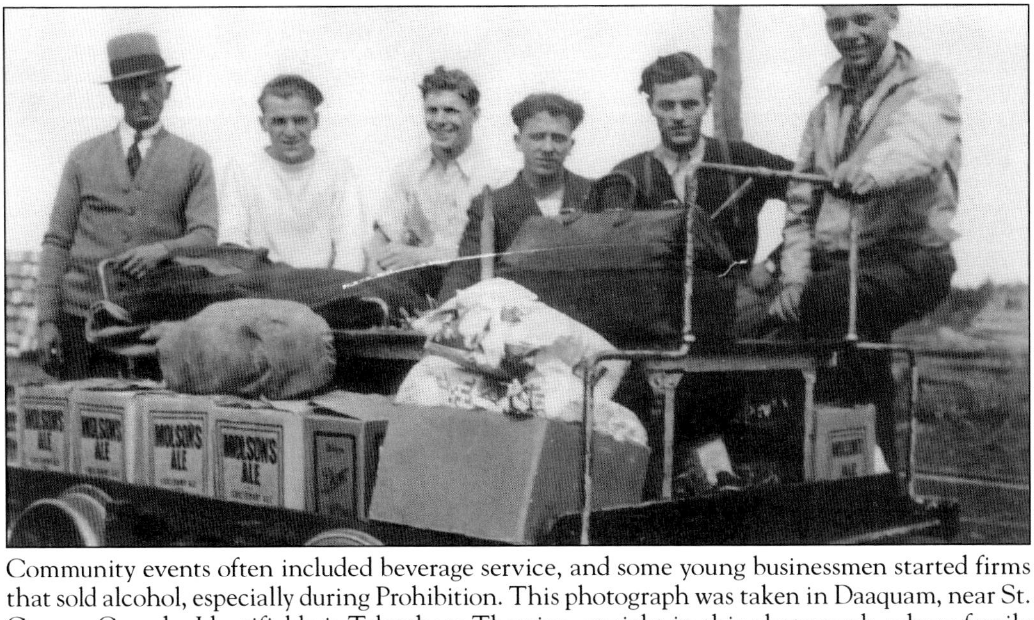

Community events often included beverage service, and some young businessmen started firms that sold alcohol, especially during Prohibition. This photograph was taken in Daaquam, near St. George, Canada. Identifiable is Telesphore Therrien, at right in this photograph, whose family settled in Lewiston. Here is a team of "distributors" during the 1930s with cases of Molson Ale. (Courtesy of the Franco-American Heritage Center at St. Mary's.)

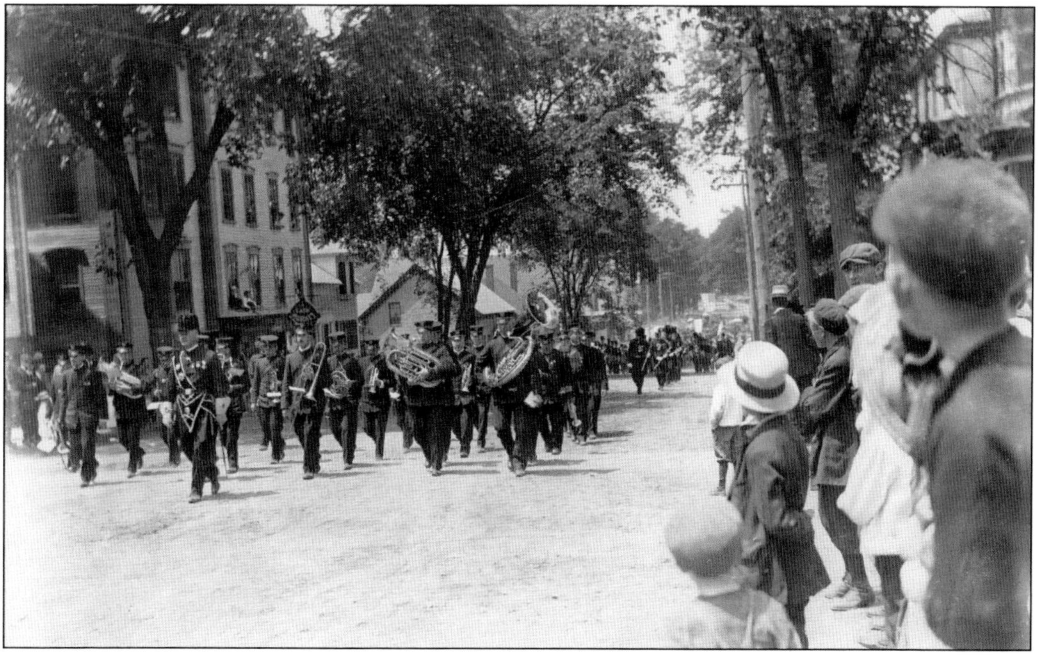

Bands and parades were the order of the day when a community had something to celebrate. Here a lengthy procession moves through the streets of Biddeford in 1915 as children at lower right watch attentively. (Courtesy of the McArthur Public Library.)

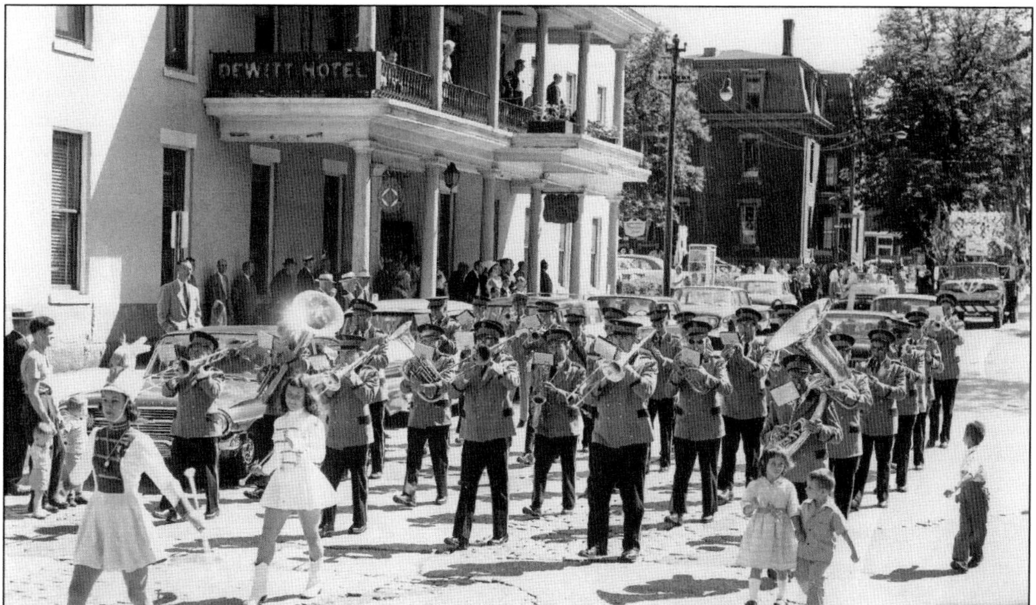

A parade passes the Dewitt Hotel in Lewiston during a community celebration in honor of St. Jean-Baptiste during the mid-1950s. A truck can be seen in the rear carrying a float and more revelers. (Courtesy of the University of Southern Maine, Lewiston-Auburn College Franco-American Collection.)

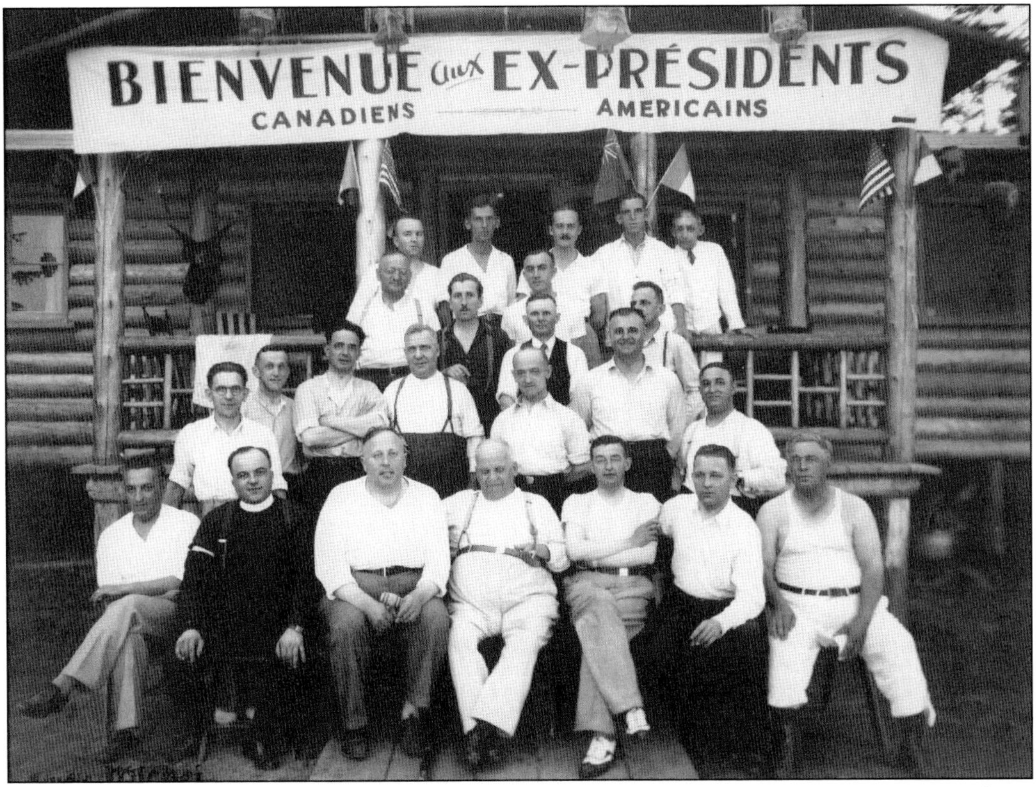

Connections with friends from Québec were ongoing, as this photograph depicting ex-presidents of community clubs suggests. Unlike immigrants from Ireland and Italy, newcomers from Canada could go back and forth easily from the new home to the old country. (Courtesy of the University of Southern Maine, Lewiston-Auburn College Franco-American Collection.)

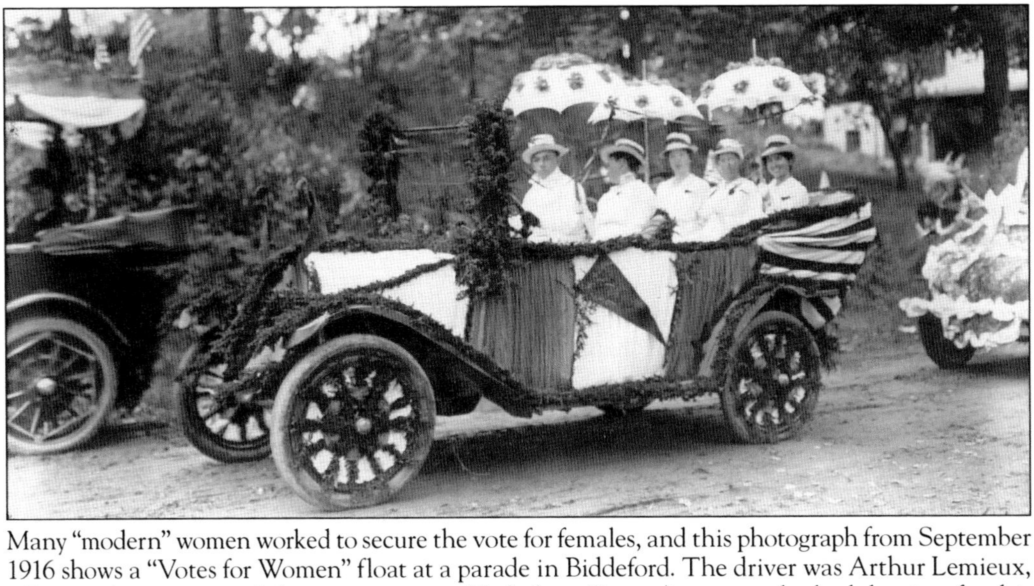

Many "modern" women worked to secure the vote for females, and this photograph from September 1916 shows a "Votes for Women" float at a parade in Biddeford. The driver was Arthur Lemieux, a Franco-American, and the passengers are likely (non-Franco) women who had the time for this type of political activity. (Courtesy of the McArthur Public Library.)

The staff at *Le Messager* in Lewiston takes a break. The newspaper was a French-language publication that united the community and kept residents informed of public events. Many first-generation Franco-Americans read little English, so it was helpful to have a French paper to provide news and commentary. (Courtesy of the University of Southern Maine, Lewiston-Auburn College Franco-American Collection.)

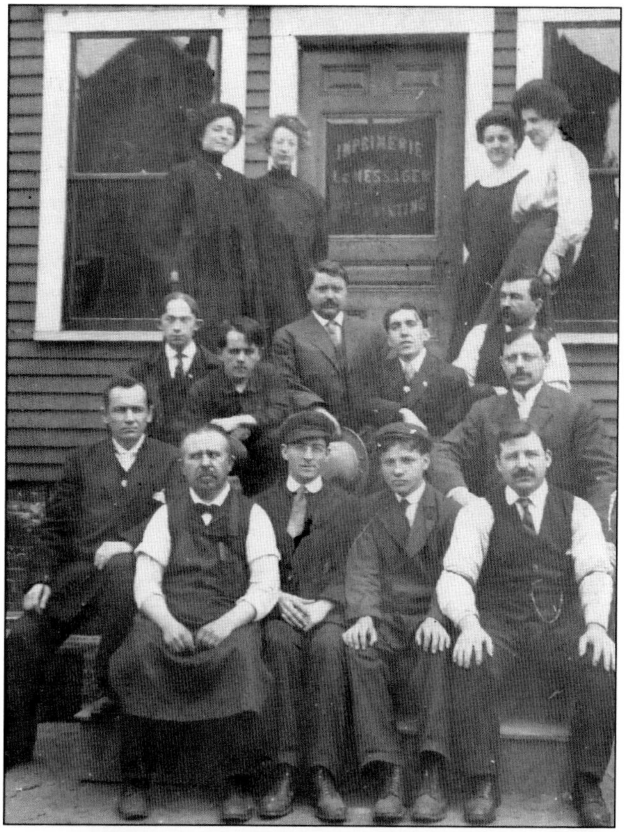

Le Club Passe-Temps Drum and Bugle Corps marches in a 1948 parade in Lewiston's Kennedy Park. One of the organizers was Bert Dutil, who played the glockenspiel. The Dutil family was a leader in planning parades and managing the activities of snowshoe clubs. (Courtesy of the University of Southern Maine, Lewiston-Auburn College Franco-American Collection.)

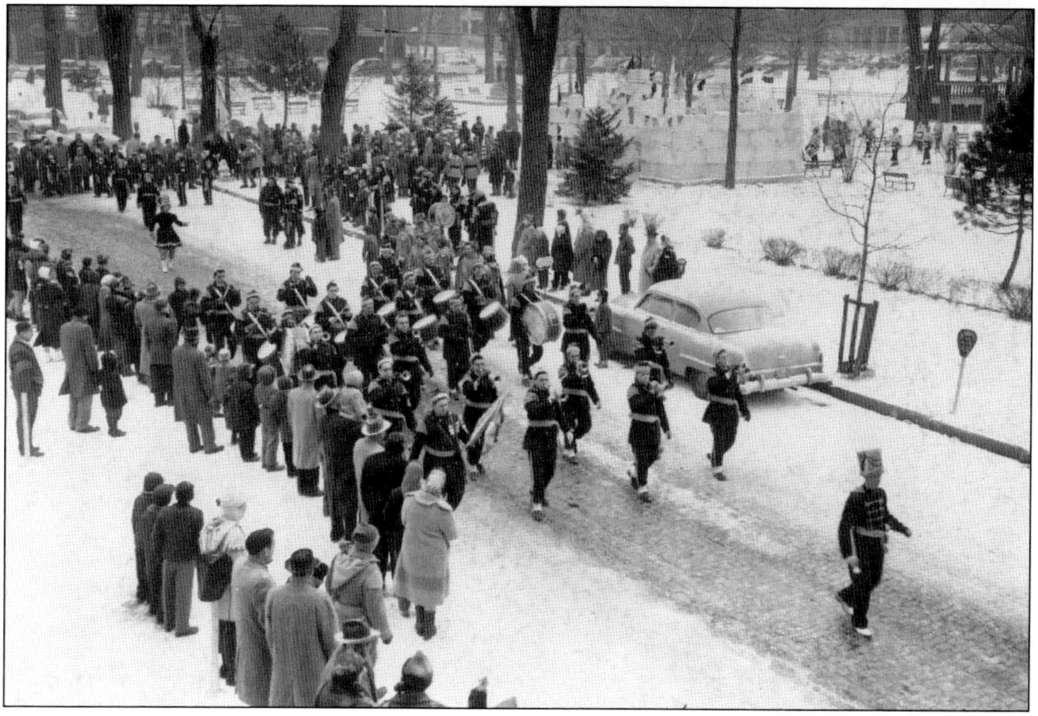

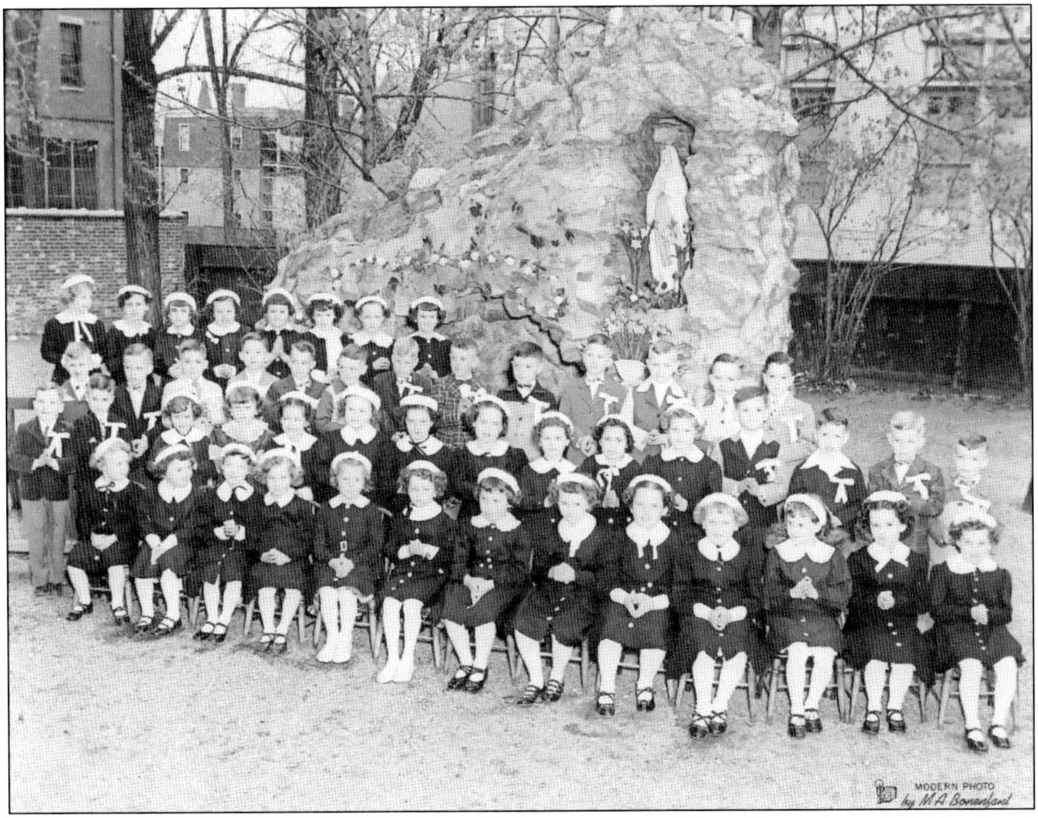

Parochial schools united youngsters, many of whom continued friendships through high school and beyond. (Courtesy of the University of Southern Maine, Lewiston-Auburn College Franco-American Collection.)

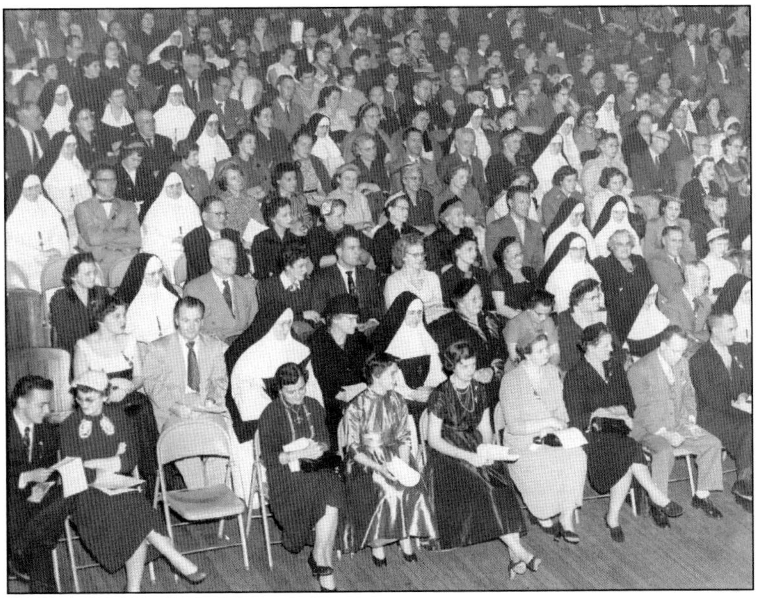

Citizens mixed with members of the church at major community events. Nuns, such as those shown here at a gathering in Lewiston, played a major role in the administration of school systems and educational activities. (Courtesy of the University of Southern Maine, Lewiston-Auburn College Franco-American Collection.)

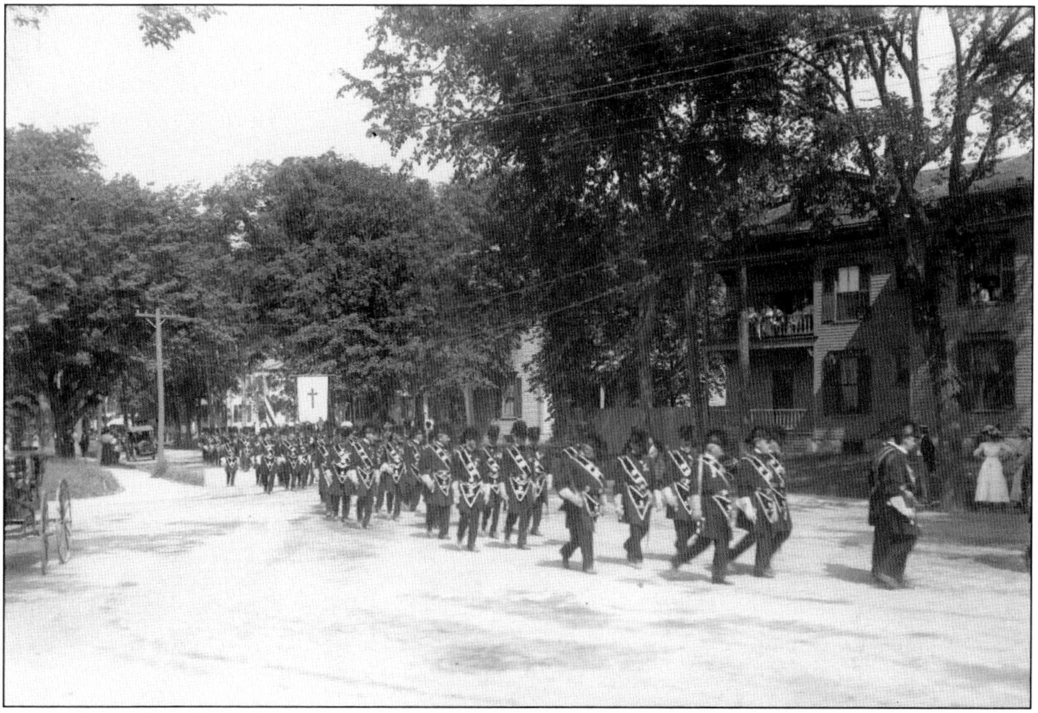

A band marches through Biddeford with a cross visible in the rear section, and spectators gather on porches or along the street. Seen at left are early models of motor cars. (Courtesy of the McArthur Public Library.)

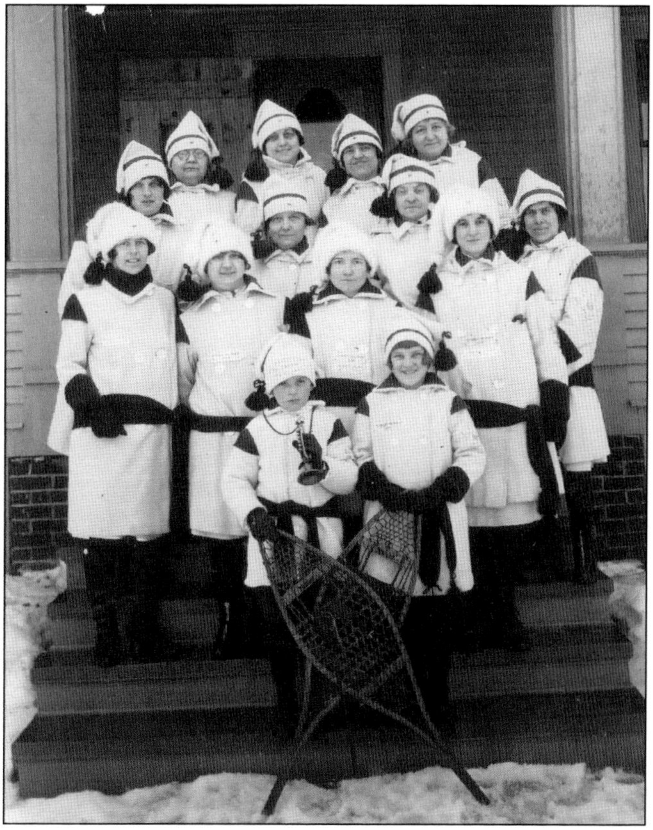

Young women were active in many community activities, including snowshoeing. Here a group poses in their club uniforms. (Courtesy of the University of Southern Maine, Lewiston-Auburn College Franco-American Collection.)

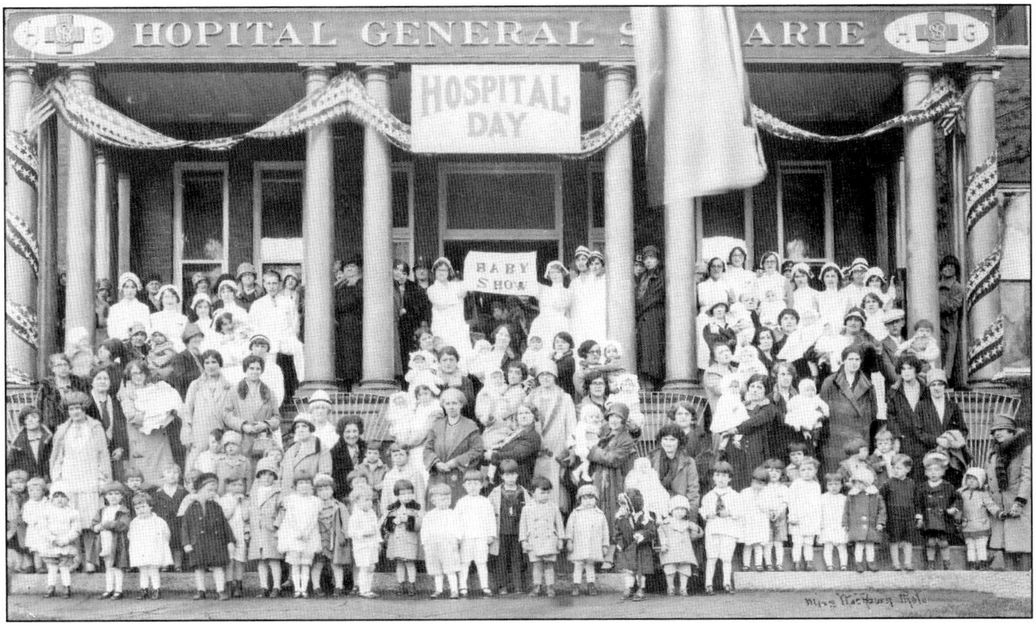

Mothers and their toddlers joined together at the Hospital Day Baby Show in 1926 hosted by the Sisters of Charity, an order from St. Hyacinthe, Québec. In 1889, they founded what was then known as the French hospital, Notre Dame de Lourdes. Today it is the modern St. Mary's Regional Medical Center. (Courtesy of the University of Southern Maine, Lewiston-Auburn College Franco-American Collection.)

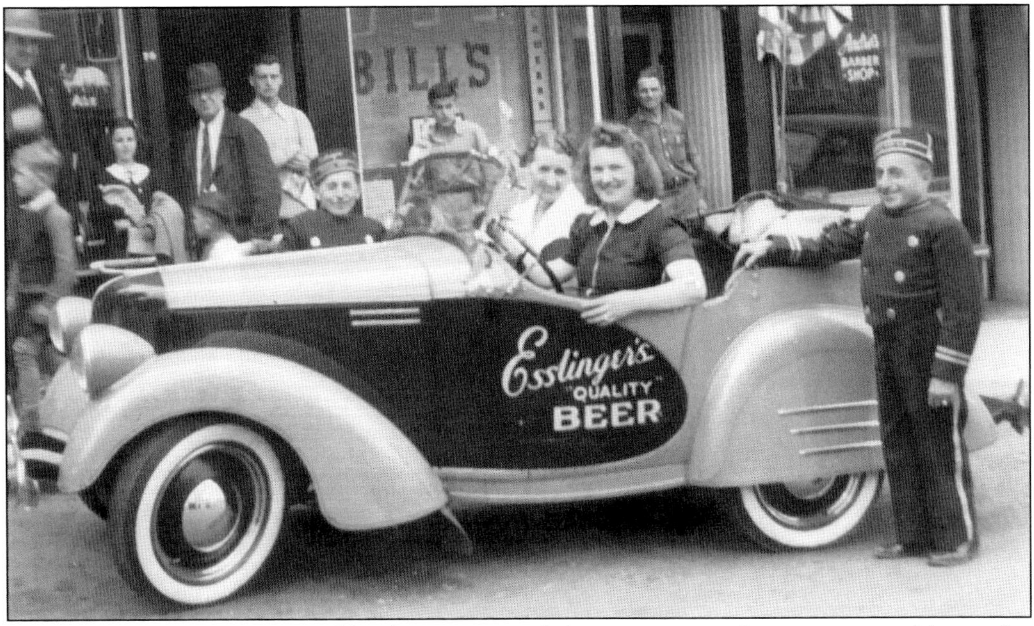

Promoting local business could take on unusual dimensions, as this event to publicize the Carpentier's Store in the 1940s shows. The store was owned by Leo and Germaine Carpentier, and Germaine can be seen at the wheel when the car visited the Broad Street commercial section in New Auburn. The undersized "extras" were imported for the day. (Courtesy of the University of Southern Maine, Lewiston-Auburn College Franco-American Collection.)

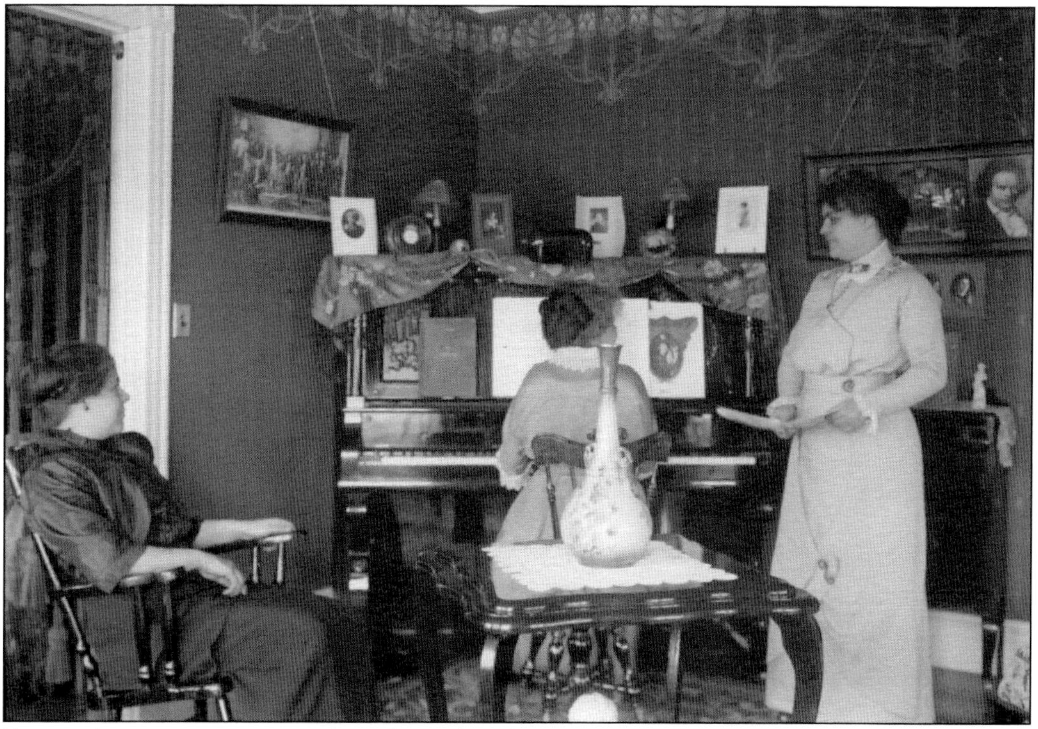

Franco-American women took pride in their homes and in domestic activity. Here are three sisters—from left to right, Marie-Anne Janelle, Victoria Janelle, and Arzelie Janelle—relaxing in a Lewiston living room. (Courtesy of the University of Southern Maine, Lewiston-Auburn College Franco-American Collection.)

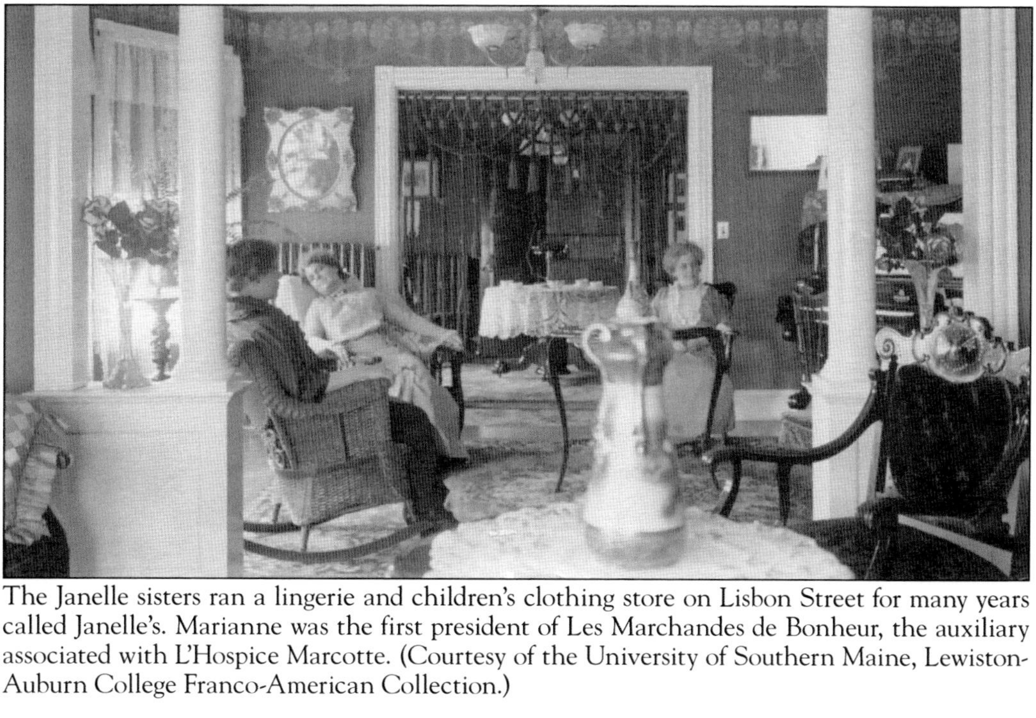

The Janelle sisters ran a lingerie and children's clothing store on Lisbon Street for many years called Janelle's. Marianne was the first president of Les Marchandes de Bonheur, the auxiliary associated with L'Hospice Marcotte. (Courtesy of the University of Southern Maine, Lewiston-Auburn College Franco-American Collection.)

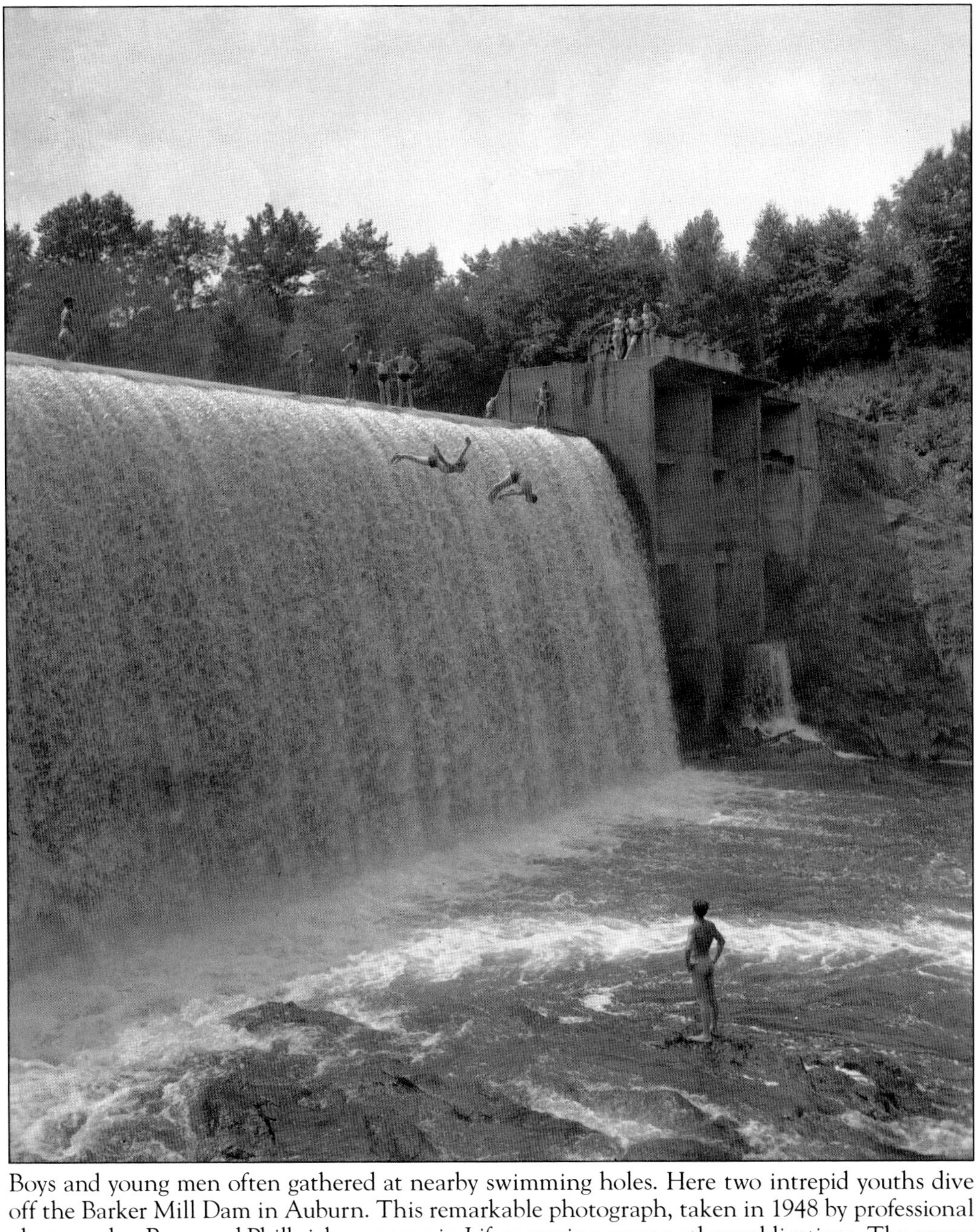

Boys and young men often gathered at nearby swimming holes. Here two intrepid youths dive off the Barker Mill Dam in Auburn. This remarkable photograph, taken in 1948 by professional photographer Raymond Philbrick, was seen in *Life* magazine among other publications. The young divers are Norman Goulet (left) and Raymond Cote. (Photograph by Raymond H. Philbrick, courtesy of Dan Philbrick.)

Five

Sports and Recreation

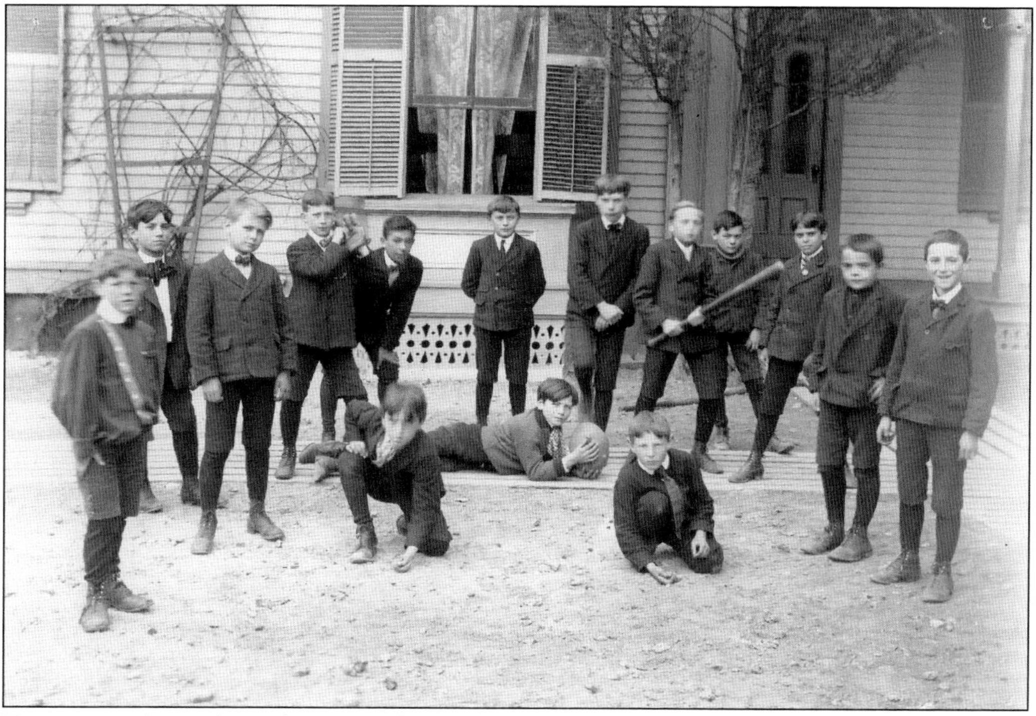

Team sports have always been popular in the Franco-American community. Here are boys at Lewiston's St. Peter's School in 1925 representing a variety of sports, including marbles, which is depicted by youngsters in the front row. (Courtesy of the University of Southern Maine, Lewiston-Auburn College Franco-American Collection.)

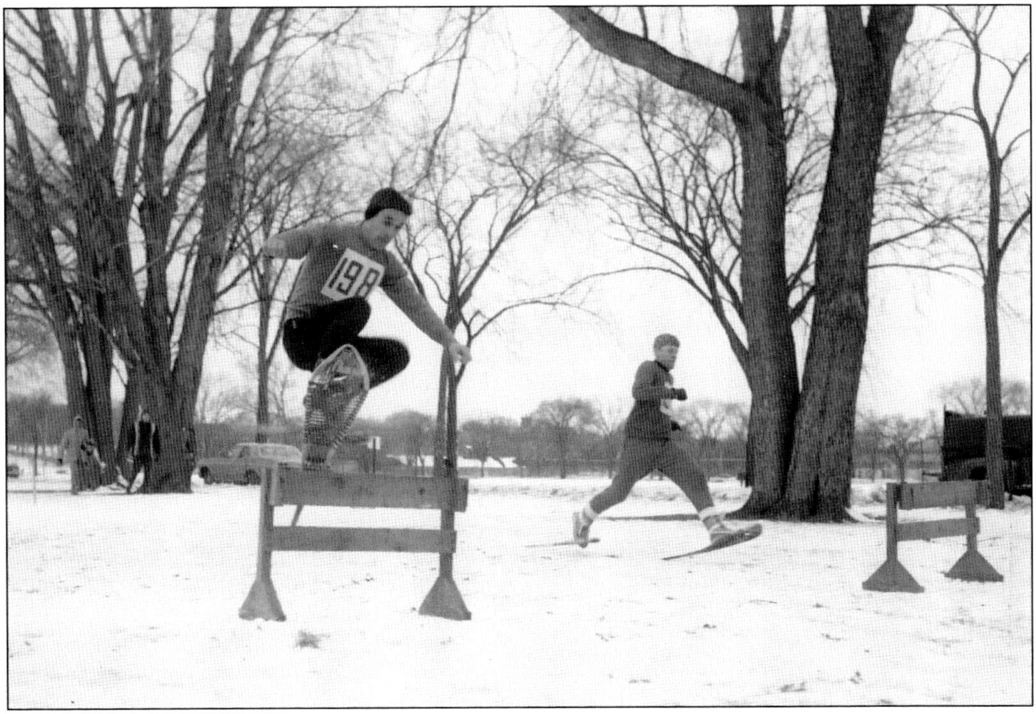

Snowshoe competitions involved sprints, distance events, and hurdle races, as shown here. Athletes came from Canada as well as other Maine towns and cities to compete. (Courtesy of the University of Southern Maine, Lewiston-Auburn College Franco-American Collection.)

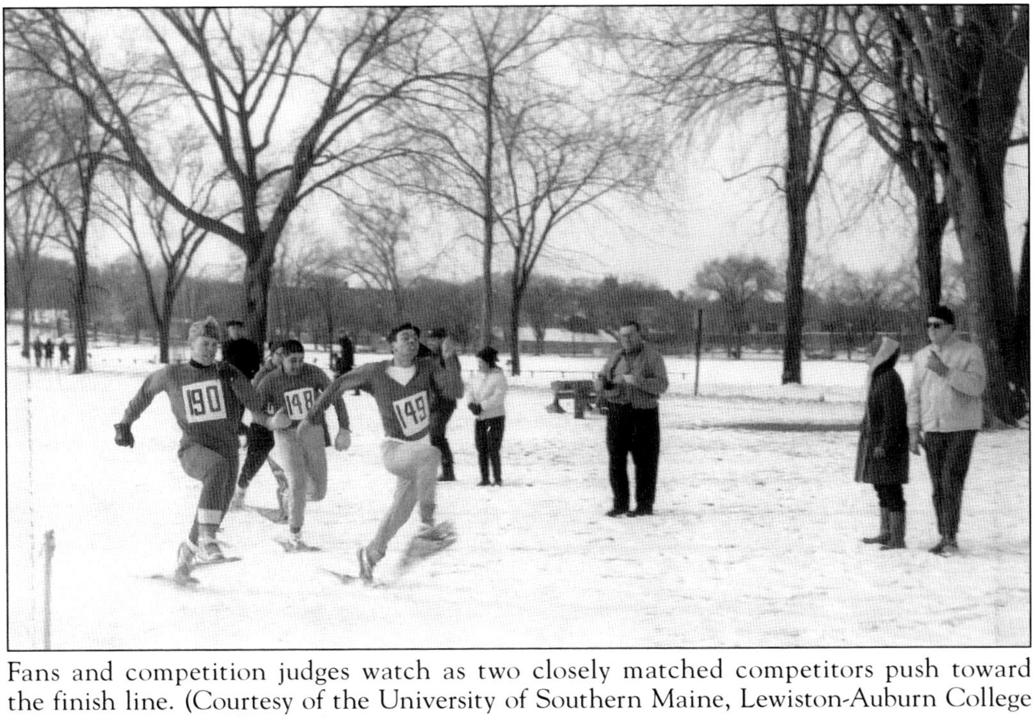

Fans and competition judges watch as two closely matched competitors push toward the finish line. (Courtesy of the University of Southern Maine, Lewiston-Auburn College Franco-American Collection.)

Hockey was a sport played throughout Maine mill cities. Dick Lecompte, captain of the 1963 St. Dominic High School (Lewiston) team, is shown here coming to a quick stop in front of teammate Mike Parent. (Photograph by Raymond H. Philbrick, courtesy of Dan Philbrick.)

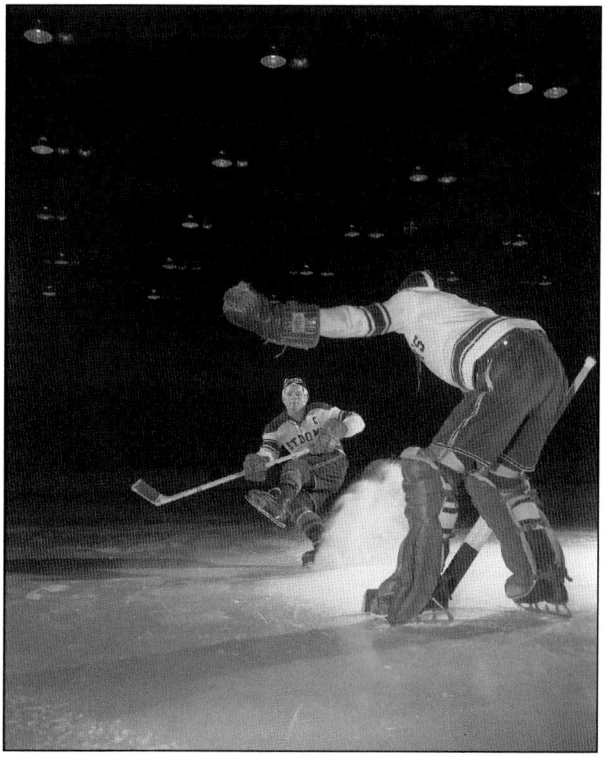

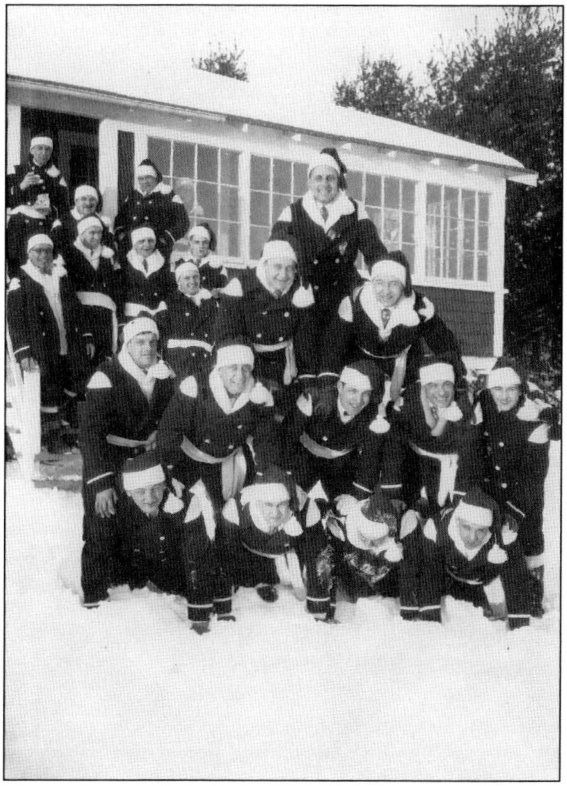

Not all activities at a snowshoe convention weekend were of a competitive nature. Here are snowshoers socializing outside a small cottage in Lewiston that was used as a hospitality center. (Courtesy of the University of Southern Maine, Lewiston-Auburn College Franco-American Collection.)

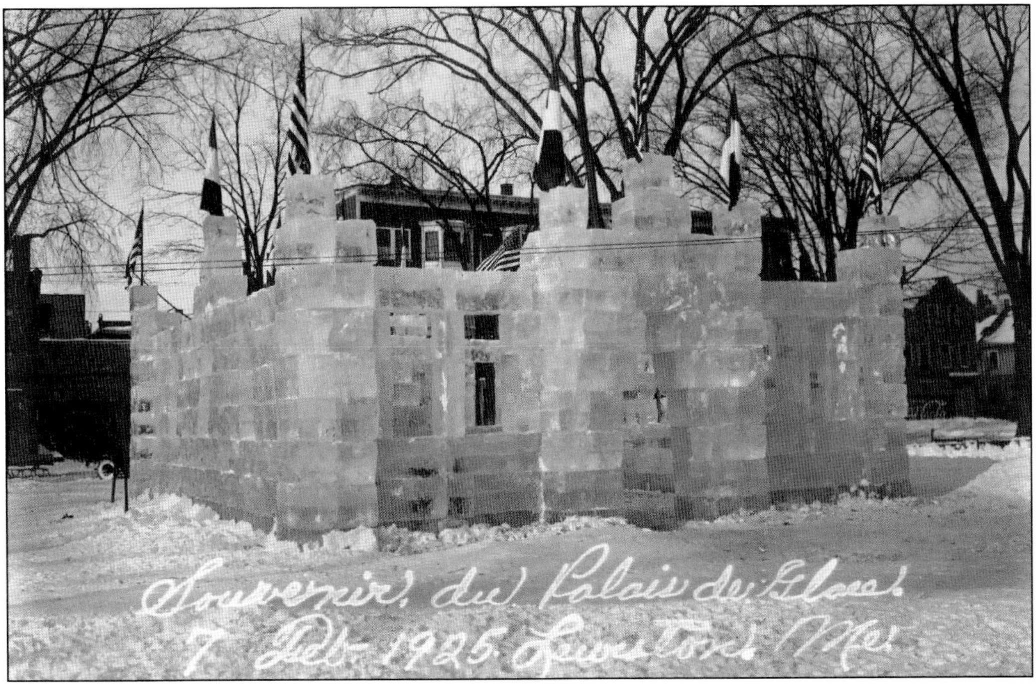

Ice palaces were sometimes built in city parks within walking distance of snowshoe competitions, such as this edifice in the snow in 1925. (Courtesy of the University of Southern Maine, Lewiston-Auburn College Franco-American Collection.)

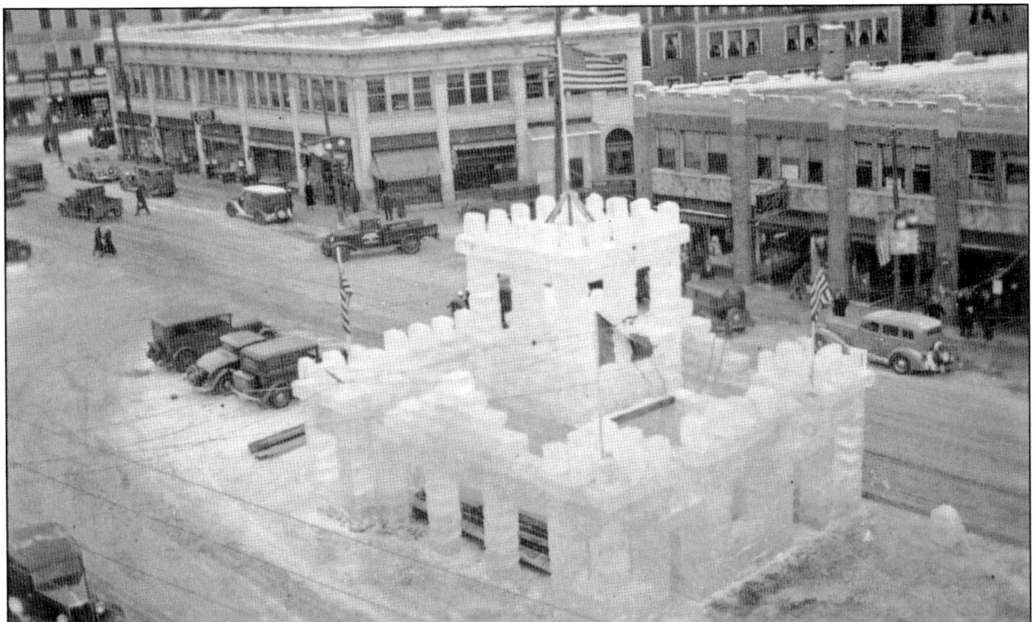

This castle was built in 1926 on Main Street in Lewiston, near the intersection of Lisbon Street. Members of snowshoe convention committees were in charge of putting up the structures, and this was an activity that could be pursued by those who did not actually do the snowshoeing. (Courtesy of the University of Southern Maine, Lewiston-Auburn College Franco-American Collection.)

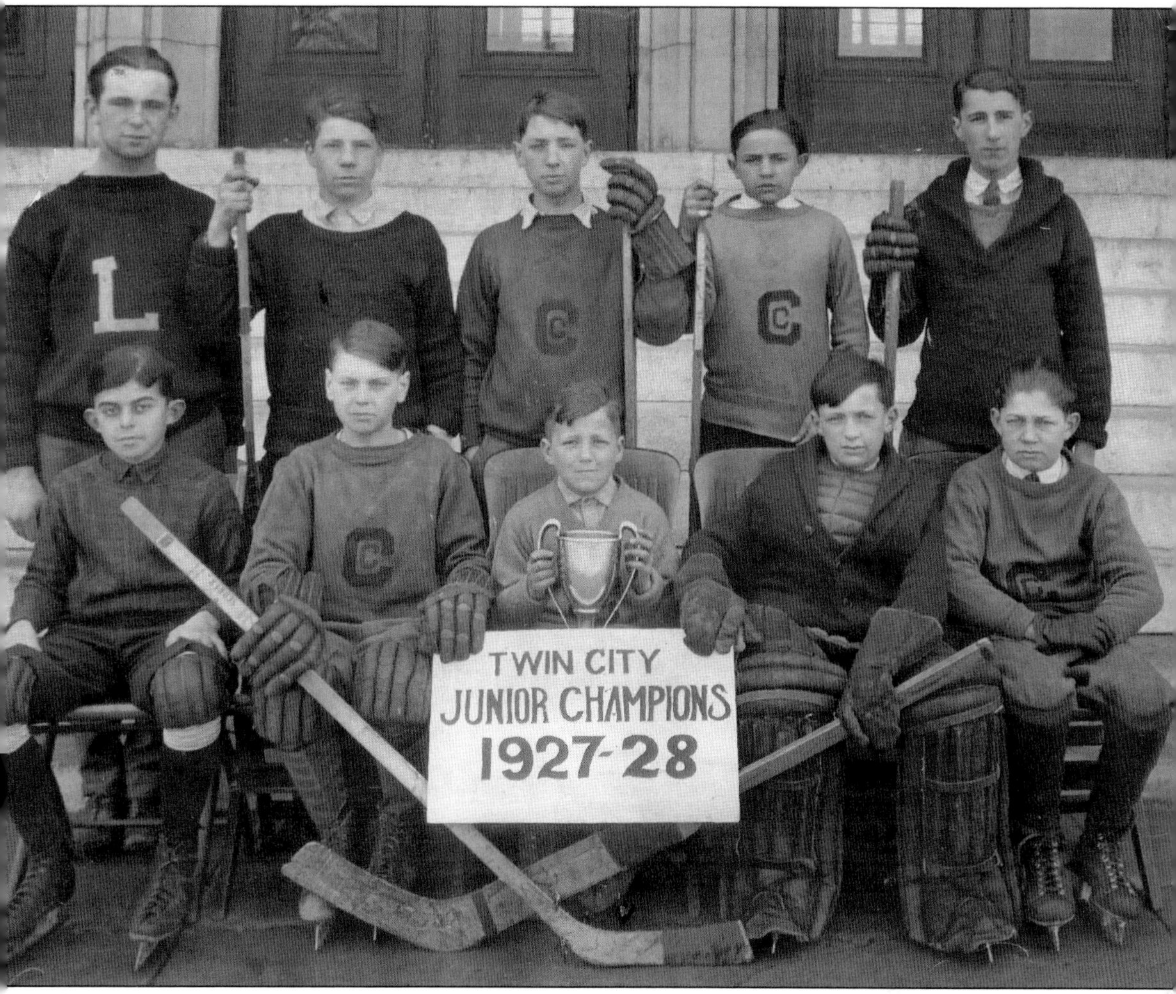

The Cyclones, a legendary Franco-American hockey team in Lewiston, was organized by J. B. Macotte in 1926. This photograph shows the squad after winning its second consecutive junior championship. (Courtesy of the University of Southern Maine, Lewiston-Auburn College Franco-American Collection.)

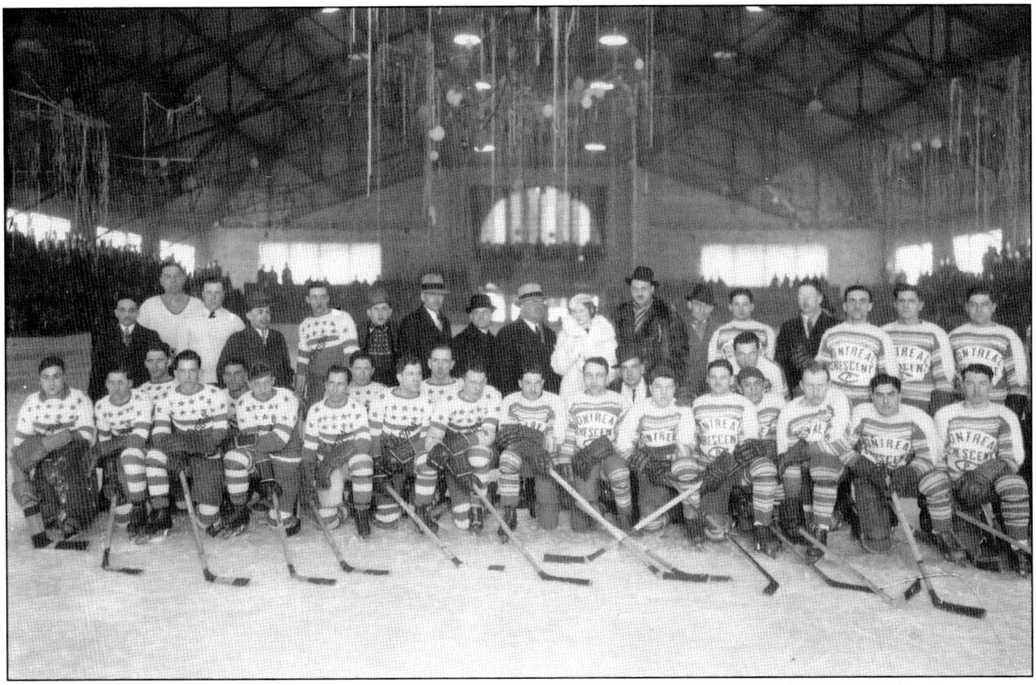

The players on the right in this photograph were from Montreal, and they played a Lewiston team at an indoor center in Lewiston. Canadian teams often came to Maine communities for games and vice versa. (Courtesy of the University of Southern Maine, Lewiston-Auburn College Franco-American Collection.)

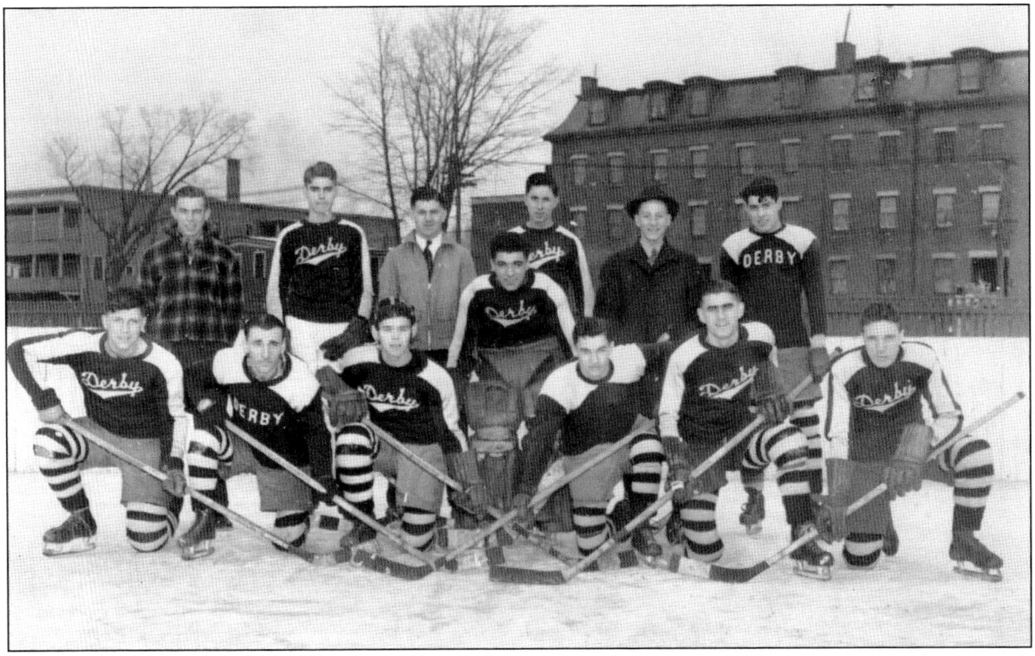

Franco-Americans were hardy athletes and often competed on outdoor rinks, as this photograph indicates. (Courtesy of the University of Southern Maine, Lewiston-Auburn College Franco-American Collection.)

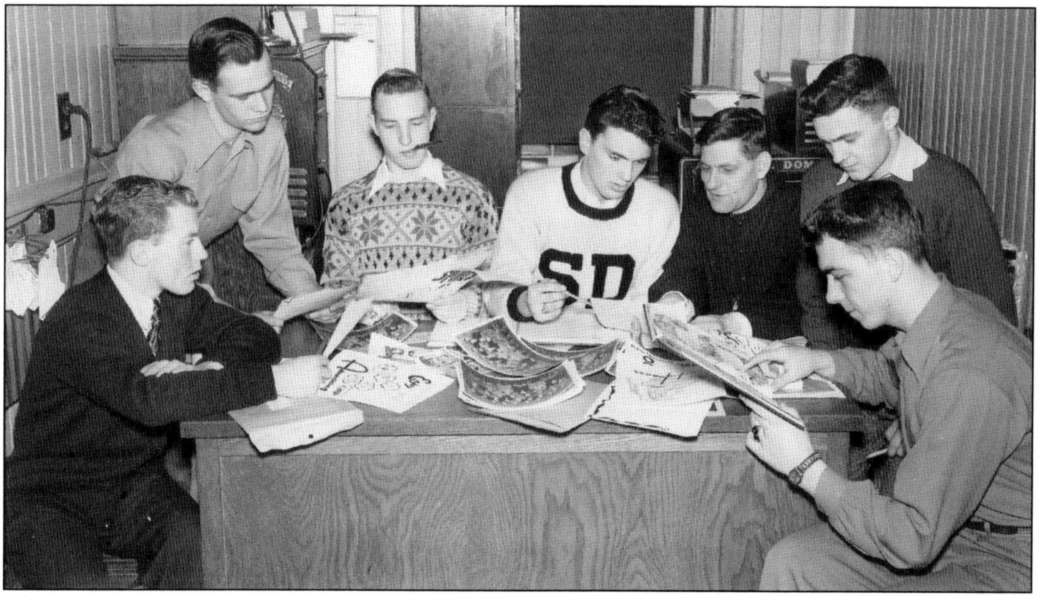

Chronicling the sports and activities at the school level were the writers of school newspapers and yearbooks. Here is the St. Dominic High School Yearbook Committee in 1950. From left to right are Donald Martin, Donald Langlois, Normand Vallee, Joseph Chabot, Brother Fernand, Gerard Tetu, and Robert Albert. (Courtesy of the University of Southern Maine, Lewiston-Auburn College Franco-American Collection.)

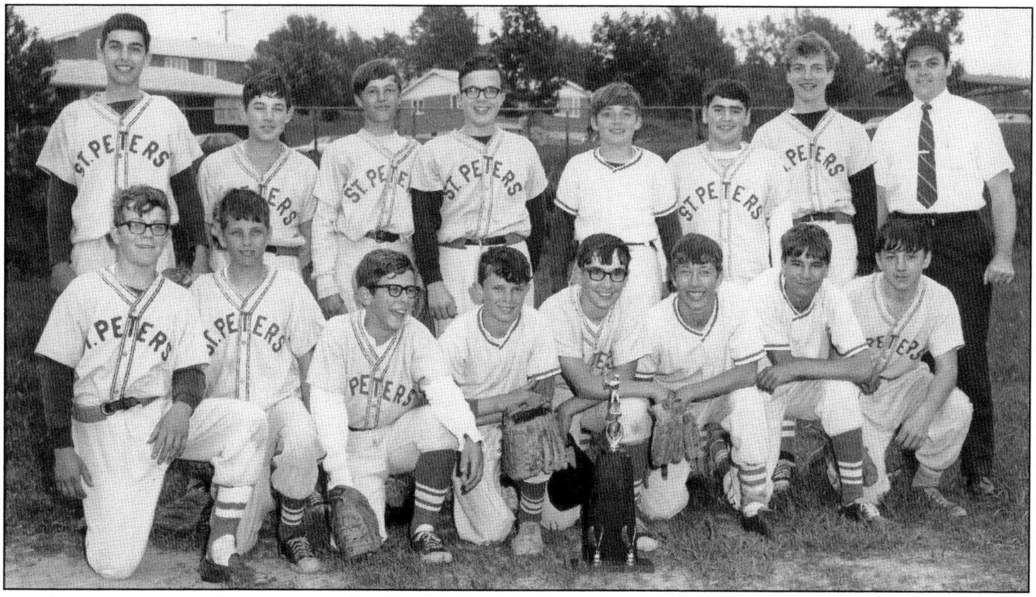

Baseball was a popular sport in the Franco-American community. Here is the St. Peter's School team of Lewiston in 1970, and just about every player has a smile on his face. From left to right are (first row) Ron Tardif, Paul Roy, Roger "Flip" Philippon, Ricky St. Laurent, Steve Ouellette, Dave Martin, Ryan Saucier, and Raymond Goulet; (second row) Mike Courschesne, Donald Mercier, Marc Casavant, Dick Perron, Paul Ouellette, Jimmy Custeau, Bob Levesque, and Roland "Junior" Perreault. (Courtesy of the University of Southern Maine, Lewiston-Auburn College Franco-American Collection.)

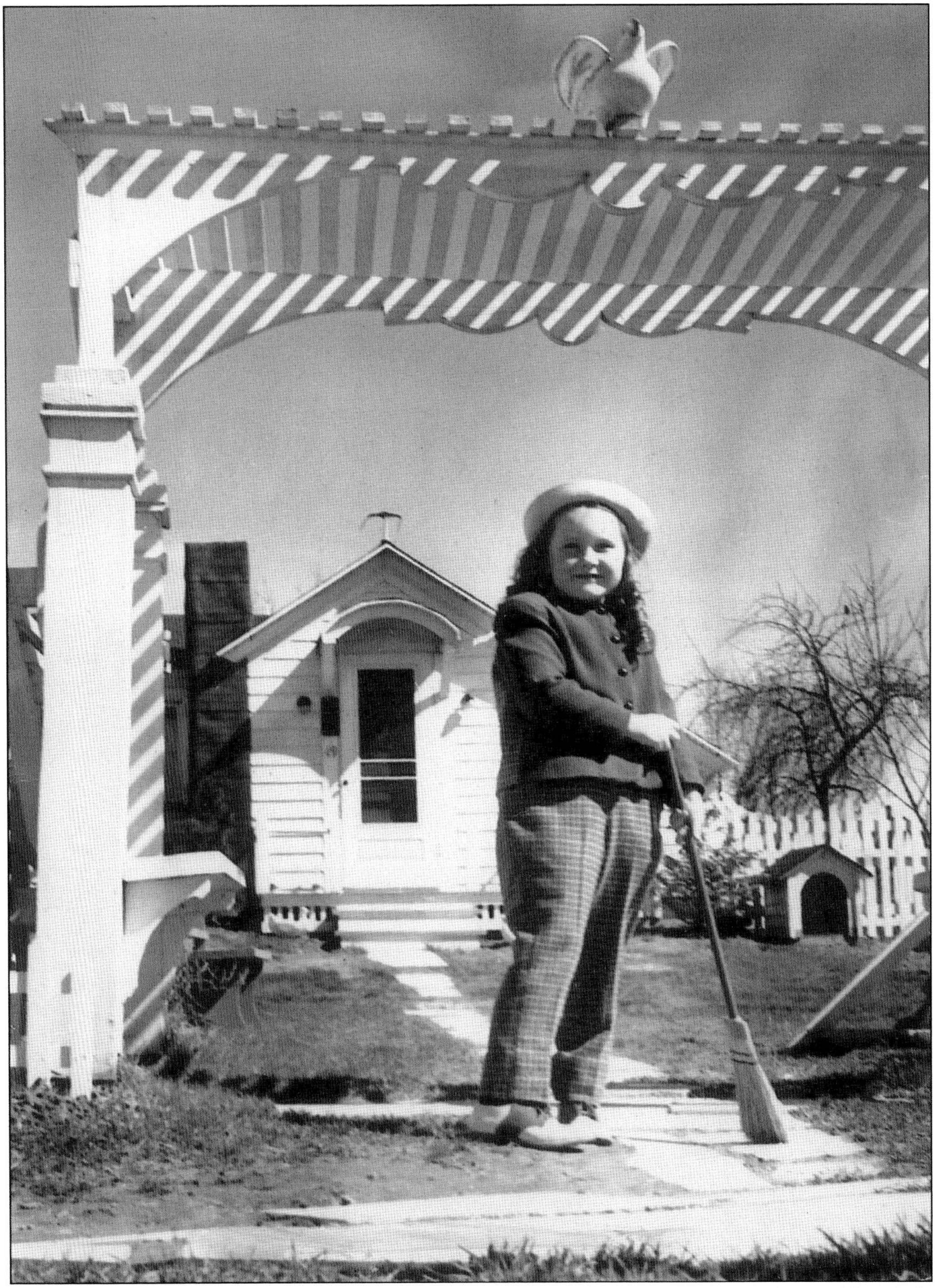

Mercedes Caron, a youngster here in 1948, stands in front of a playhouse built for her and her dolls in Lewiston. However, the rental market was so tight after World War II that the child never got to use the structure for recreation. It was leased to local workers who needed housing. (Courtesy of the University of Southern Maine, Lewiston-Auburn College Franco-American Collection.)

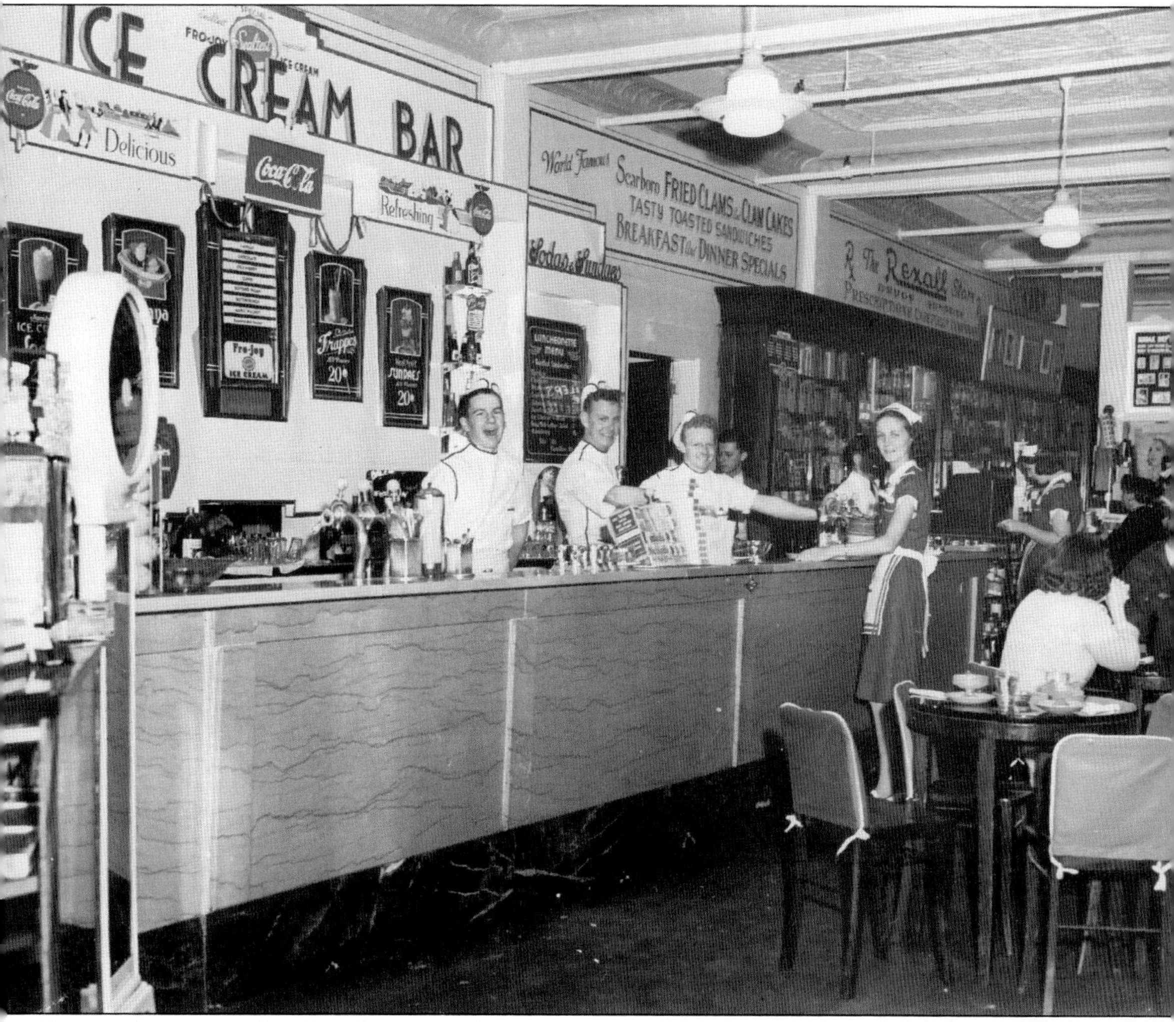

Franco-American families frequented restaurants and ice-cream shops like this one in Lewiston (1940) as they became more prosperous. Many teenagers held after-school jobs at such establishments. (Courtesy of the University of Southern Maine, Lewiston-Auburn College Franco-American Collection.)

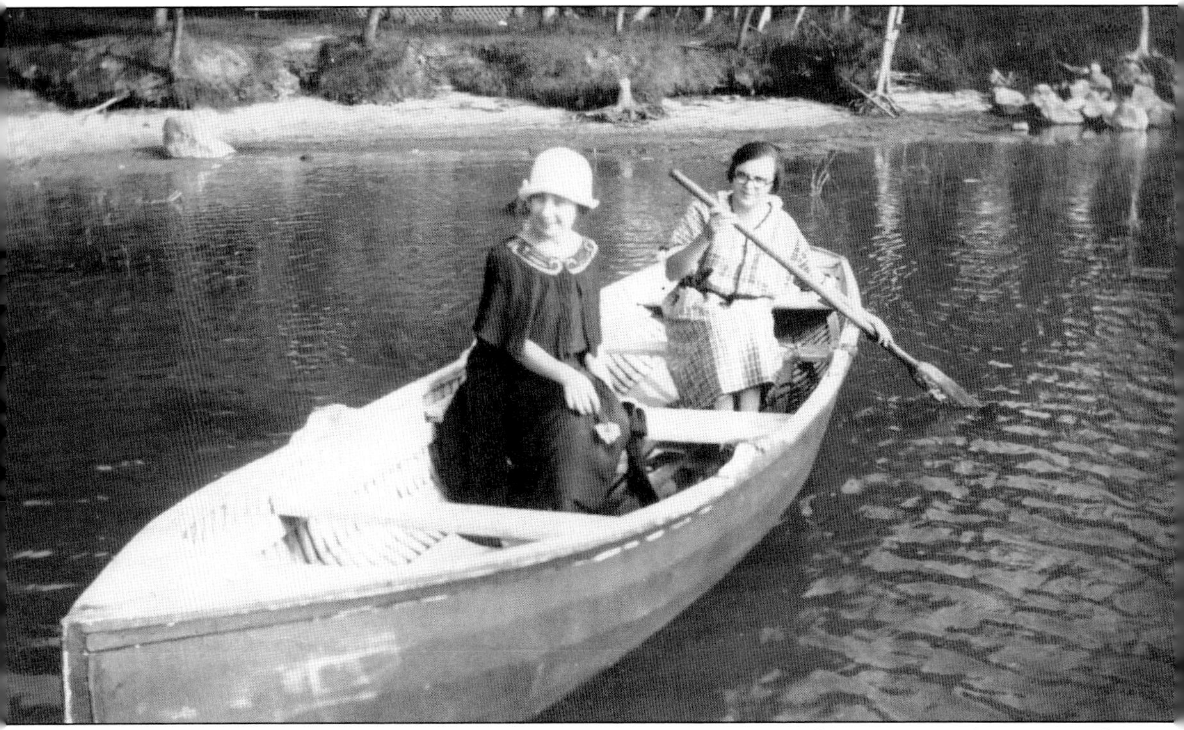

Maine mill communities were adjacent to water, a perfect spot for recreational outings. This 1925 photograph shows Liliane Laurendeau (right), age 17, with Alice Levesque at Lake Grove, a popular recreational site by Lake Auburn. (Courtesy of the University of Southern Maine, Lewiston-Auburn College Franco-American Collection.)

Six

Arts and Entertainment

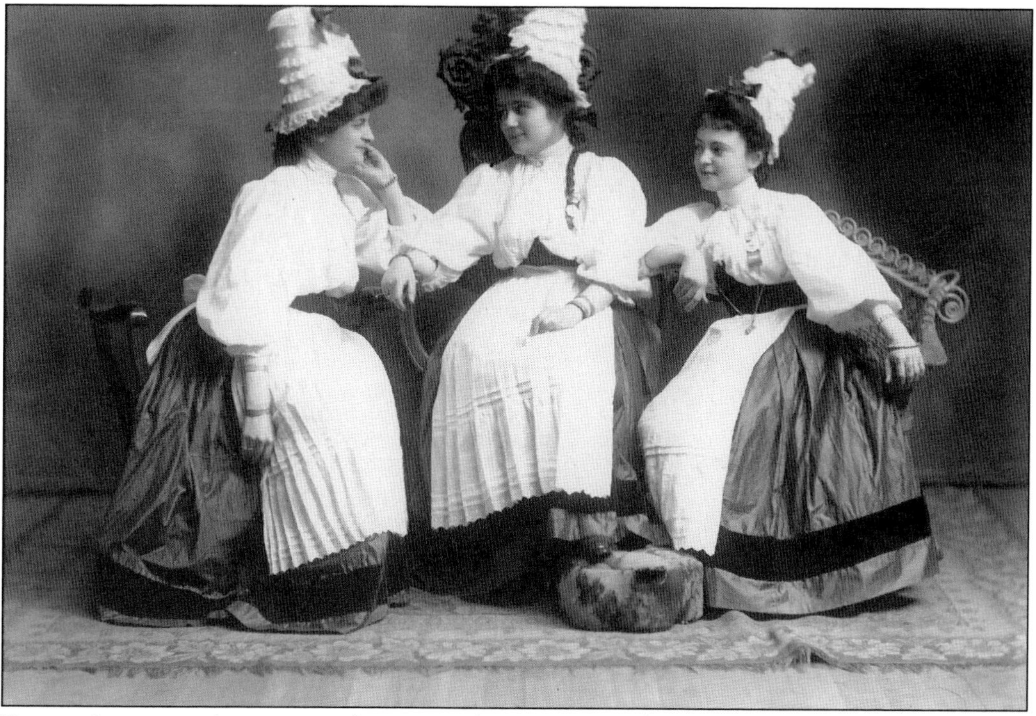

Franco-Americans have enjoyed stage productions since the early days of immigration. Here are three actresses in *Les Cloches de Corneville*, produced in Lewiston in 1896. (Courtesy of the University of Southern Maine, Lewiston-Auburn College Franco-American Collection.)

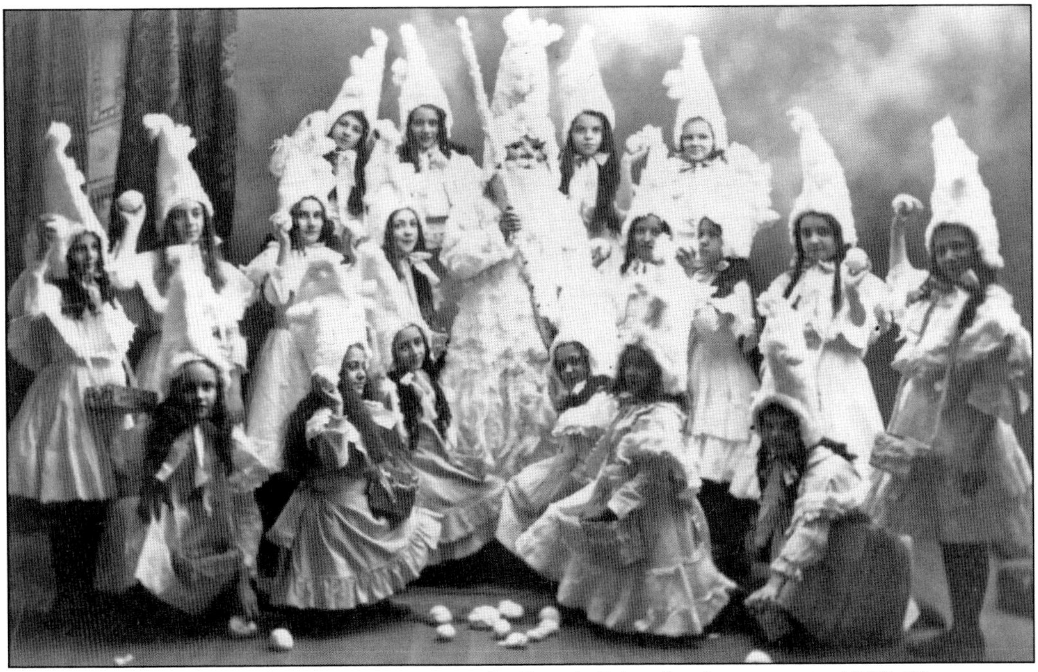

Children dressed for a Christmas pageant at St. Peter's School in Lewiston in 1900. Theater was part of the curriculum at the bilingual school. (Courtesy of the University of Southern Maine, Lewiston-Auburn College Franco-American Collection.)

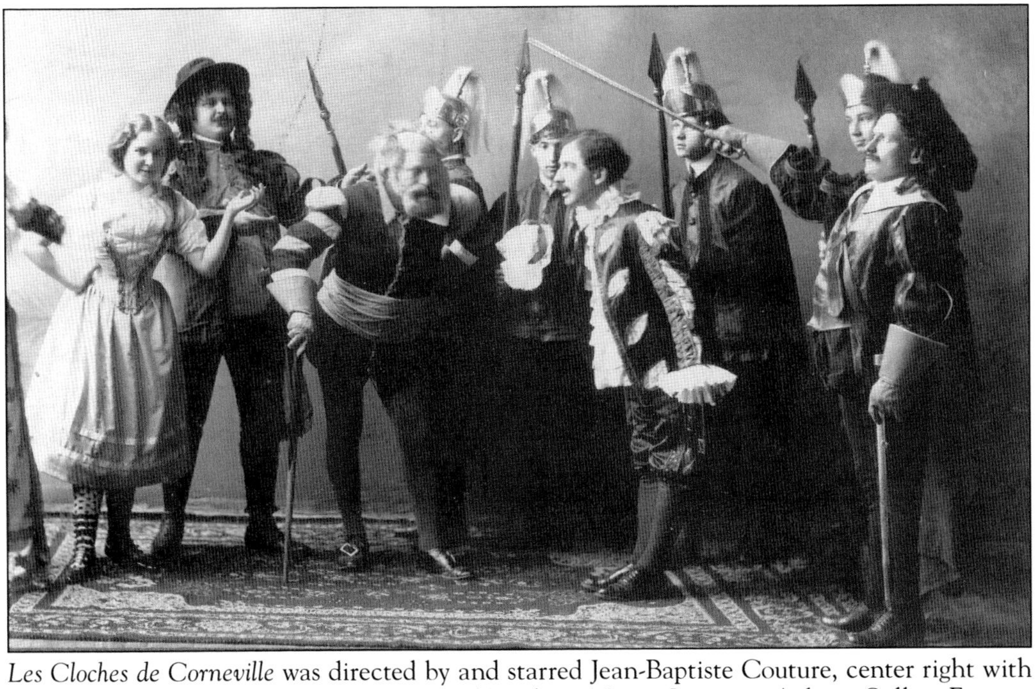

Les Cloches de Corneville was directed by and starred Jean-Baptiste Couture, center right with ruffled sleeves. (Courtesy of the University of Southern Maine, Lewiston-Auburn College Franco-American Collection.)

Jean-Baptiste Couture, seen here without the greasepaint, was a native of Québec. In 1883, he came to the United States, where he joined the French-language newspaper *Le Messager.* Couture (1866–1943) was a leader in the Franco-American arts community of Lewiston-Auburn for five decades. (Courtesy of the University of Southern Maine, Lewiston-Auburn College Franco-American Collection.)

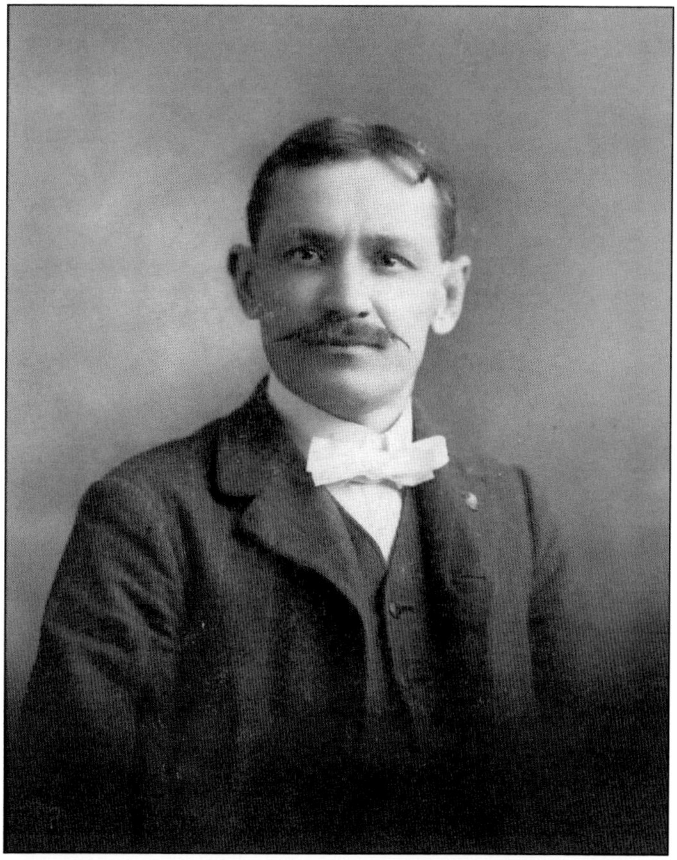

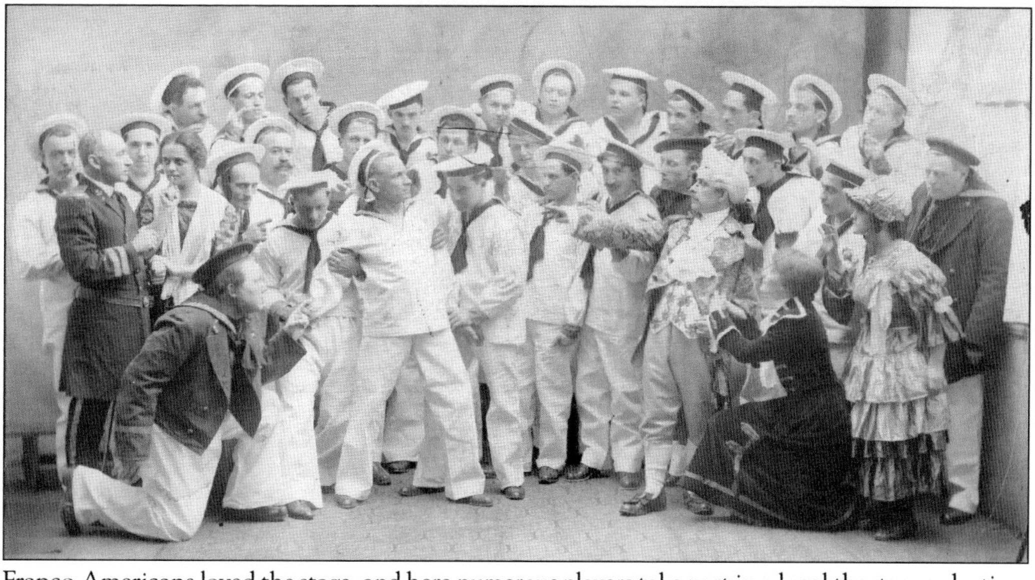

Franco-Americans loved the stage, and here numerous players take part in a local theater production. This is a scene from *L'Amour a Bord*, a 1930s French version of Gilbert and Sullivan's *H.M.S. Pinafore*. (Courtesy of the University of Southern Maine, Lewiston-Auburn College Franco-American Collection.)

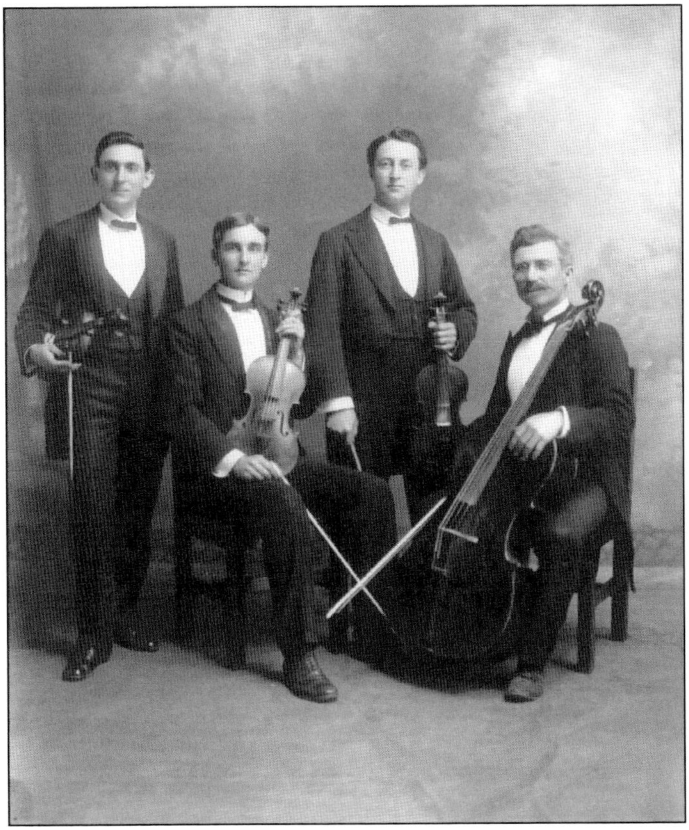

The appreciation of music took many forms in the Franco-American community. Shown here is a Biddeford quartet in the early 20th century: (from left to right) William Simard, Edward Murphy, Frederick Lavigne, and Pierre Painchaud. (Courtesy of the McArthur Public Library.)

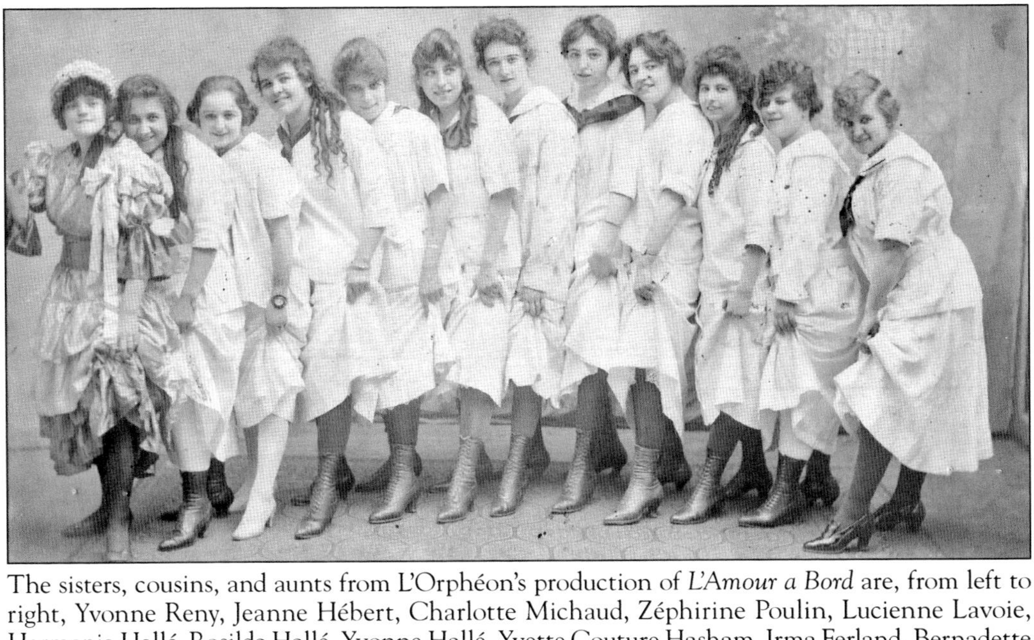

The sisters, cousins, and aunts from L'Orphéon's production of *L'Amour a Bord* are, from left to right, Yvonne Reny, Jeanne Hébert, Charlotte Michaud, Zéphirine Poulin, Lucienne Lavoie, Harmonia Hallé, Rosilda Hallé, Yvonne Hallé, Yvette Couture Hasham, Irma Ferland, Bernadette Desjardins, and Marie Guilbeault. (Courtesy of the University of Southern Maine, Lewiston-Auburn College Franco-American Collection.)

Alphonse Coté was a professional musician and the organist and choir director at St. Louis Church in New Auburn. Coté (1876–1933) sang the tenor lead in several local operas, including *Romeo and Juliette*, *Il Trovatore*, *La Traviata*, and *Rigoletto*. He was also an early recording artist for Victor Records. (Courtesy of the University of Southern Maine, Lewiston-Auburn College Franco-American Collection.)

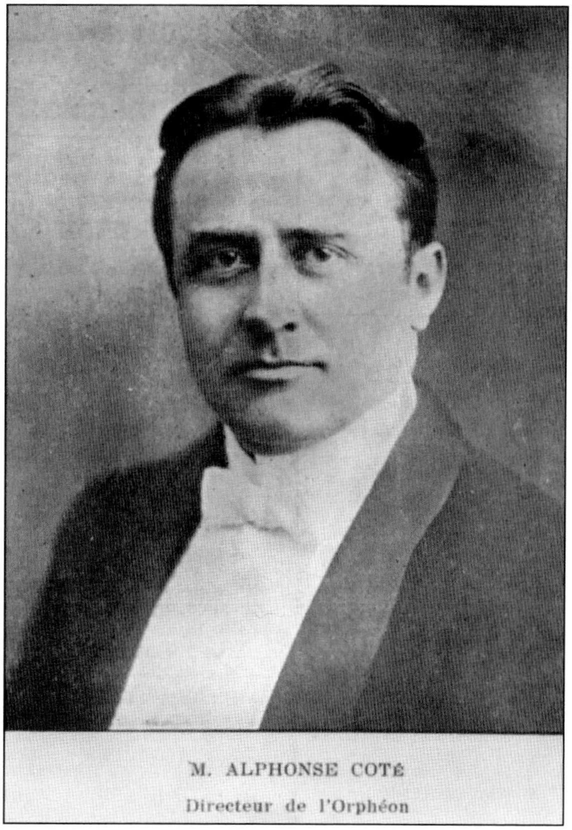

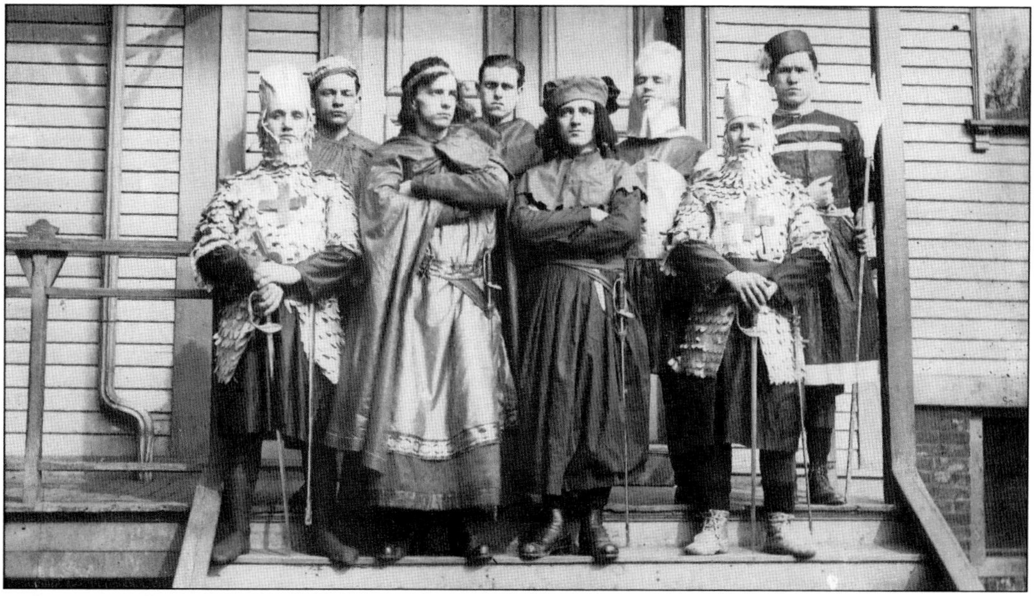

Robert Rumilly, a noted Canadian historian, once referred to Lewiston as "the French Athens of New England" because of its large number of literary and cultural organizations. Les Défenseurs, shown here, was a French Catholic organization that put on many productions. (Courtesy of the University of Southern Maine, Lewiston-Auburn College Franco-American Collection.)

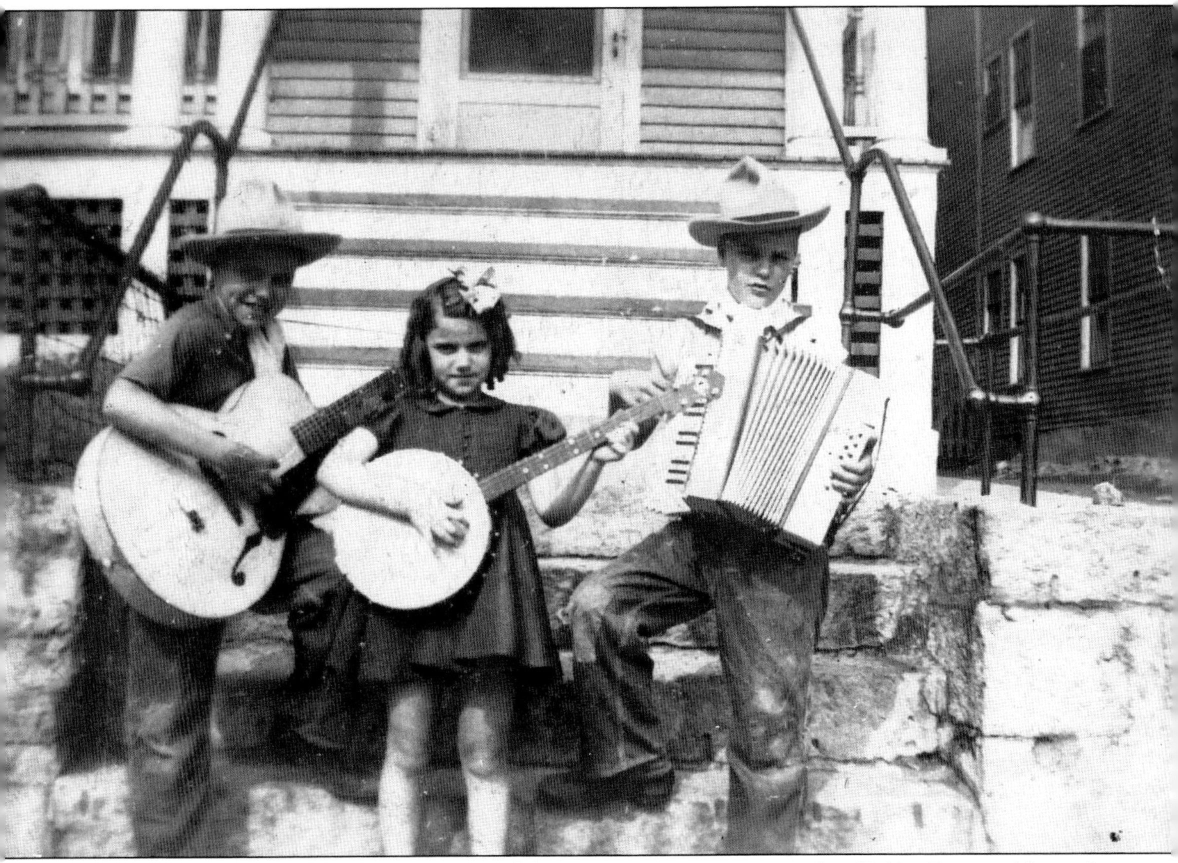

A trio of Tanguays performed at local functions in Lewiston in the 1940s. Pictured here from left to right are Raymond, Giselle, and Maurice Tanguay at the Tanguay residence at 250 Park Street, Lewiston. (Courtesy of the University of Southern Maine, Lewiston-Auburn College Franco-American Collection.)

Fernand Despins, born in 1896, was a gifted performer even as a child. He was a Lewiston native who graduated from St. Charles Borromeo College in Québec and Bates College in Lewiston and from Boston University Law School. He was involved in many stage productions and was a member of Le Club Musical Litteraire, Le Cercle Canadian, and other groups. He was mayor of Lewiston in 1939–1940. (Courtesy of the University of Southern Maine, Lewiston-Auburn College Franco-American Collection.)

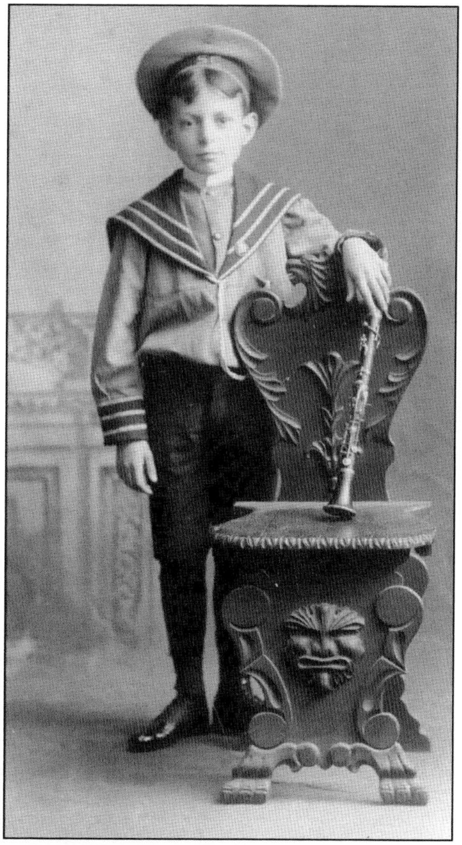

The Jalbert family of Lewiston created the Jalbert Orchestra, shown here in the 1920s. They were the well-trained children of Arthur and Celina Simard Jalbert of Lewiston. In an era before television, children often entertained at home. From left to right are Fern, Germaine, Conrad, Judy, Gertrude, and Gabriel. Not pictured is Louis Jalbert, who later became a major political figure in Maine's Democratic Party. (Courtesy of the University of Southern Maine, Lewiston-Auburn College Franco-American Collection.)

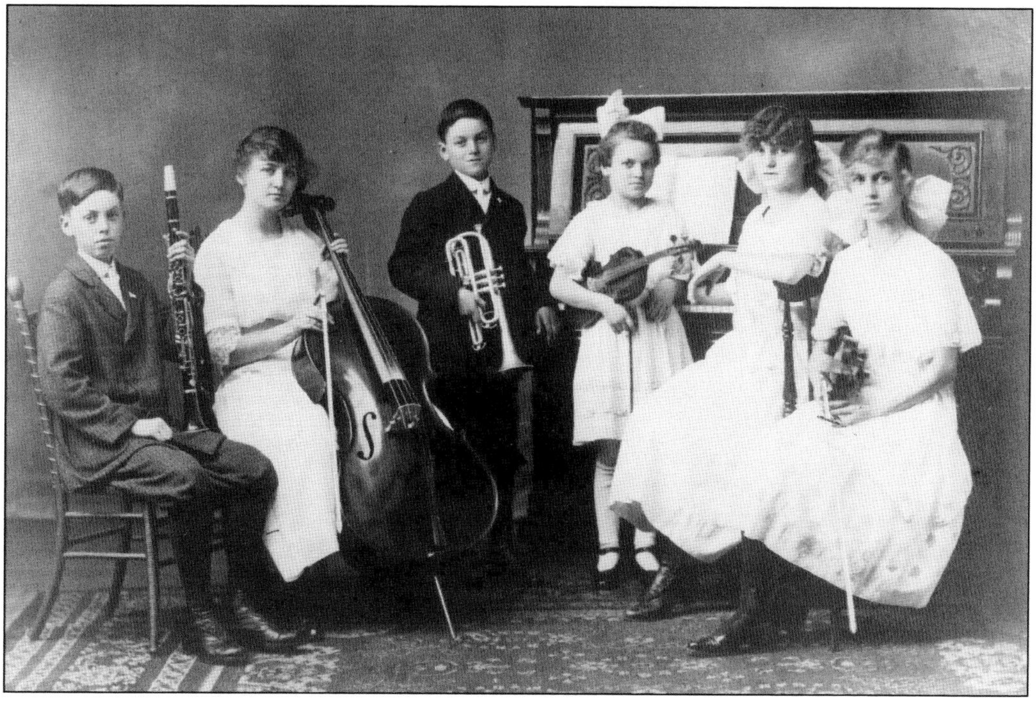

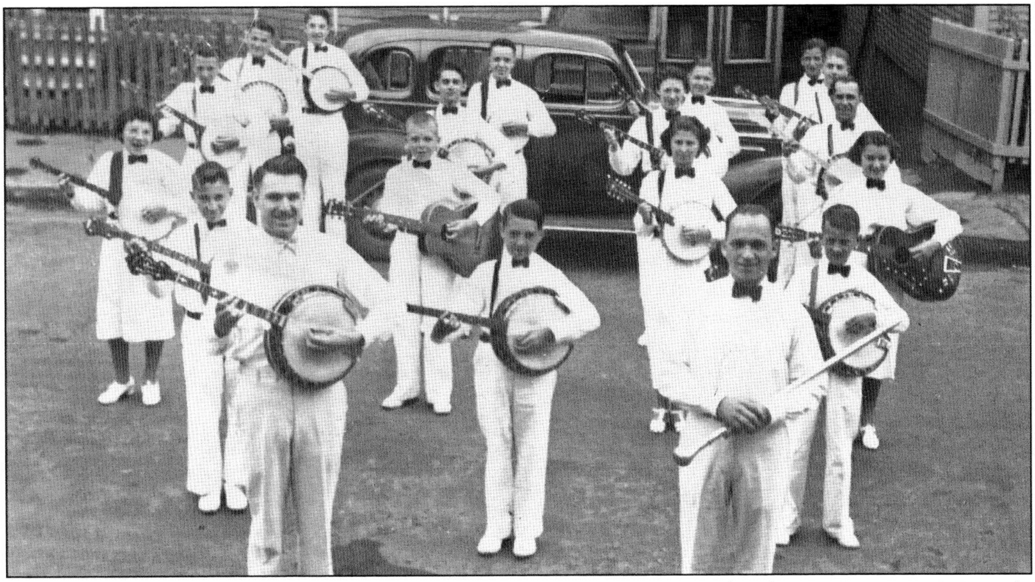

Music was in demand in the 1930s, and here is a 1939 photograph of Leo Gaumont's Parade String Band. Gaumont (1911–1963) taught guitar, banjo, and mandolin to adults and children. His students frequently performed in parades, and the Leo Gaumont Orchestra played French and country tunes for parties and weddings. (Courtesy of the University of Southern Maine, Lewiston-Auburn College Franco-American Collection.)

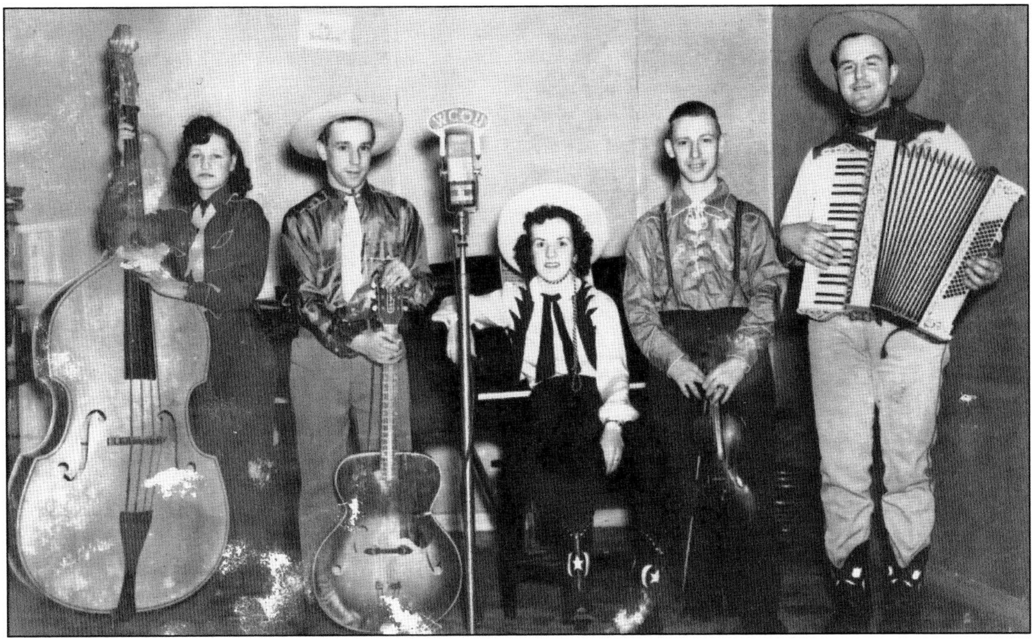

Sylvia and Rosaire Roy were popular musicians in the central Maine area for many years, and their musical group is pictured here in 1949. From left to right are Julie Vallée, Rosaire Labbé, Sylvia Roy (seated), Albert Cyr, and Rosaire Roy. Many young musicians were self-taught and earned extra money playing at weddings, parties, and venues such as the Maple Leaf Club on Lisbon Street in Lewiston. (Courtesy of the University of Southern Maine, Lewiston-Auburn College Franco-American Collection.)

Seven

EDUCATION

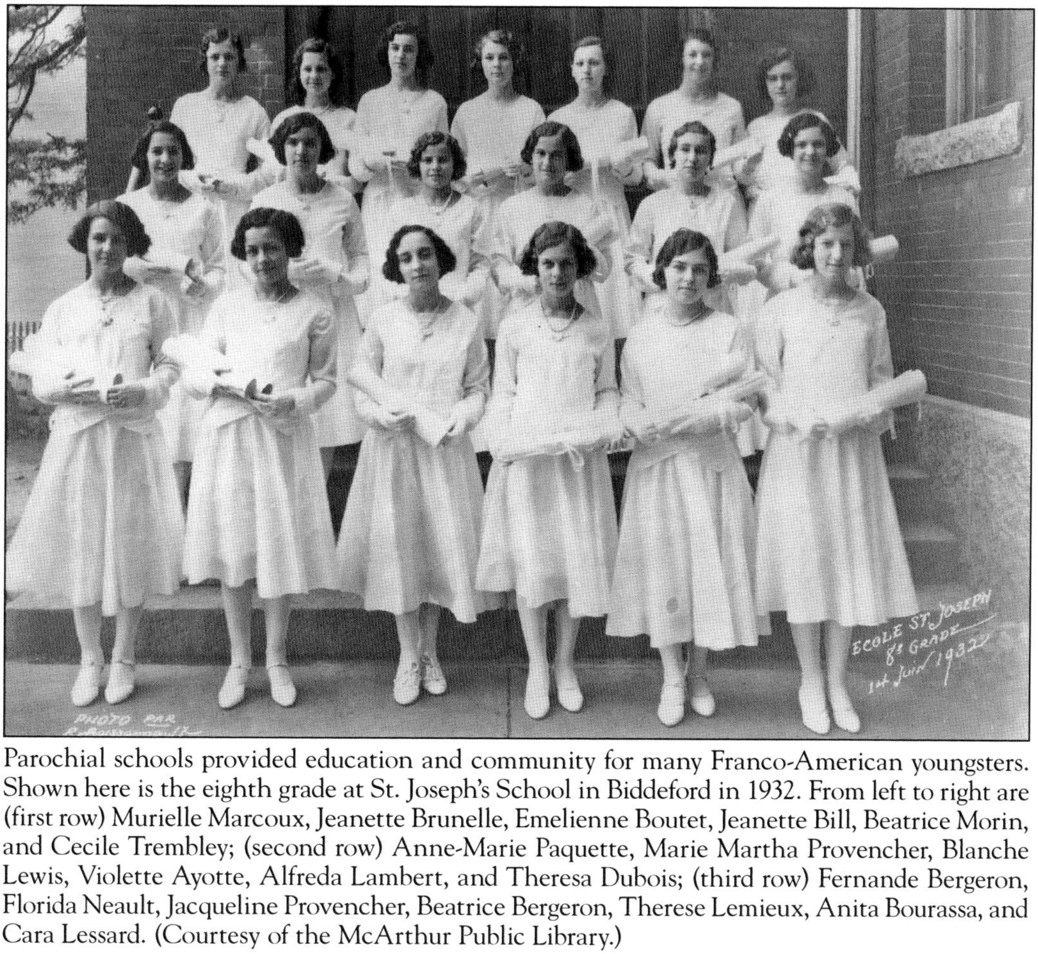

Parochial schools provided education and community for many Franco-American youngsters. Shown here is the eighth grade at St. Joseph's School in Biddeford in 1932. From left to right are (first row) Murielle Marcoux, Jeanette Brunelle, Emelienne Boutet, Jeanette Bill, Beatrice Morin, and Cecile Trembley; (second row) Anne-Marie Paquette, Marie Martha Provencher, Blanche Lewis, Violette Ayotte, Alfreda Lambert, and Theresa Dubois; (third row) Fernande Bergeron, Florida Neault, Jacqueline Provencher, Beatrice Bergeron, Therese Lemieux, Anita Bourassa, and Cara Lessard. (Courtesy of the McArthur Public Library.)

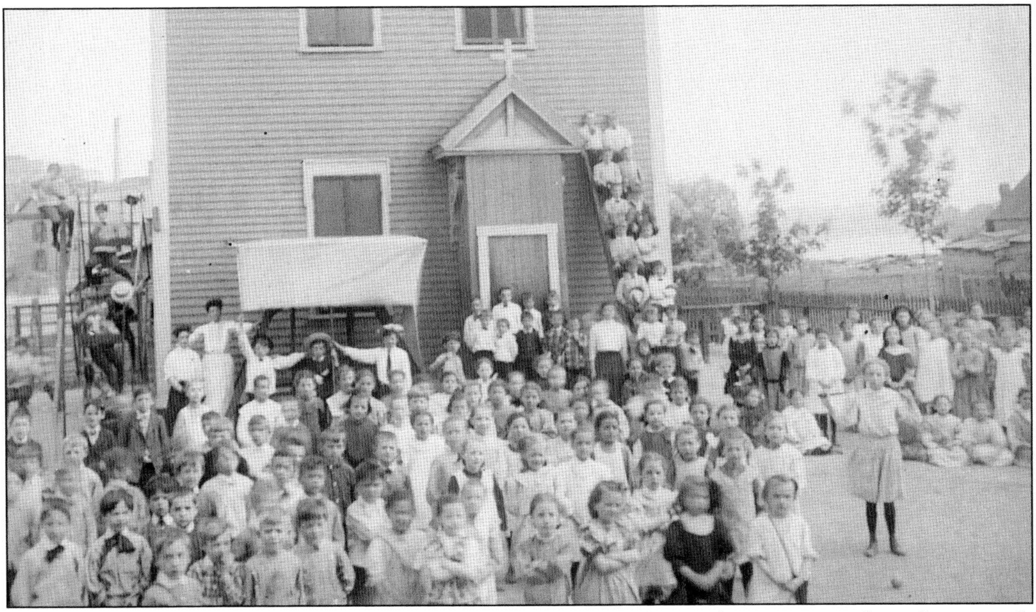

The Lincoln Street French School was well attended in the early 1900s, as this photograph indicates. Lincoln Street was located near Petit Canada or Little Canada. The neighborhood's proximity to the Grand Trunk Railroad Station on Lincoln Street and the textile mills made it easier for new immigrants from Canada to adjust. (Courtesy of the University of Southern Maine, Lewiston-Auburn College Franco-American Collection.)

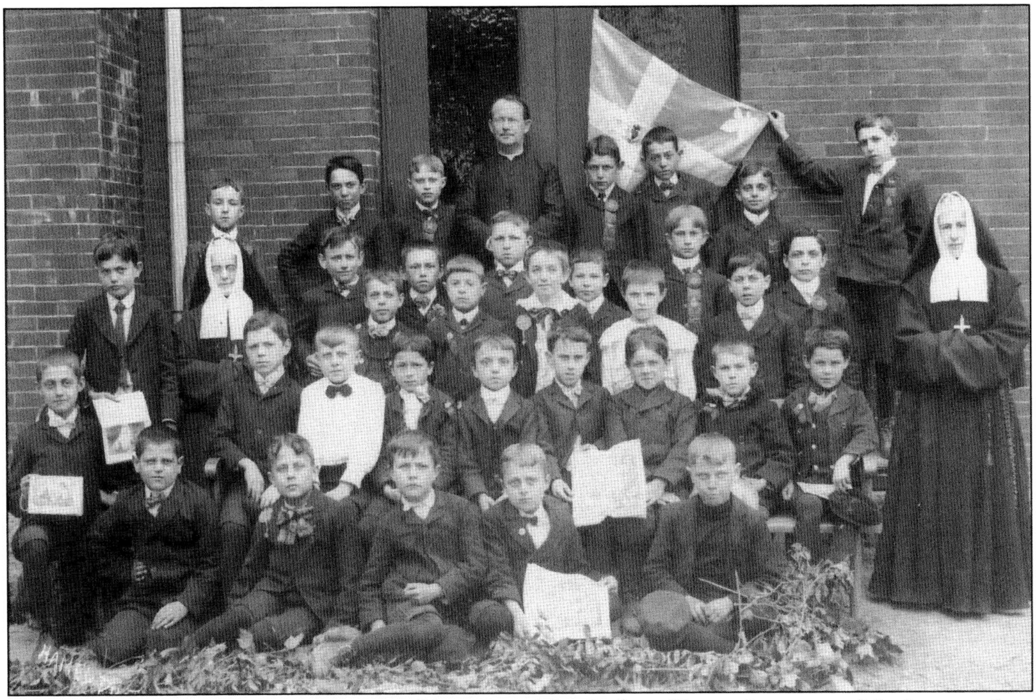

St. Andre School pupils were supervised by nuns of the Order of Sister Servants of the Immaculate Heart of Mary. A flag reflecting appreciation of their French heritage can be seen in the background of this 1900 photograph. (Courtesy of Dr. Norman Beaupre and the McArthur Public Library.)

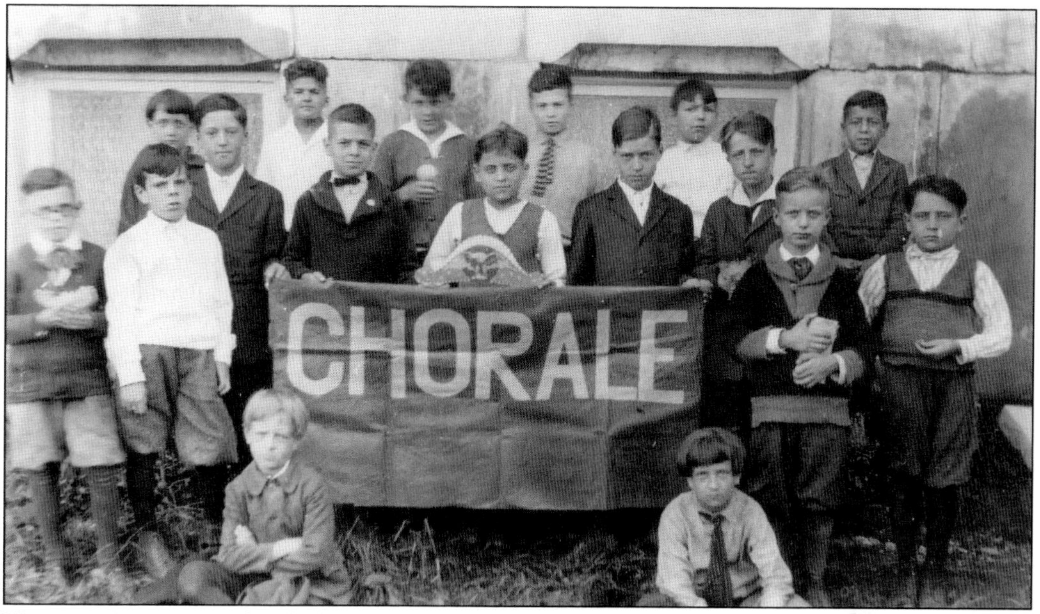

Here is a St. Peter's School chorale in Lewiston. Many youngsters found recreation activities at school and church. (Courtesy of the University of Southern Maine, Lewiston-Auburn College Franco-American Collection.)

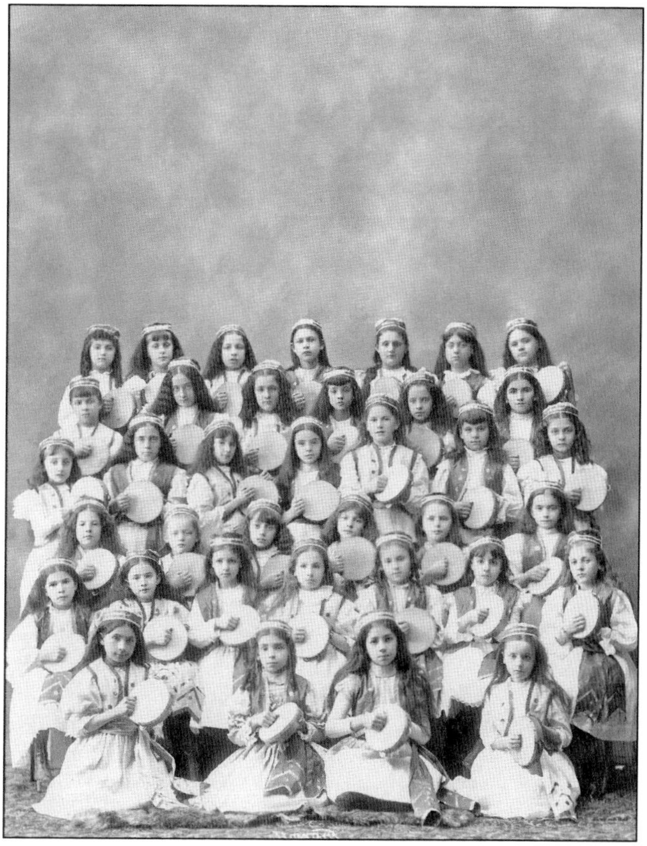

Here is a tambourine group at St. Peter's School in Lewiston in 1903. From left to right are (first row) Alida Rancourt, unidentified, Imelda Thibault, and Clara Langelier; (second row) Imelda Dutil, Rose Croteau, Anna Laplante, Alexina Monreuil, Zelpha Samson, Blanche Verville, and Antoinette Doucette; (third row) Florida Lacroix, Sadie Dostie, Alice Bard, Dora Desmarais, Fedora Langelier, and Marie Croteau; (fourth row) Salome Jacque Barriault, unidentified, Nellie Bard, Eva Caye, ? Laplante, unidentified, and Melanie Beaudette; (fifth row) ? Fortin, Ernestine Lemaire, unidentified, ? Saucier, Blanche Beaudette, and Marianne Simard; (sixth row) L. Laroche, Jenny Jacques, two unidentified, Albine Voyer, unidentified, and Aurore Morneau. (Courtesy of the University of Southern Maine, Lewiston-Auburn College Franco-American Collection.)

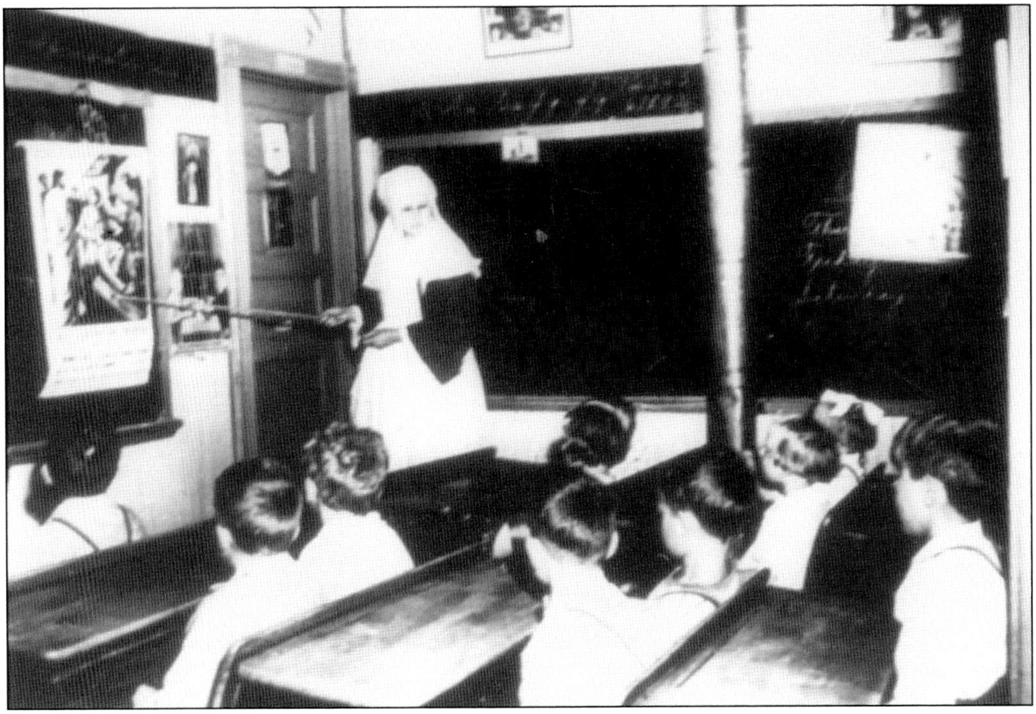

Classes might have been smaller in the rural St. John Valley than in other Franco-American communities, but students were just as serious when the nuns addressed them. Sister Ernest taught in Lille in the 1940s. (Courtesy of the Acadian Archives, University of Maine at Fort Kent.)

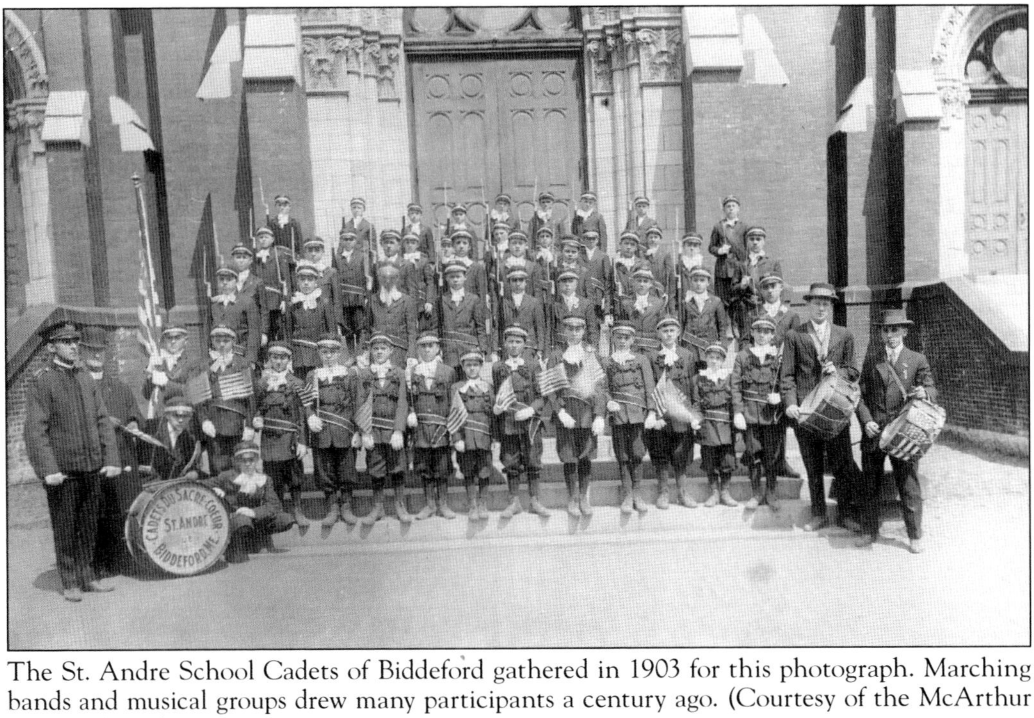

The St. Andre School Cadets of Biddeford gathered in 1903 for this photograph. Marching bands and musical groups drew many participants a century ago. (Courtesy of the McArthur Public Library.)

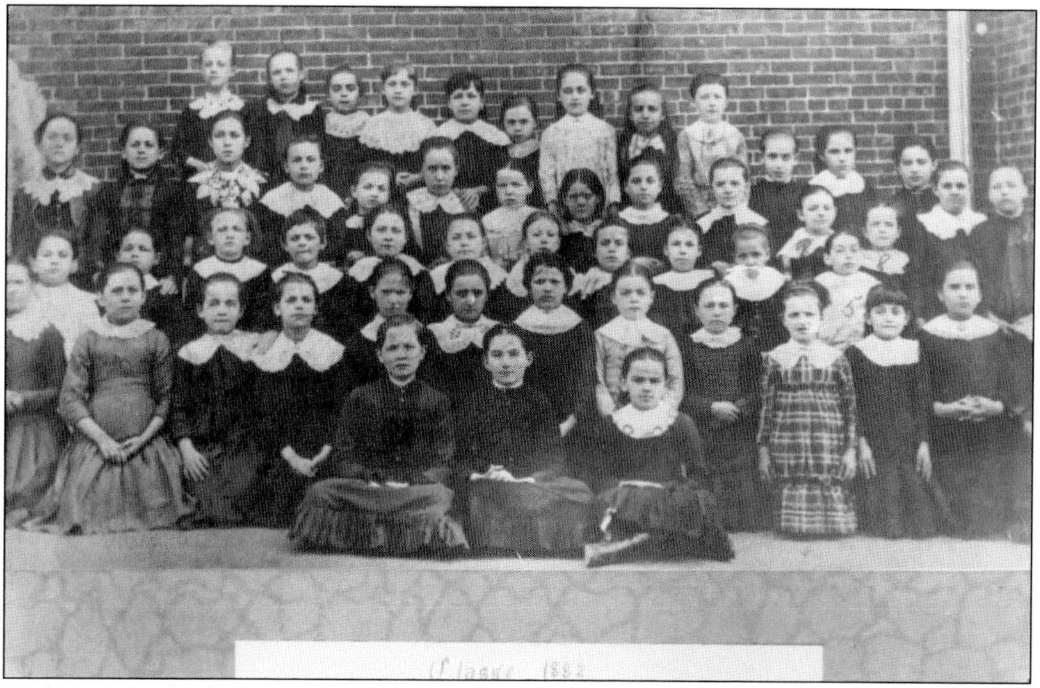

Catholic schools that were sympathetic to French-speaking youngsters were well attended, as this photograph of St. Joseph's School of Biddeford in the late 19th century indicates. Local historians say that when St. Joseph's School opened in 1888, it had 860 pupils. (Courtesy of the McArthur Public Library.)

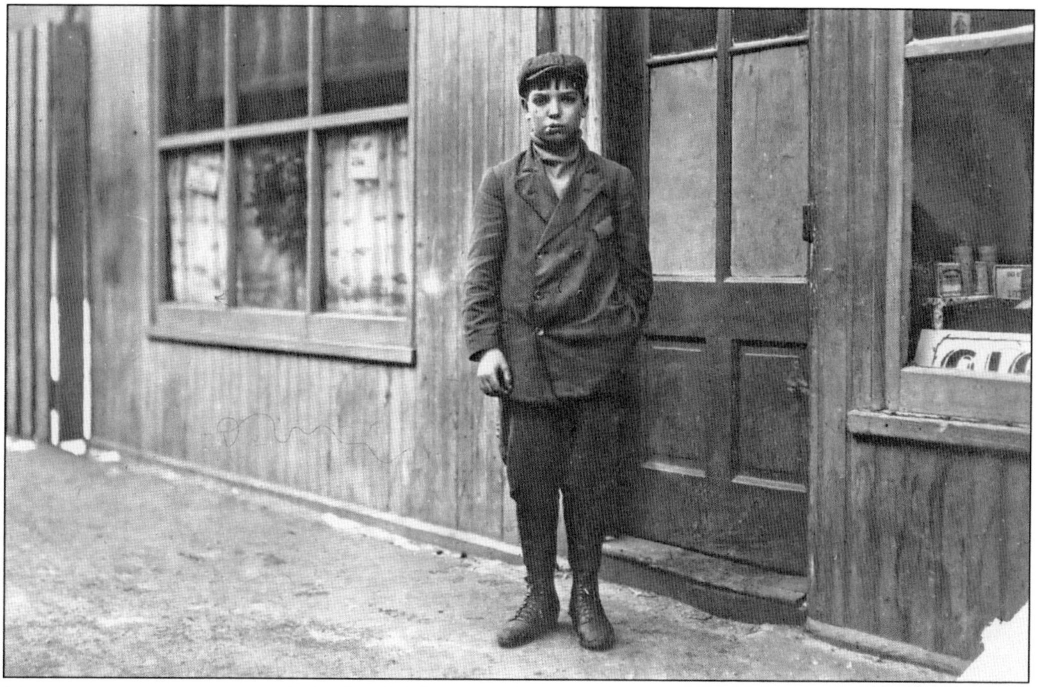

Not every youngster attended school. Here is a Lewiston boy in 1906 who worked in the mills to support his family. (Courtesy of the Library of Congress.)

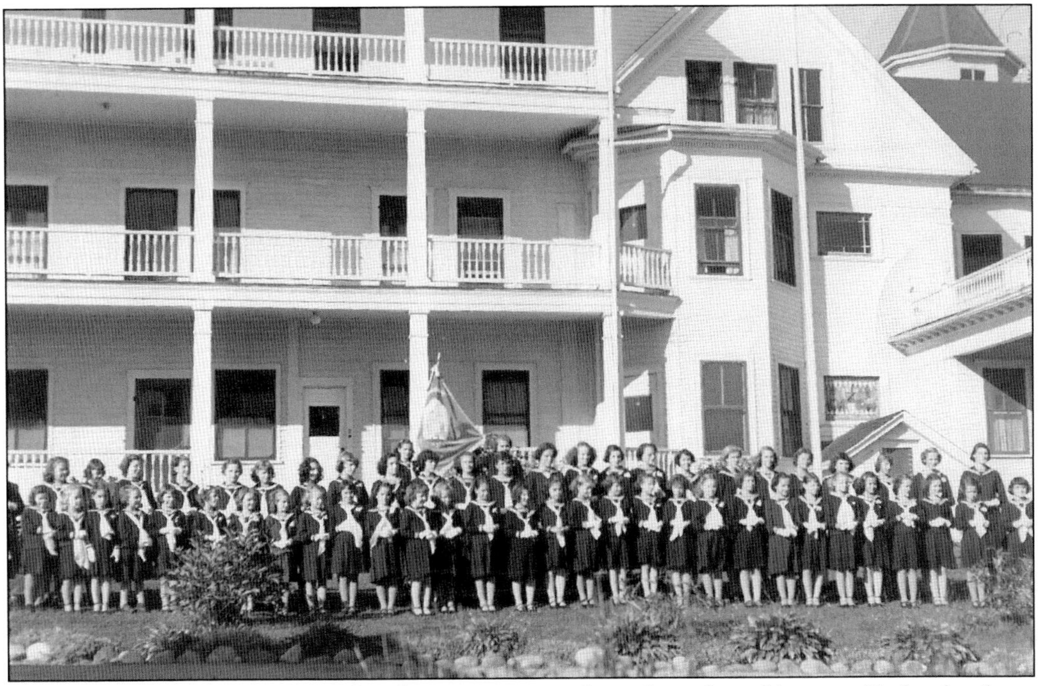

Catholic school systems often offered separate curriculums for girls and boys and helped to keep down costs of the public school system. Here are several classes in Lewiston. (Courtesy of the University of Southern Maine, Lewiston-Auburn College Franco-American Collection.)

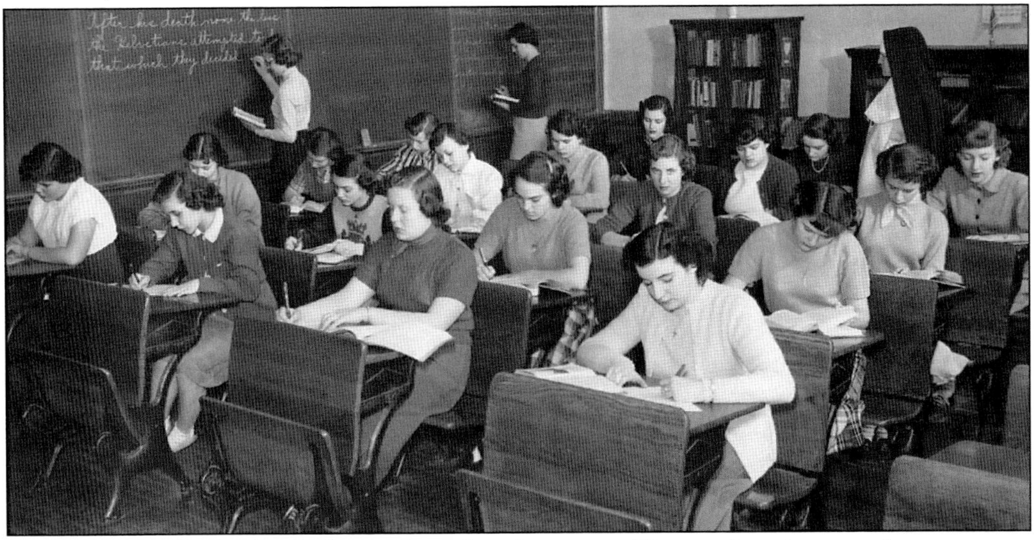

Catholic high schools played a large role in the educations of Franco-Americans until recent years. Here is a sophomore class at St. Dominic's High School, girls division, in 1950. At the blackboard are Jackie Dubois and Yvette Chalifoux. Shown from left to right are (first row) Jacqueline Gouse, Thérèse Lévesque, Diane Breton, and Yolande Talbot; (second row) Violette Hébert, Madeleine Dumont, Louise Brochu, and Patricia Dupont; (third row) Joline Langlois, Dolores Bannister, Irène Turcotte, Joan Paradis, Thérèse Poitras, and Sister Mari Aline; (fourth row) Lorraine Morency, Marguerite Paré, Madeleine Délorge, and Pauline Bégin. (Courtesy of the University of Southern Maine, Lewiston-Auburn College Franco-American Collection.)

Eight

Franco-American Pride

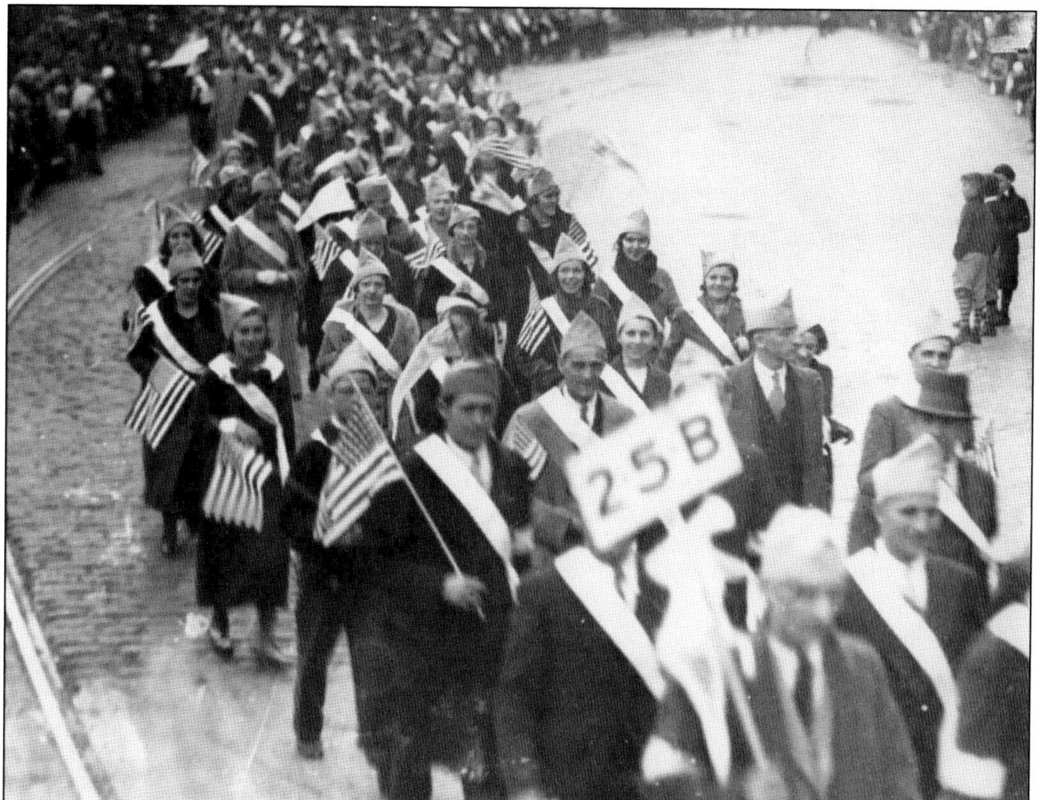

Franco-Americans enjoyed parades and processions years ago, and here are the Knights of Columbus and Painchaud's Band marching up Main Street in Biddeford with American flags in hand. (Courtesy of the McArthur Public Library.)

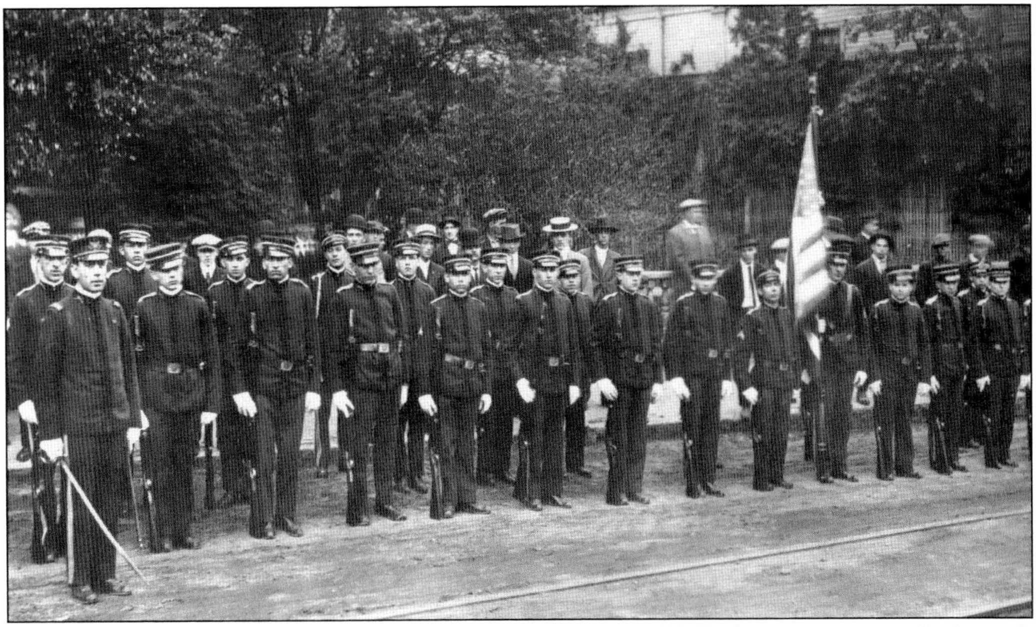

Members of the Fusiliers Lautier of the St. John Club in Biddeford prepare to march through Biddeford during a parade in 1910. The group was active from 1901 to 1918 but disbanded as young men went overseas for World War I. (Courtesy of the McArthur Public Library.)

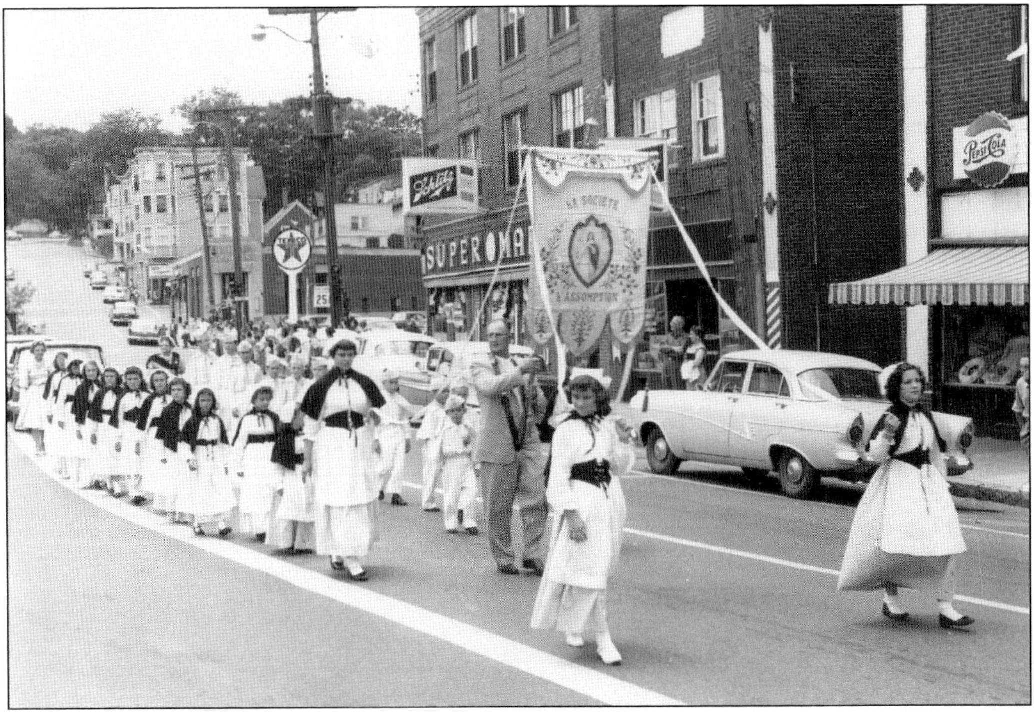

Parades celebrating St. Jean-Baptiste (St. John the Baptist) were common in Franco-American communities. Here La Société l'Assumption marches in the St. Jean-Baptiste parade in 1962 in New Auburn. (Courtesy of the University of Southern Maine, Lewiston-Auburn College Franco-American Collection.)

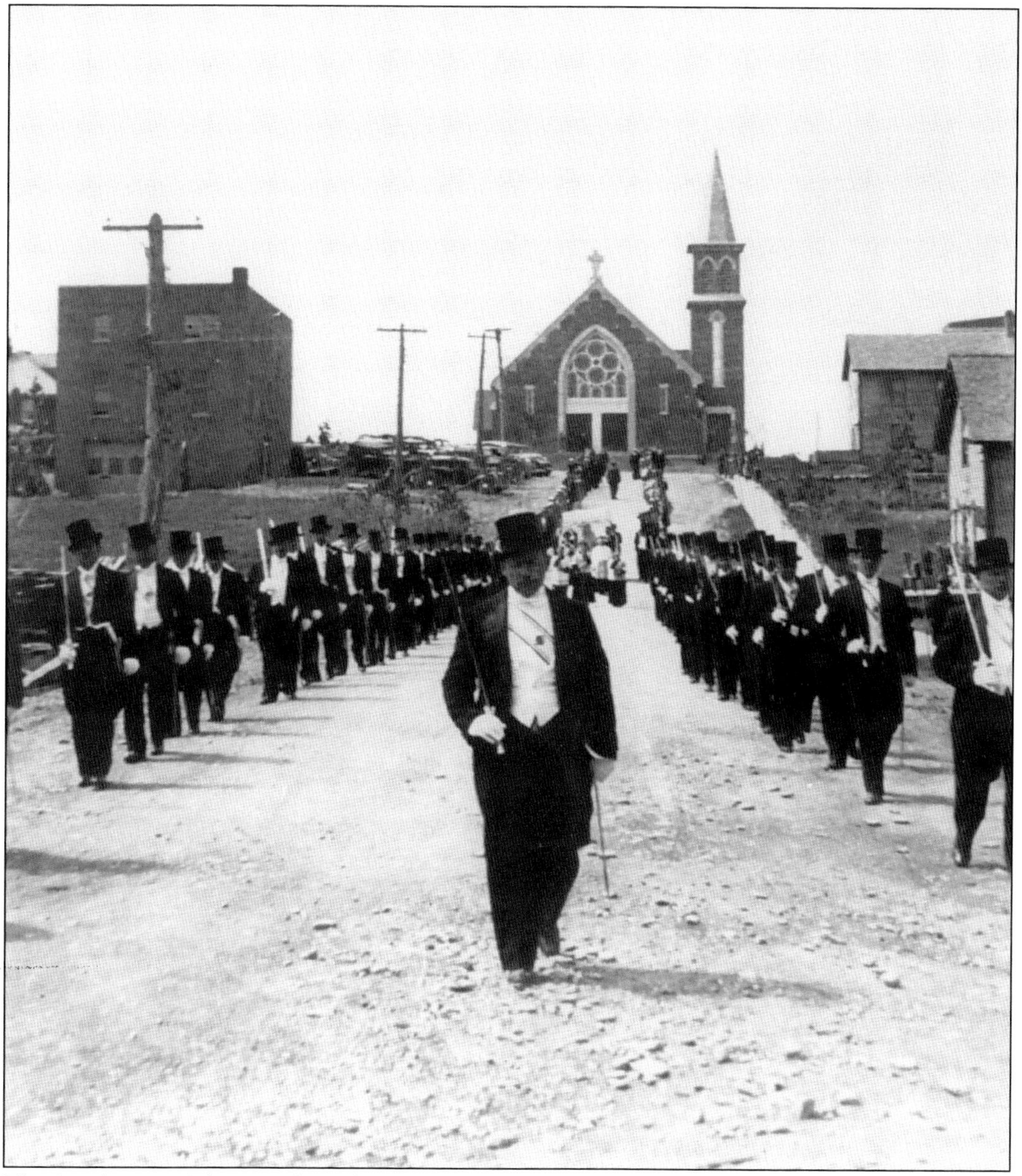

The local unit of the Knights of Columbus marches in a parade over a dirt-covered street in Madawaska in the 1930s as organization members display pride in the church and their organization. (Courtesy of the Madawaska Historical Society.)

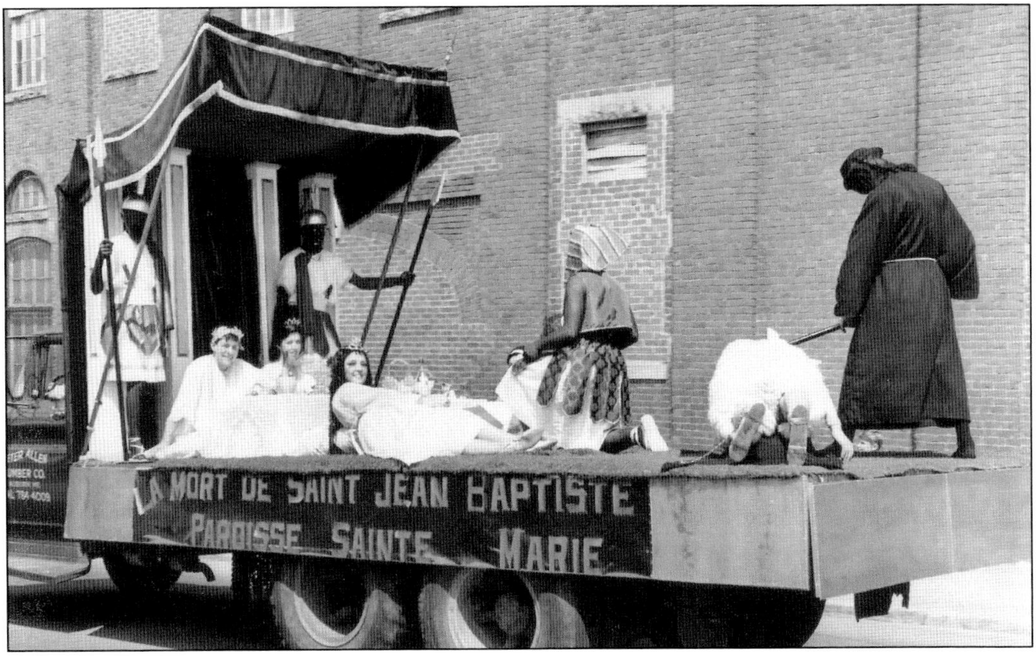

The depiction of the sacrifice of St. John the Baptist could be quite graphic. Here an "ax" is directed at the neck of a lamb to symbolize sacrifice. (Courtesy of the University of Southern Maine, Lewiston-Auburn College Franco-American Collection.)

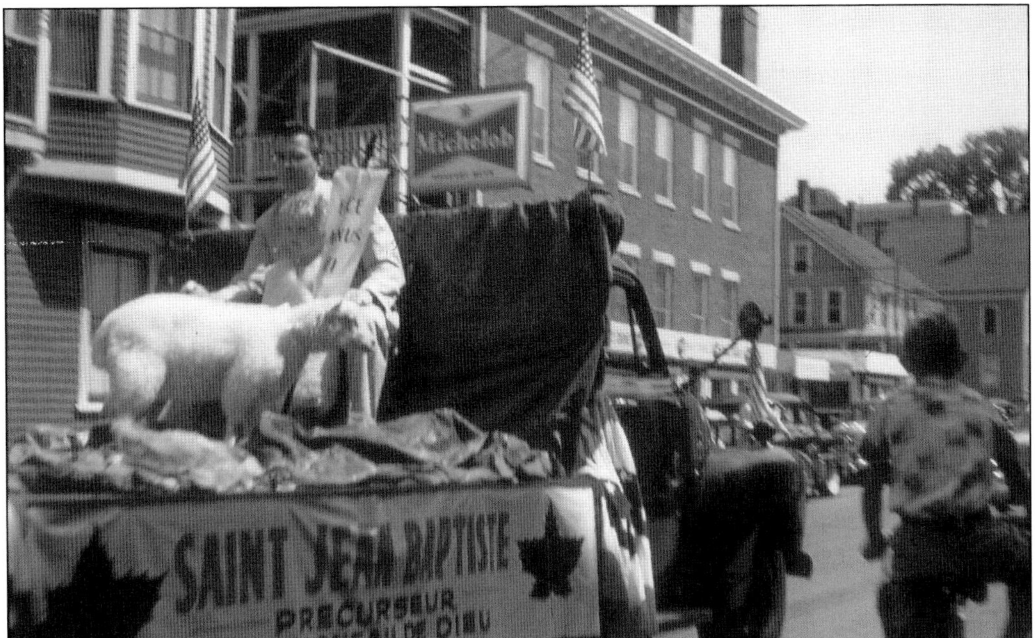

St. Jean-Baptiste Day is June 24, celebrating the patron saint of the French in North America. In Lewiston, huge popular parades celebrating St. Jean-Baptiste Day and local ethnic culture were held from 1875 to 1966 with ornate floats, marching bands, and decorated buildings. Parade floats such as this one in the 1950s often featured a sheep, either live or mounted. (Courtesy of the University of Southern Maine, Lewiston-Auburn College Franco-American Collection.)

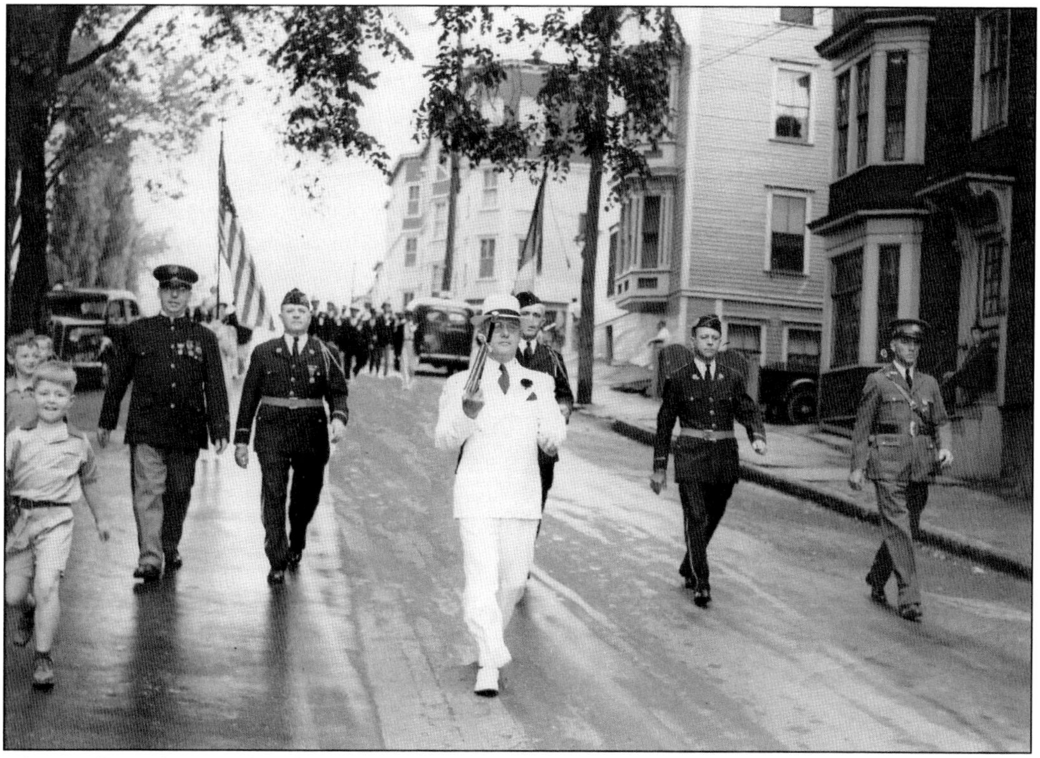

Those of French-Canadian heritage were very patriotic Americans and were often part of military parades such as this one in Lewiston in 1941. (Courtesy of University of Southern Maine, Lewiston-Auburn College Lewiston Heritage Collection.)

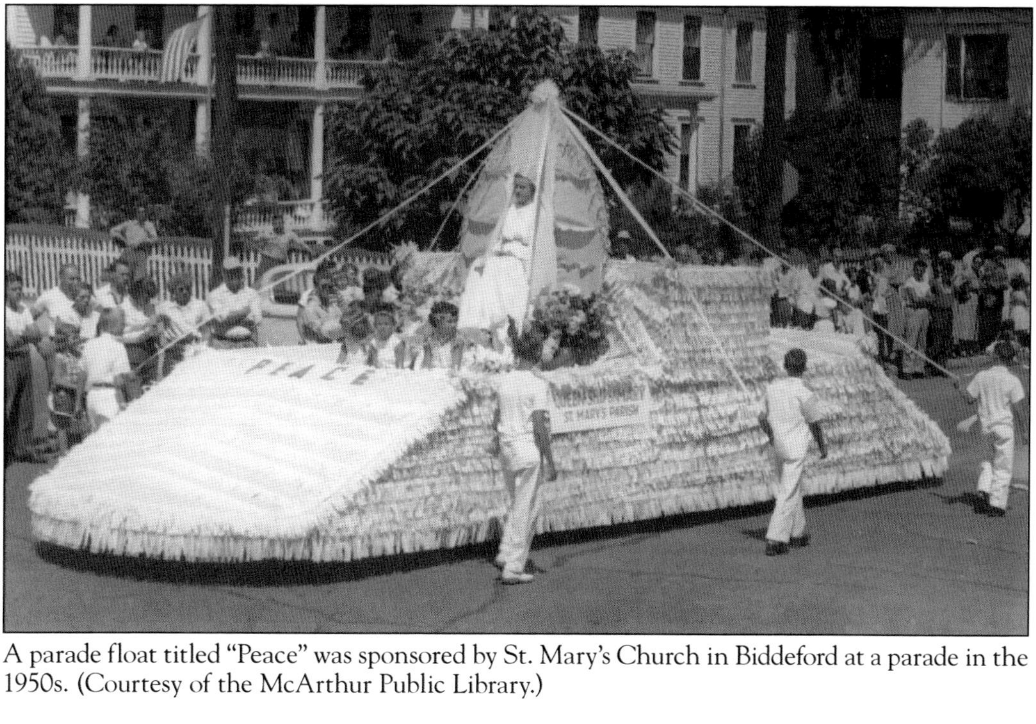

A parade float titled "Peace" was sponsored by St. Mary's Church in Biddeford at a parade in the 1950s. (Courtesy of the McArthur Public Library.)

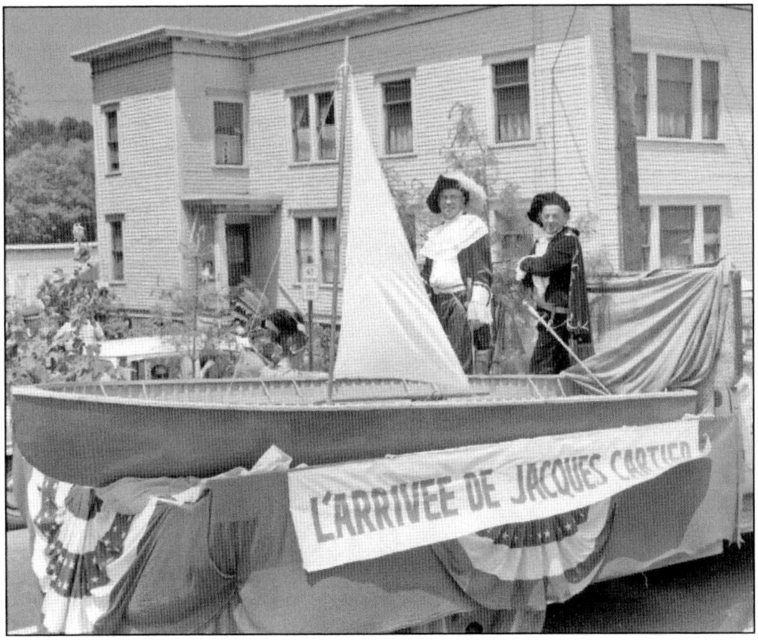

The arrival in North America of Jacques Cartier in 1604 was celebrated for years in Franco-American communities. Here is a float with two costumed reenactors in Lewiston in the 1950s. (Courtesy of the University of Southern Maine, Lewiston-Auburn College Franco-American Collection.)

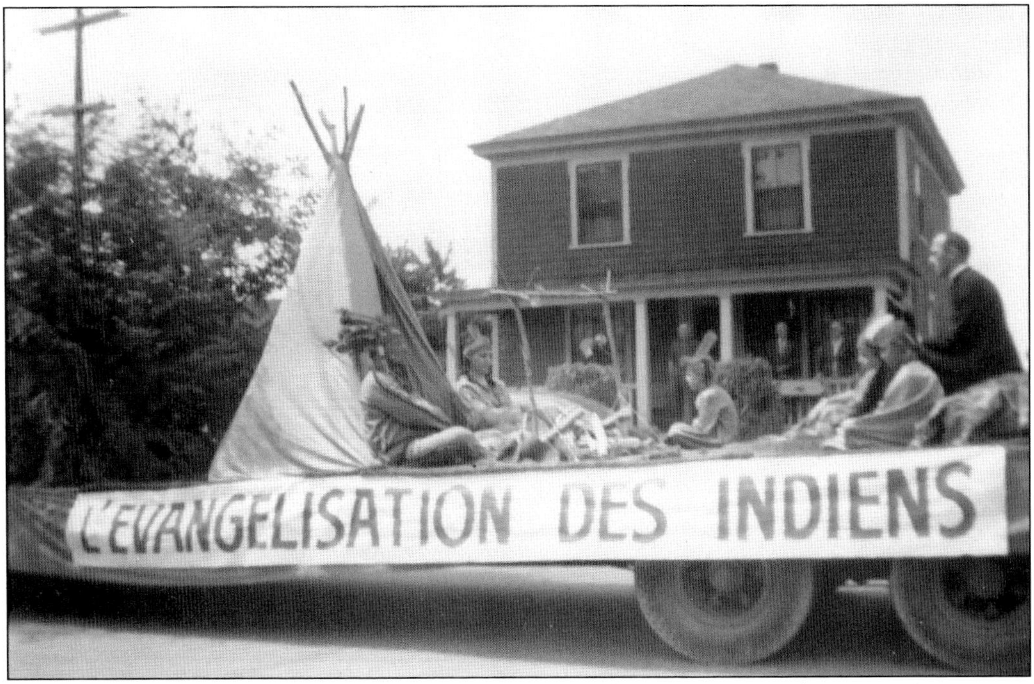

When the French arrived in this country, one of their goals was to convert the Native Americans. Here is a float that noted that effort. (Courtesy of the University of Southern Maine, Lewiston-Auburn College Franco-American Collection.)

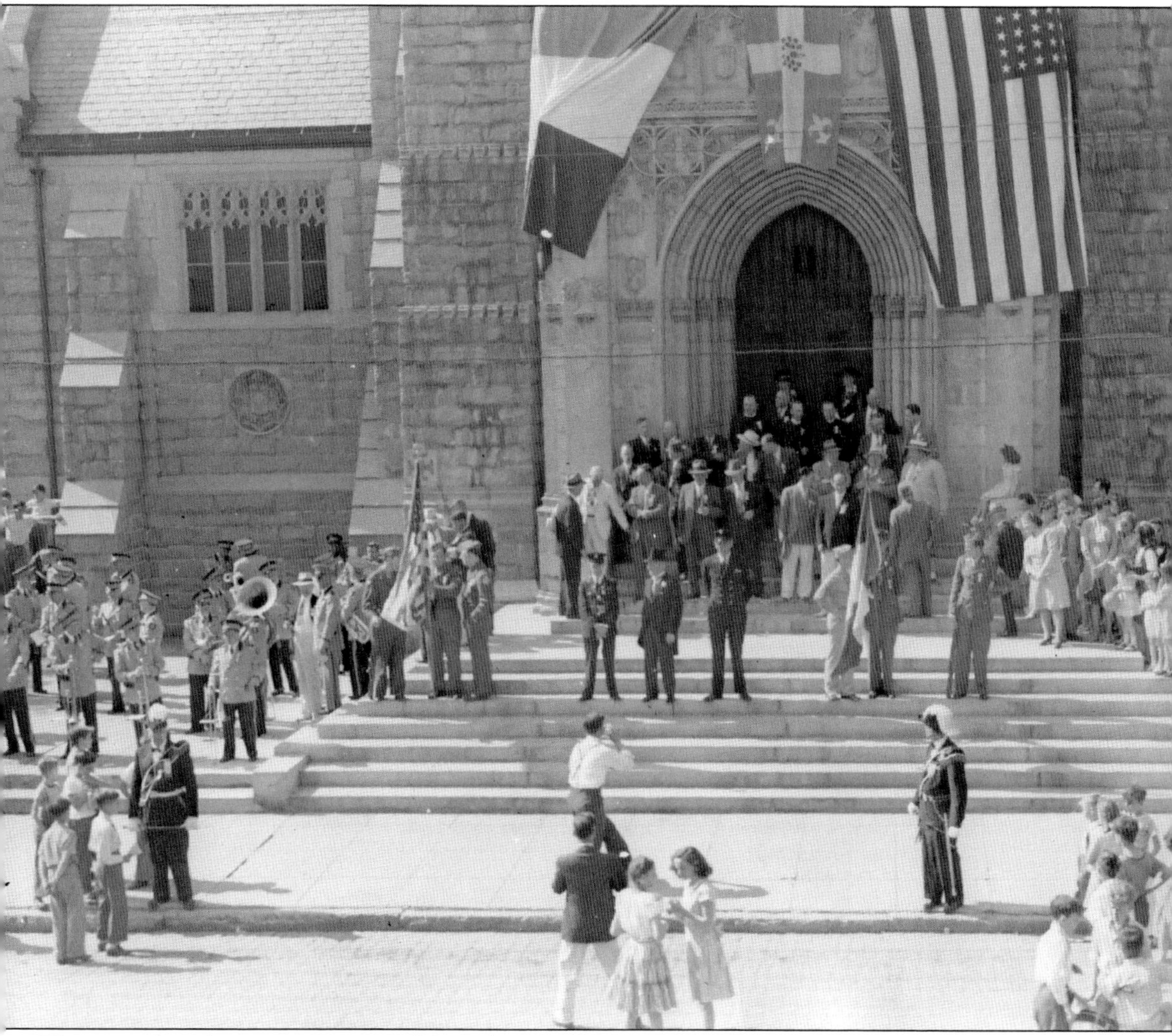

Three staples of Franco-American life—church, country, and community—are captured in this photograph taken in Lewiston during the mid-20th century. Pride in French roots often intertwined with activities of the church. (Courtesy of the University of Southern Maine, Lewiston-Auburn College Franco-American Collection.)

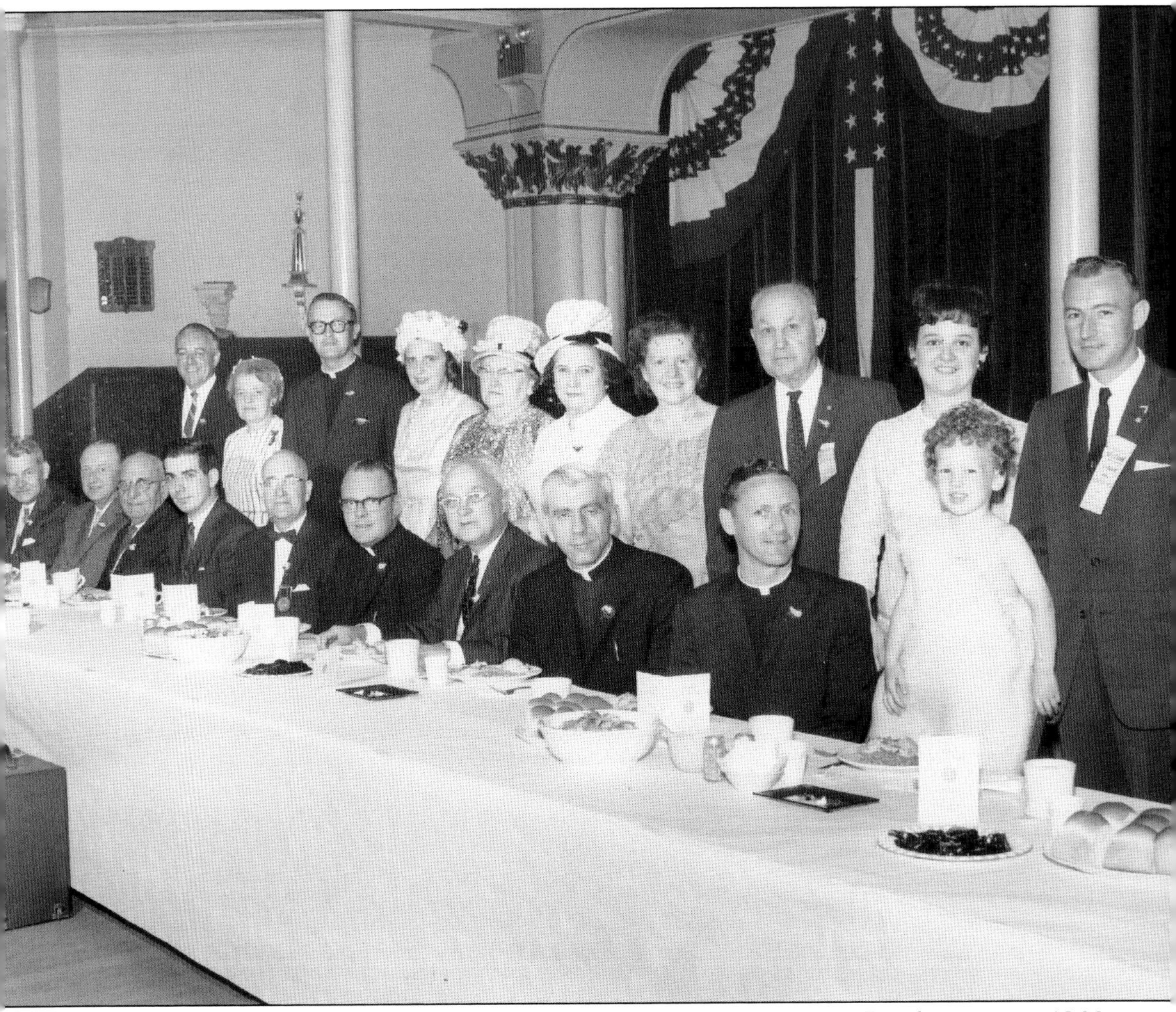

Leading Franco-American citizens gathered at a St. Jean-Baptiste Day banquet in 1966 in Lewiston. Sitting, from left to right, are community leaders including Dr. Paul Fortier, Justice Armand Dufresne, Fernand Despins, Robert Couturier, Gaston Dumais, and the Reverend Marcel Chouinard. Justice Dufresne served as chief justice of the Maine Supreme Judicial Court from 1970 to 1977. (Courtesy of the University of Southern Maine, Lewiston-Auburn College Franco-American Collection.)

John Martin of Eagle Lake has been an influential advocate for the Franco-Americans during his lengthy tenure as a (Democratic) leader in the state house and senate. Here he is seen as Speaker of the House in 1990. (Courtesy of the Clerk of the House of Representatives.)

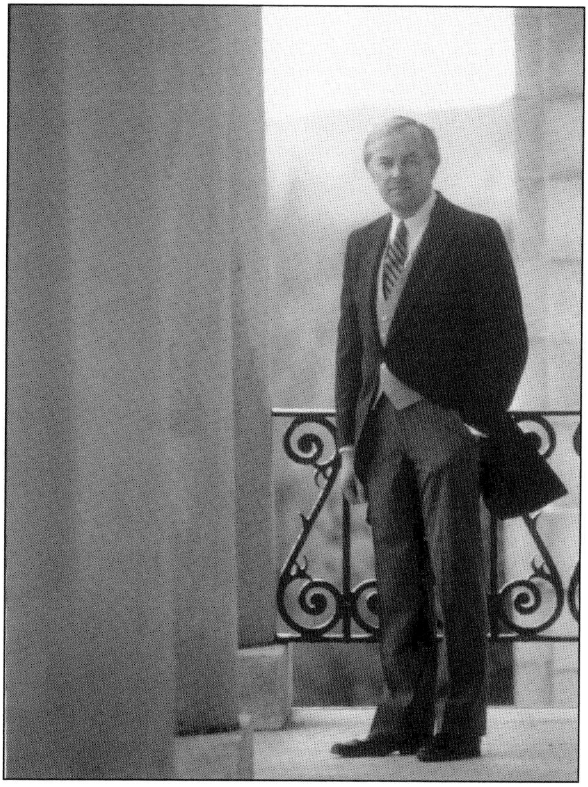

Margaret Chase Smith, who served Maine in the House and Senate from 1940 to 1973, traveled the state helping Mainers of all occupations. Here she is meeting with loggers on the St. Croix River in the 1960s. At right is an aide. She was French on her mother's side (Morin) and was among the most influential Mainers of the 20th century. (Courtesy of the Margaret Chase Smith Library.)

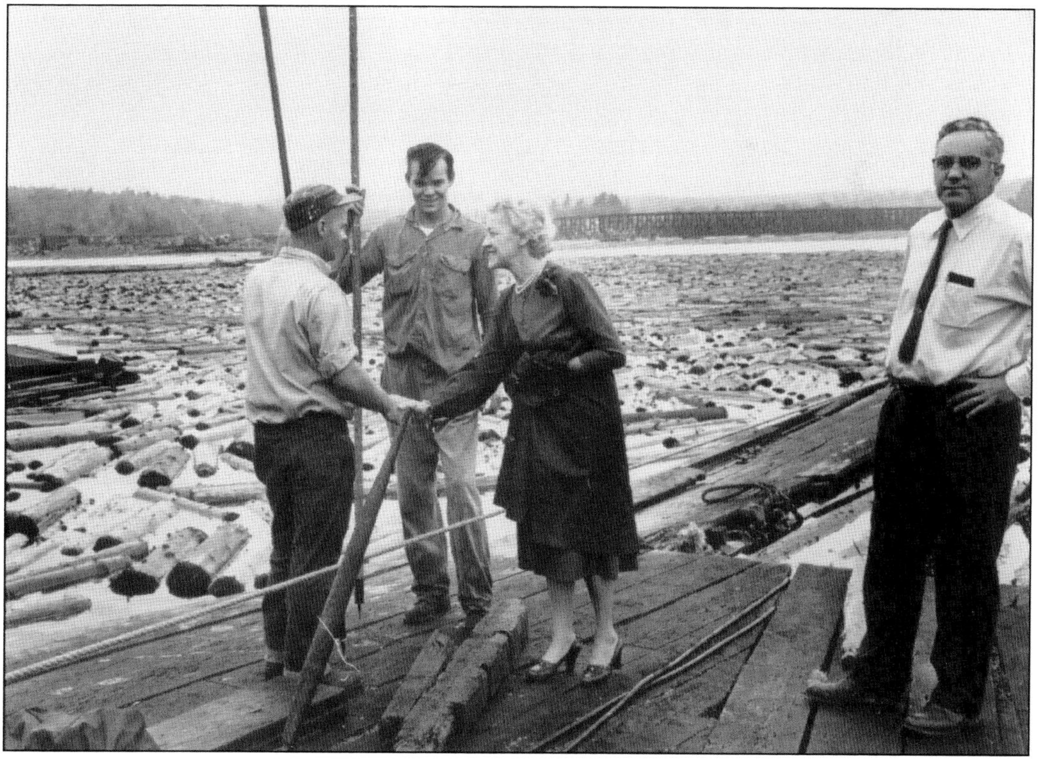

A LA DOUCE MÉMOIRE DE

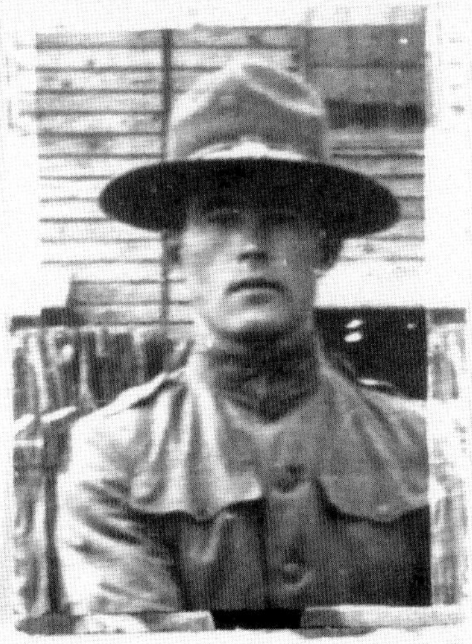

VICTORIE GENDREAULT

Fils de Raymond Gendreault

Mort en France, le 4 novembre 1918, à l'âge de 26 ans.

Mourir pour la patrie, c'est mourir pour Dieu espérons qu'il est allé cueillir là-haut les lauriers de la victoire, car sur sa fosse encore entrouverte la paix et la justice se sont entre-baisées, son sang généreusement versé nous a mérité l'ère de liberté dont nous jouissons.

Many Franco-Americans served in the armed forces, and some families never saw their boys again. Here is a remembrance of Victorie Gendreault of Madawaska, who was killed in World War I. The inscription says, in part, "In sweet memory of Victorie Gendreault, dead in France November 4, 1918, at the age of 26. To die for your country is to die for God." (Courtesy of Madawaska Historical Society.)

Nine
The Acadians

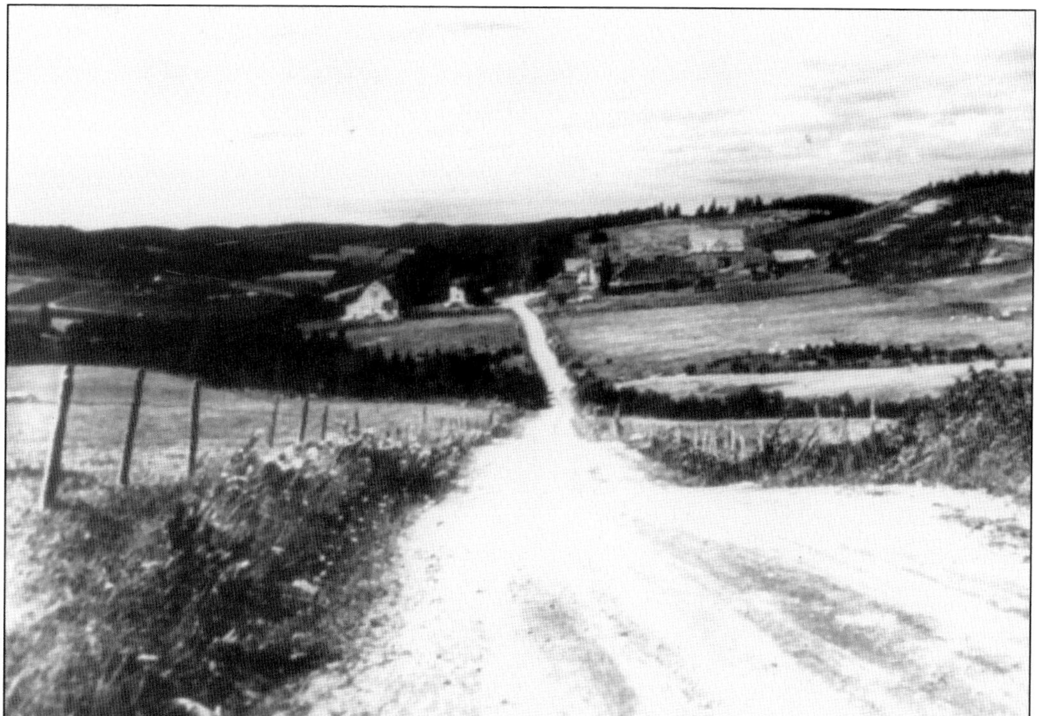

Ancestors of families who dwell in the St. John Valley generally arrived in the 18th and early 19th centuries. Because many had lived in Acadia (New Brunswick, Nova Scotia, and Prince Edward Island), they were called Acadians. This photograph shows the vast rural expanse of the St. John Valley in northern Maine in contrast to mill towns in southern Maine that were set on rivers. (Courtesy of the Acadian Archives, University of Maine at Fort Kent.)

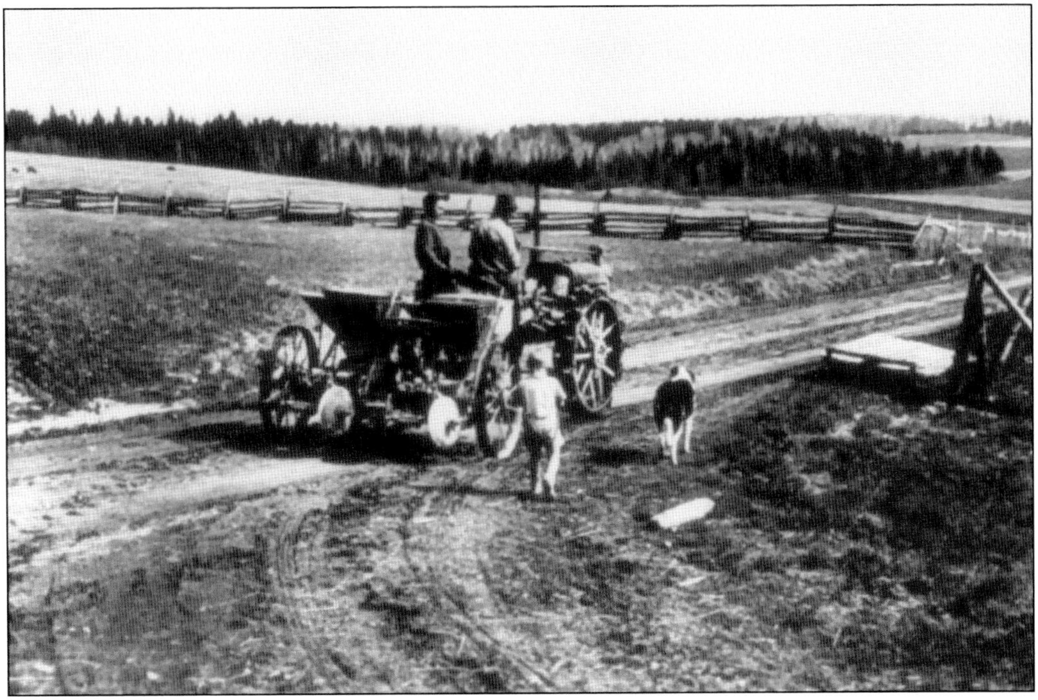

A young boy follows a tractor out to the fields to help with the chores on the farm of Leonard Gagnon in Frenchville in 1943. Children assisted on the farm, as many youngsters did in the mills. (Courtesy of the Acadian Archives, University of Maine at Fort Kent.)

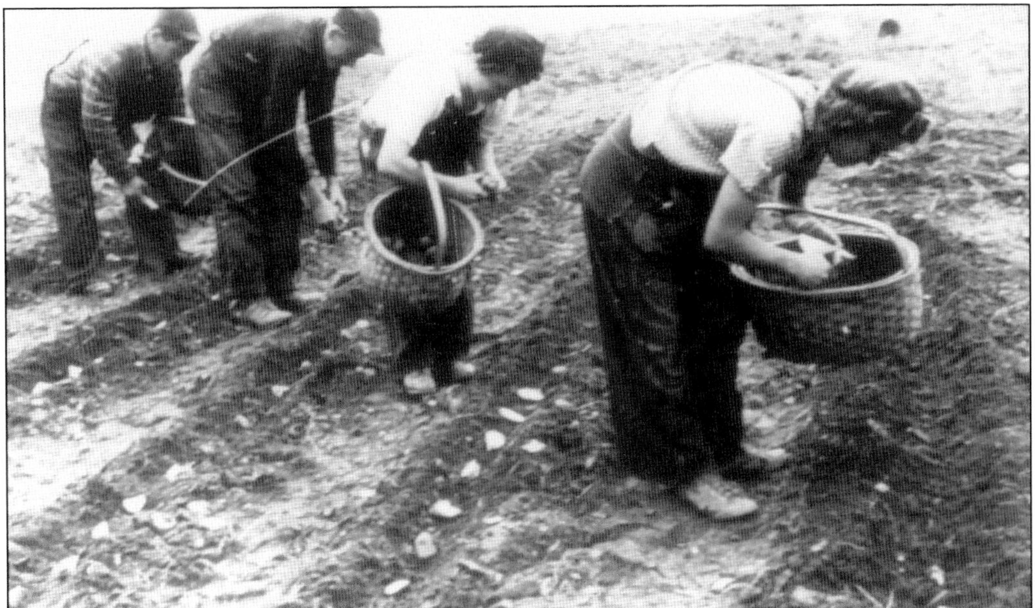

Farmers and helpers plant potatoes. Maine was a leader in the production of potatoes for many years, and the state still sends spuds all over the country. Here farmer Claude Levesque (left) and others demonstrate planting practices in Van Buren in 1940. (Courtesy of the Acadian Archives, University of Maine at Fort Kent.)

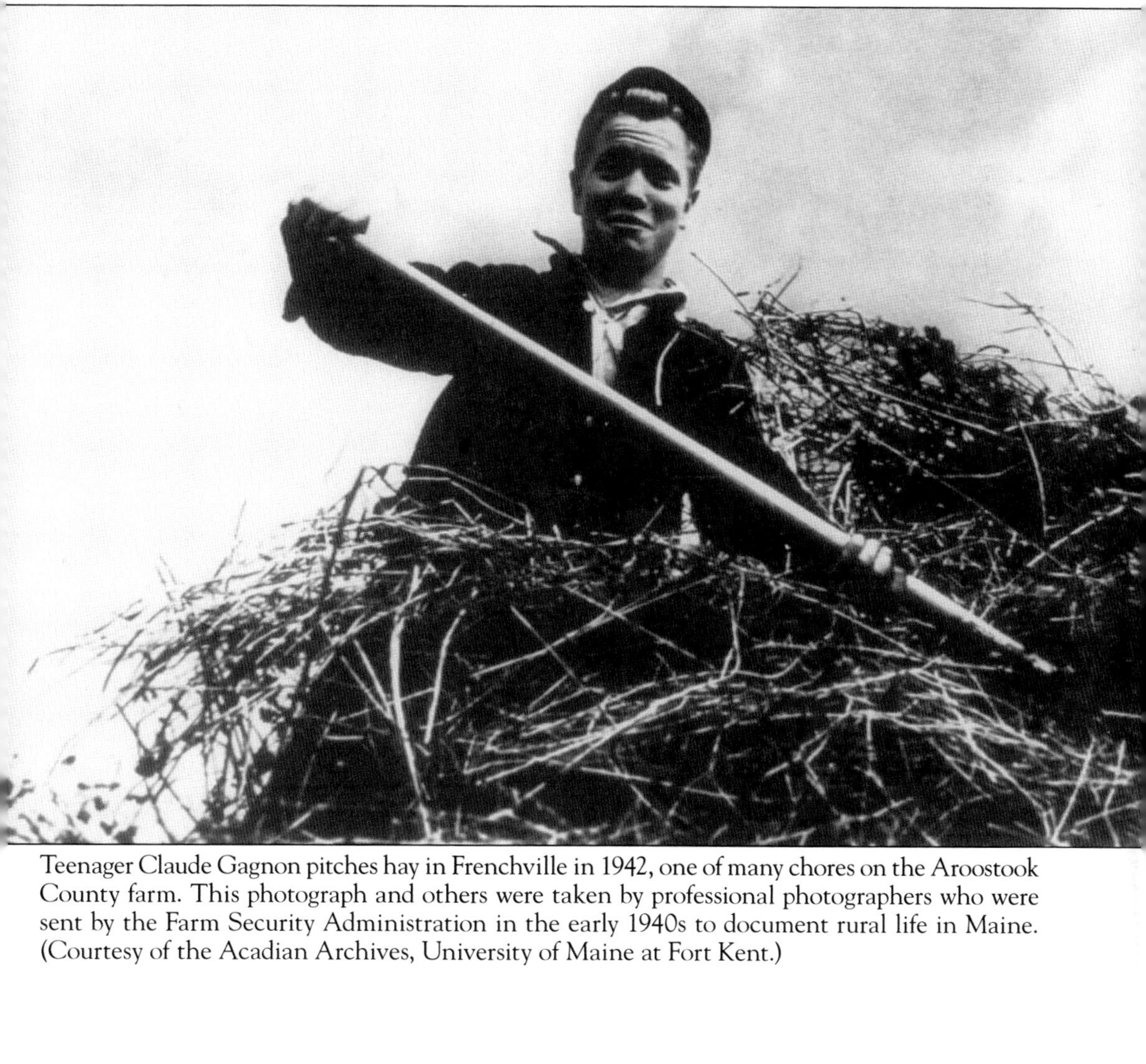

Teenager Claude Gagnon pitches hay in Frenchville in 1942, one of many chores on the Aroostook County farm. This photograph and others were taken by professional photographers who were sent by the Farm Security Administration in the early 1940s to document rural life in Maine. (Courtesy of the Acadian Archives, University of Maine at Fort Kent.)

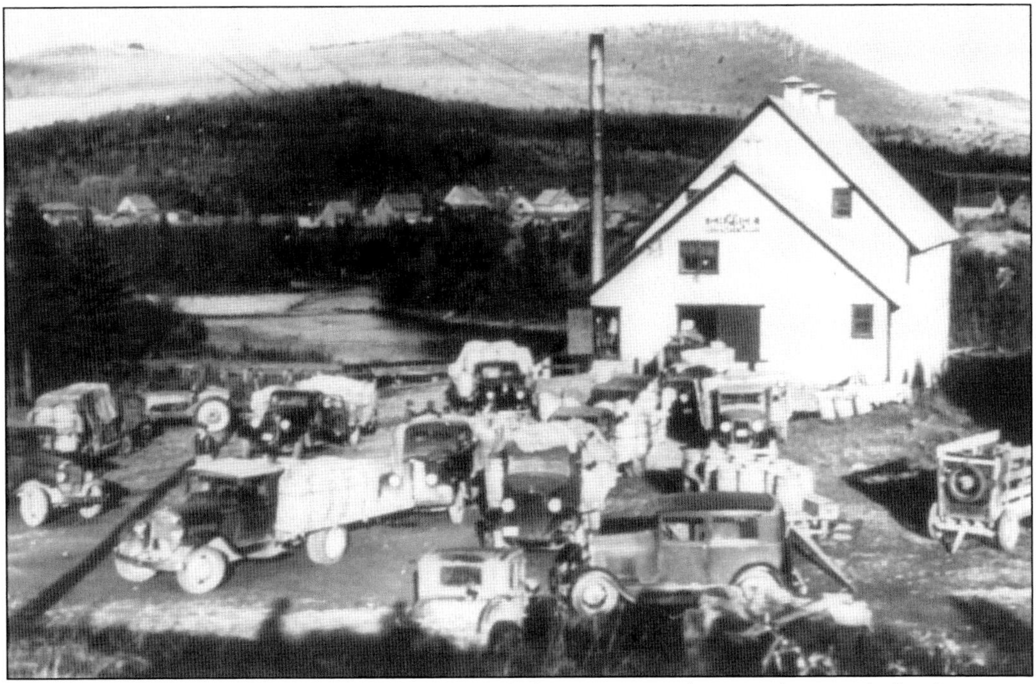

Potato farmers brought their trucks to the starch factory to get their product ready for shipment. This photograph was taken in Fort Kent in 1942. (Courtesy of the Acadian Archives, University of Maine at Fort Kent.)

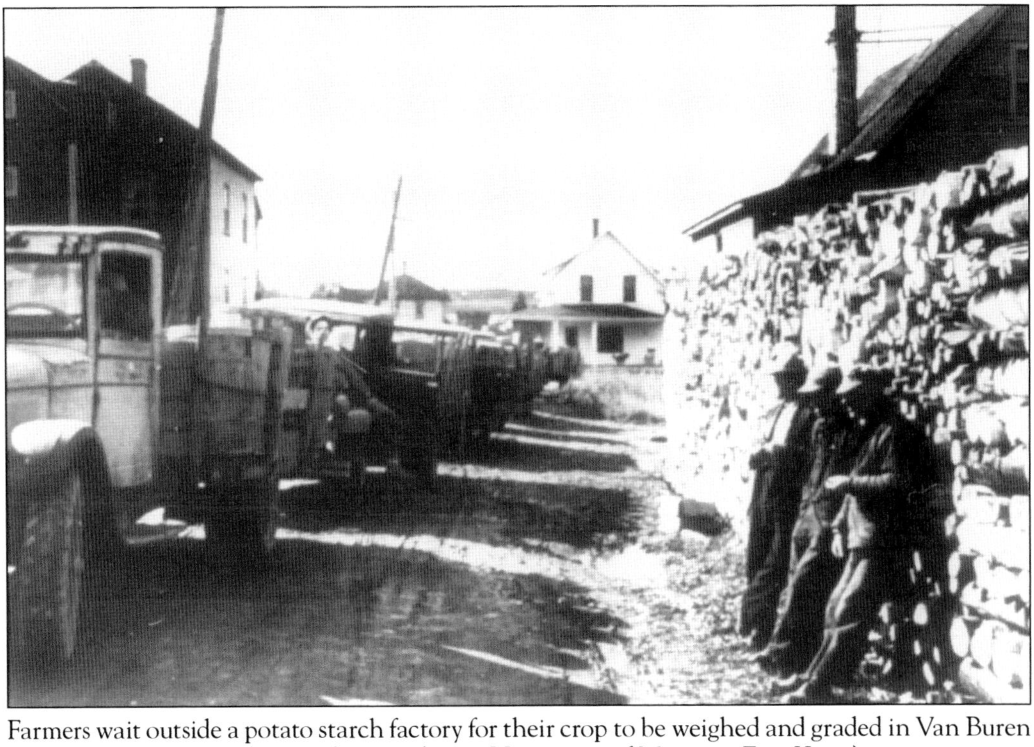

Farmers wait outside a potato starch factory for their crop to be weighed and graded in Van Buren in 1940. (Courtesy of the Acadian Archives, University of Maine at Fort Kent.)

Spring brought new tasks and activities in the St. John Valley, and many women collected maple sap even if they had to wear snowshoes to reach the trees. (Courtesy of the Madawaska Historical Society.)

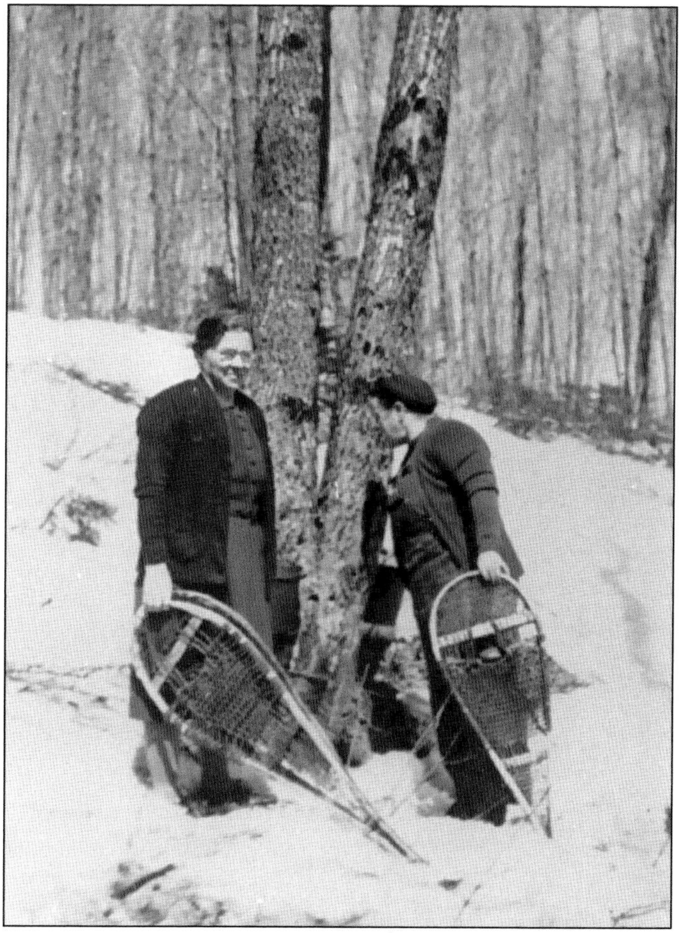

Farmer Leonard Gagnon milks a cow in the open field in Frenchville in 1942. Local historians say this photograph may have been posed, as cattle were usually milked in the barn and often by the children. (Courtesy of the Acadian Archives, University of Maine at Fort Kent.)

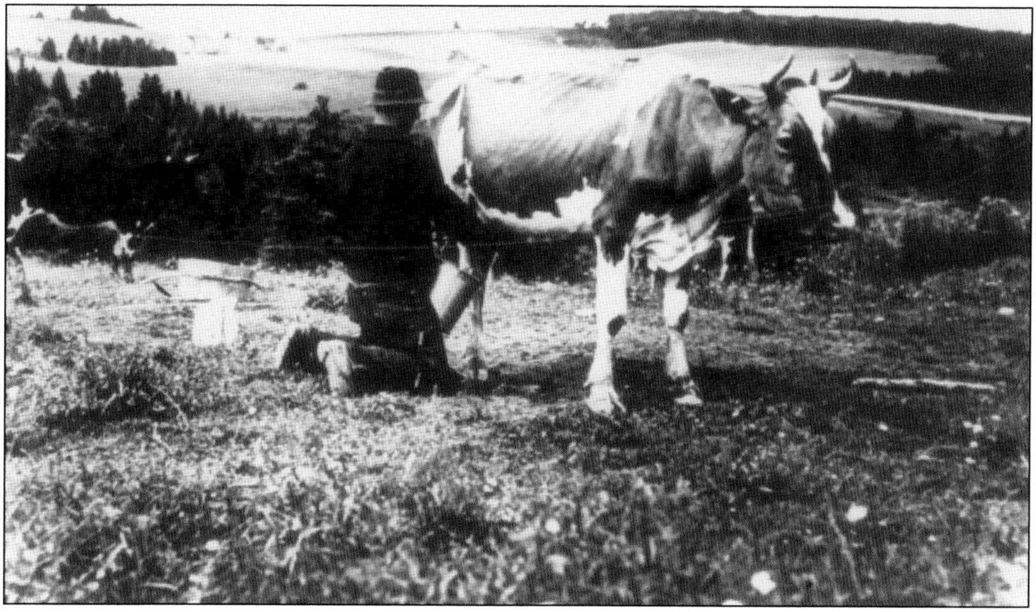

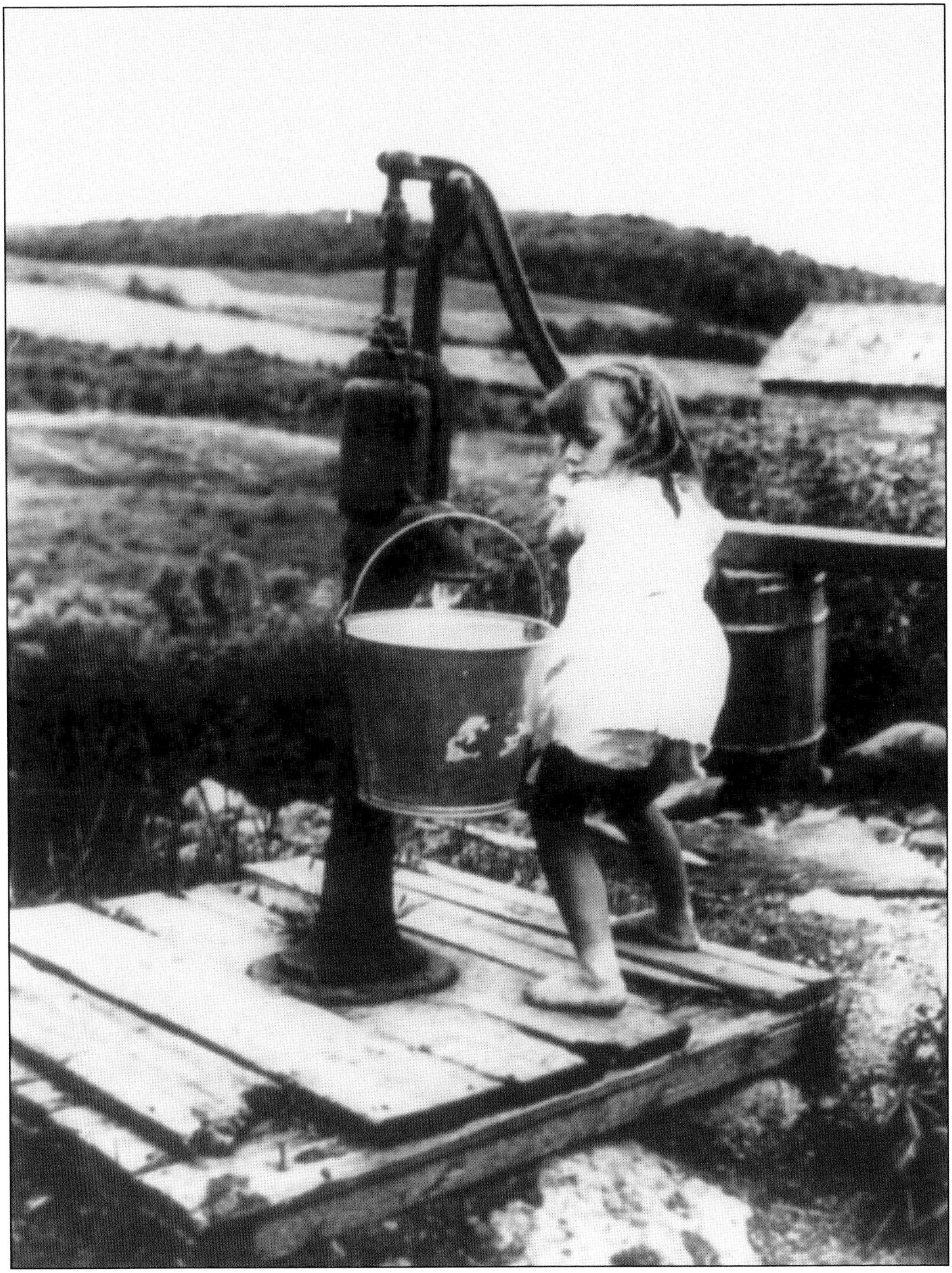

This was tiny, shoeless, but energetic Doris Daigle pumping water in Fort Kent in 1942. Youngsters were expected to run errands for their mothers at meal time. (Courtesy of the Acadian Archives, University of Maine at Fort Kent.)

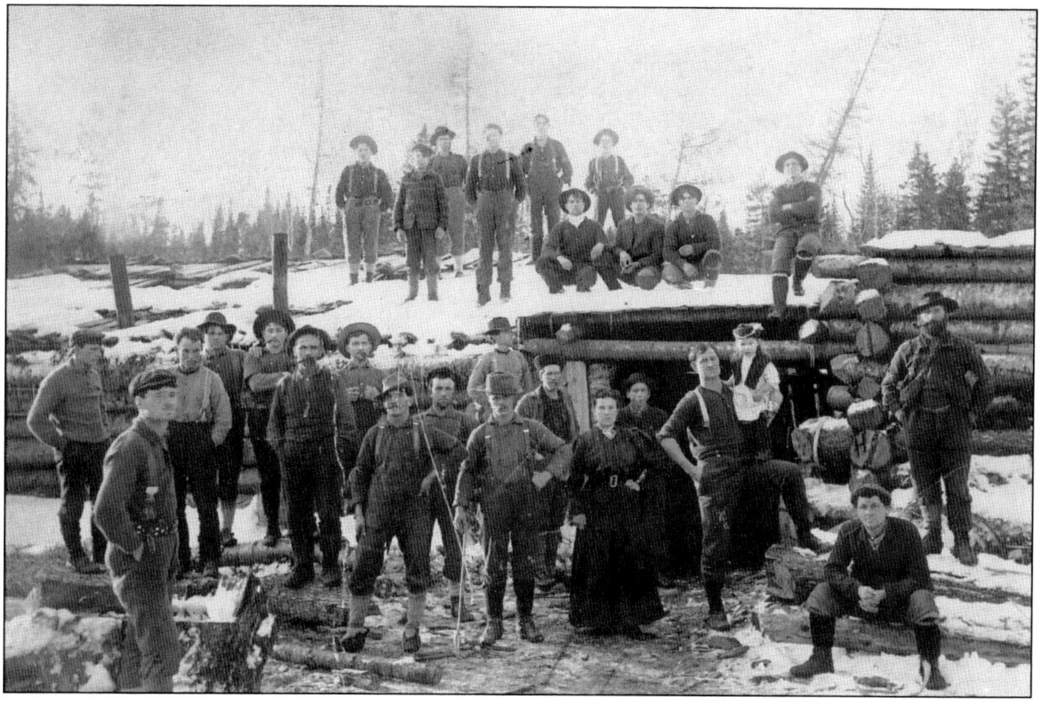

Many Francos worked in lumber camps, often through the winter, when it was easier to move the mammoth logs. Here is a camp in Allagash in 1899. (Courtesy of the Madawaska Historical Society.)

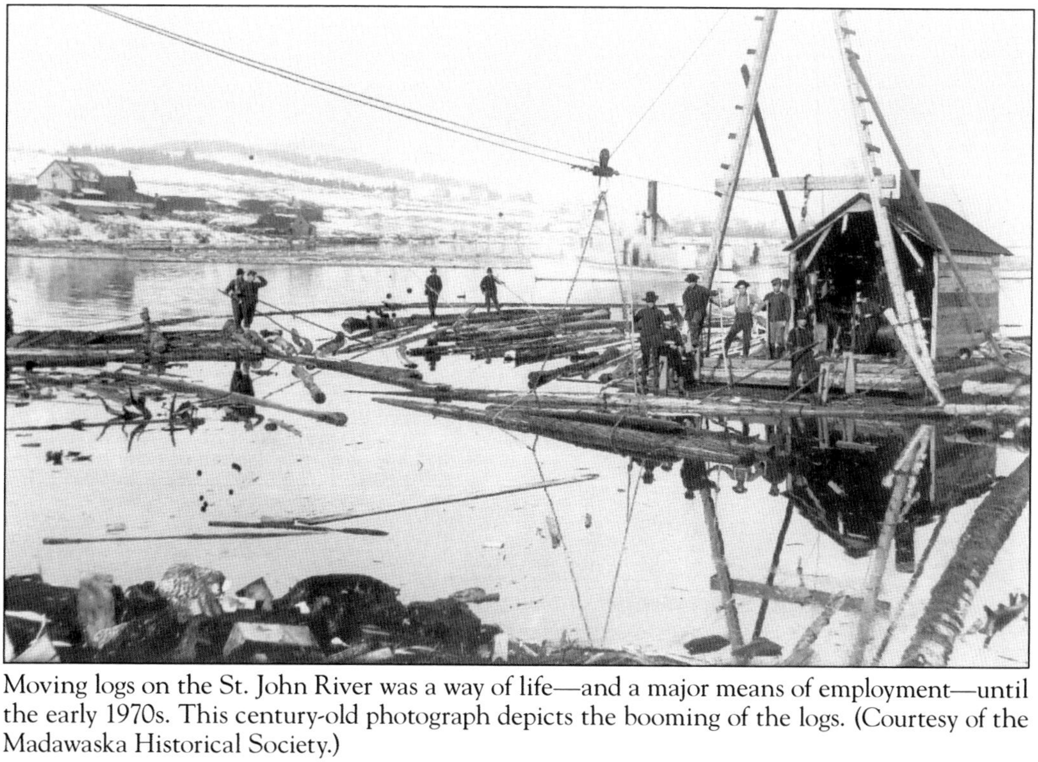

Moving logs on the St. John River was a way of life—and a major means of employment—until the early 1970s. This century-old photograph depicts the booming of the logs. (Courtesy of the Madawaska Historical Society.)

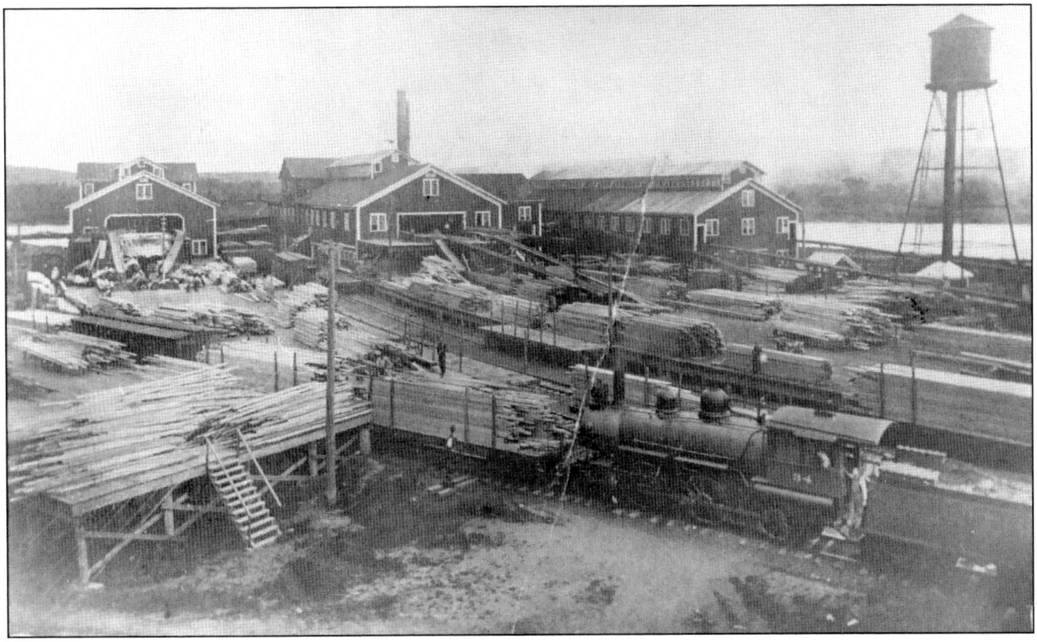

Lumber was big business a century ago, as this image from the St. John Lumber Company in Van Buren shows. (Courtesy of the Madawaska Historical Society.)

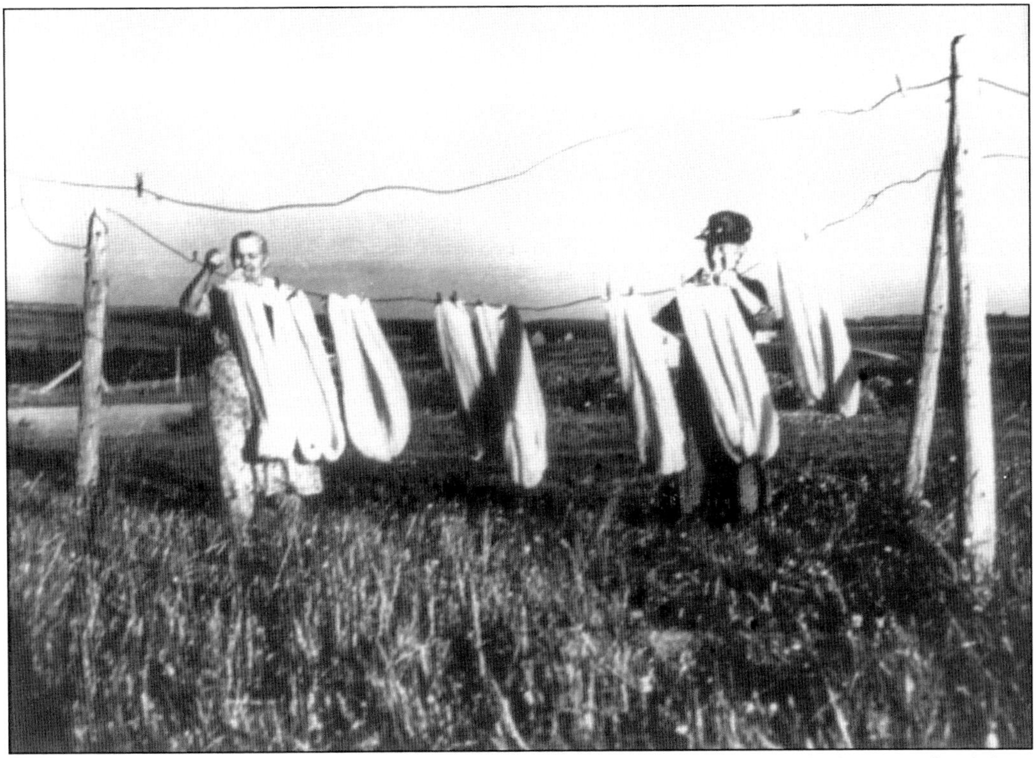

Women had many duties on the farm, including cleaning and drying the clothes. Much of their apparel was self-made in the 1930s and 1940s. (Courtesy of the Acadian Archives, University of Maine at Fort Kent.)

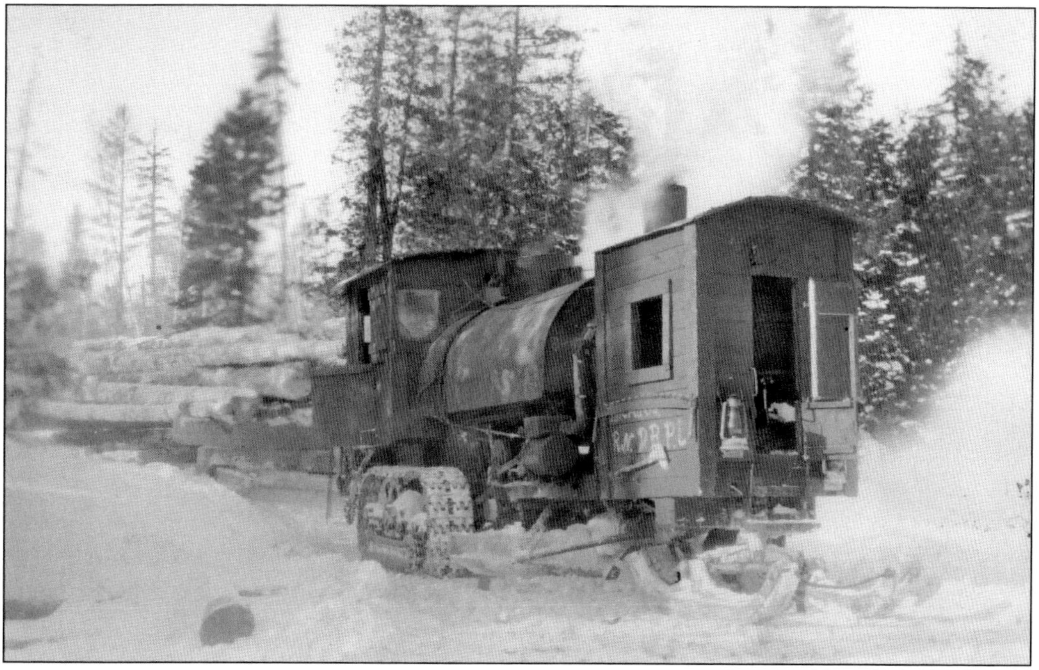

Powerful engines could traverse Aroostook County even in winter, and such reliable transportation helped the lumber and paper industries to thrive. (Courtesy of the Madawaska Historical Society.)

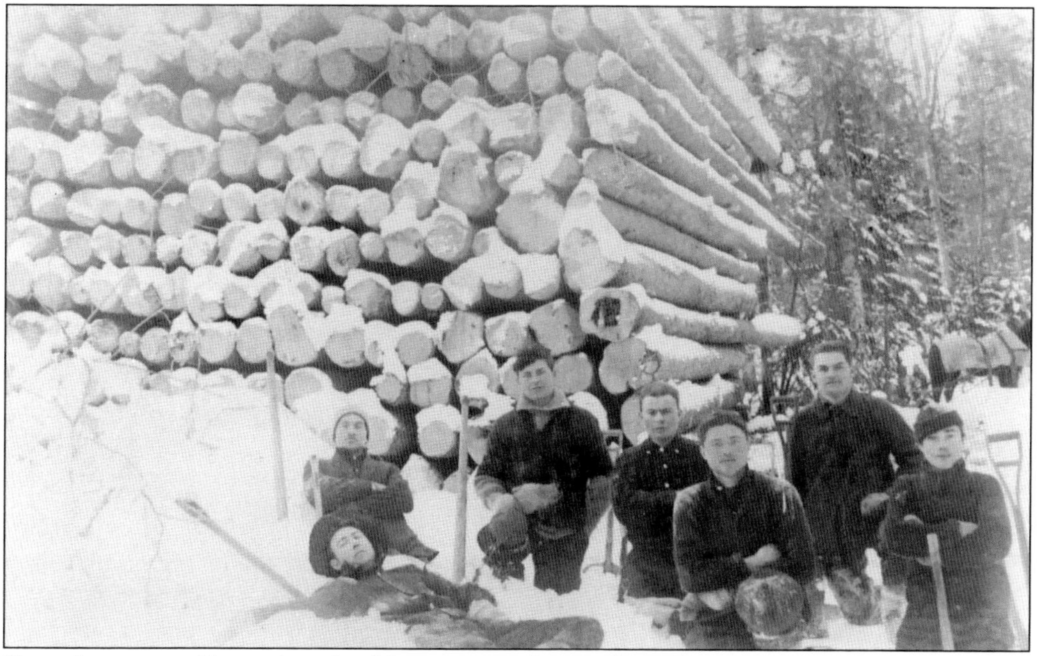

Young loggers would spend much of the winter in the woods, and priests would travel a rural circuit to celebrate mass and offer communion. (Courtesy of the Madawaska Historical Society.)

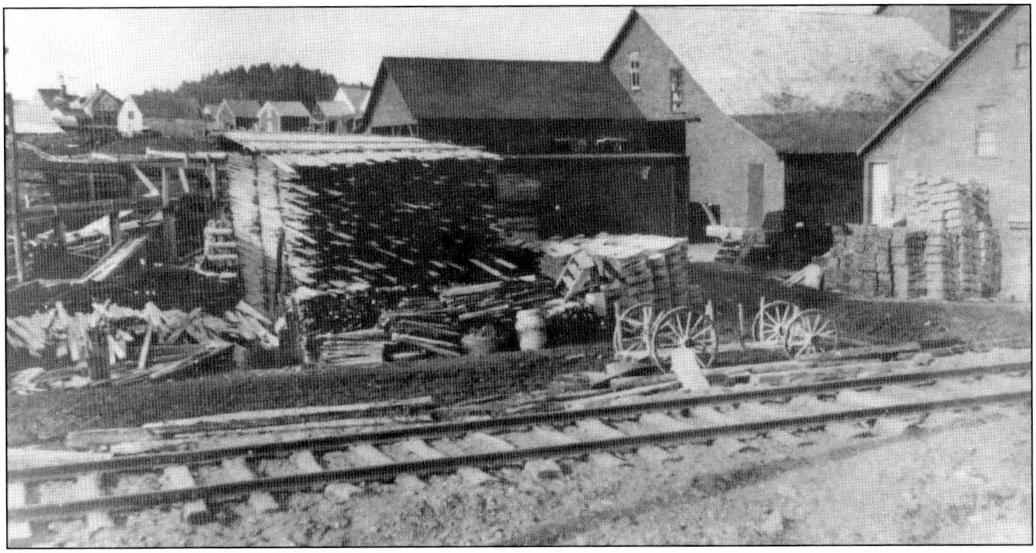

Lumberyards were huge sprawling operations that served the needs of local builders and also buyers from points south. (Courtesy of the Madawaska Historical Society.)

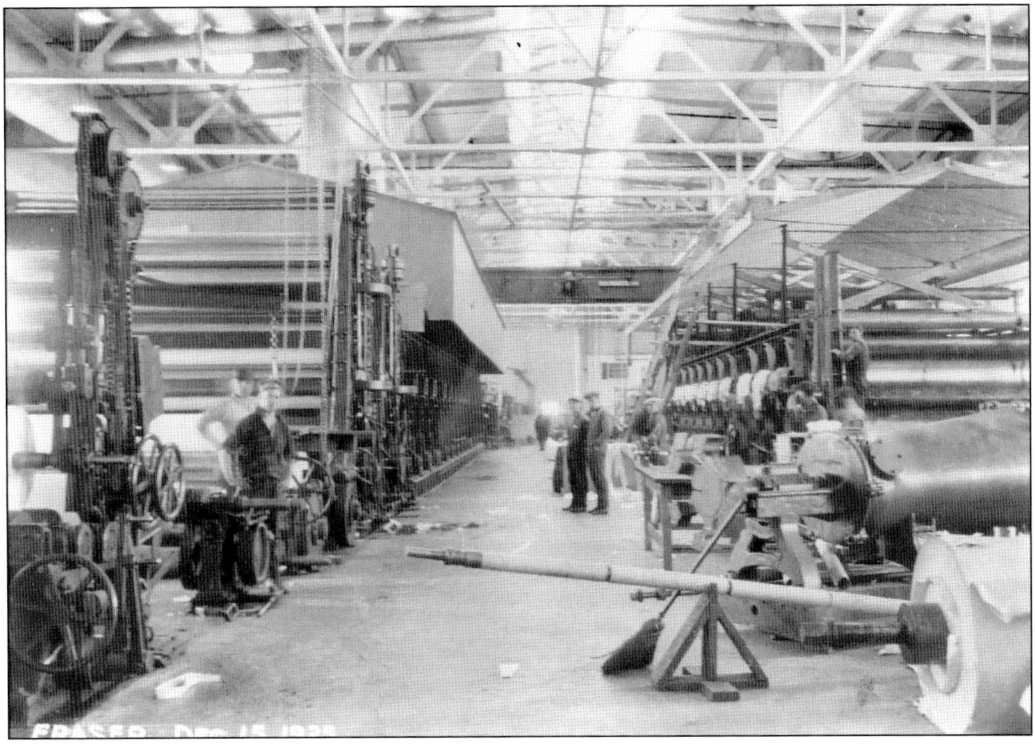

Lumber mills ordered and installed some of the largest machinery in Maine. Here is new hardware coming to Fraser Papers during the 1920s. (Courtesy of the Madawaska Historical Society.)

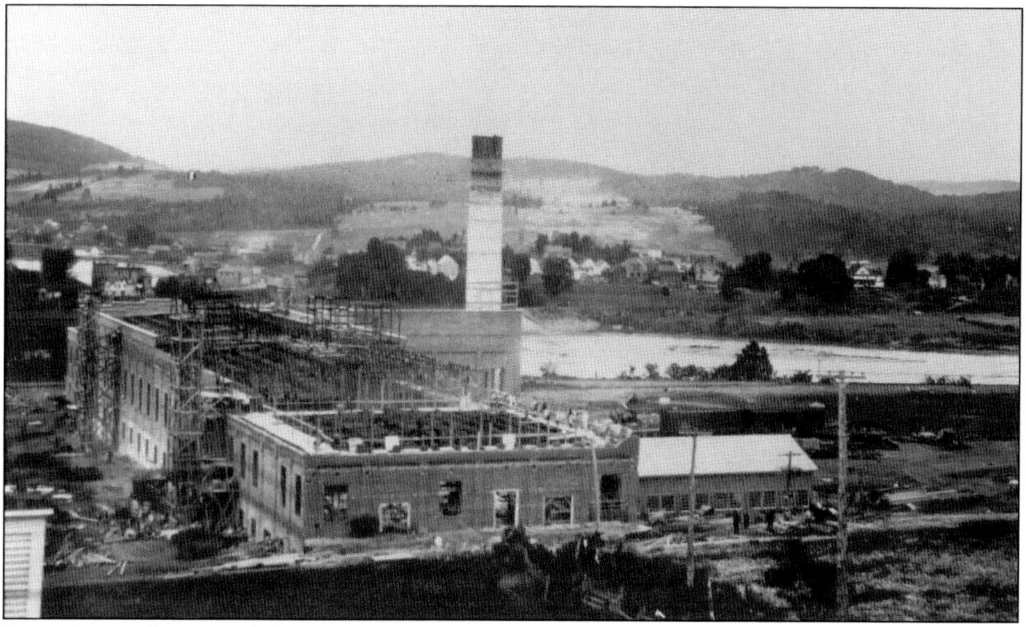

Fraser Papers dominated the Madawaska-Edmundston area for decades. Here is a Fraser mill being constructed in 1925. (Courtesy of the Madawaska Historical Society.)

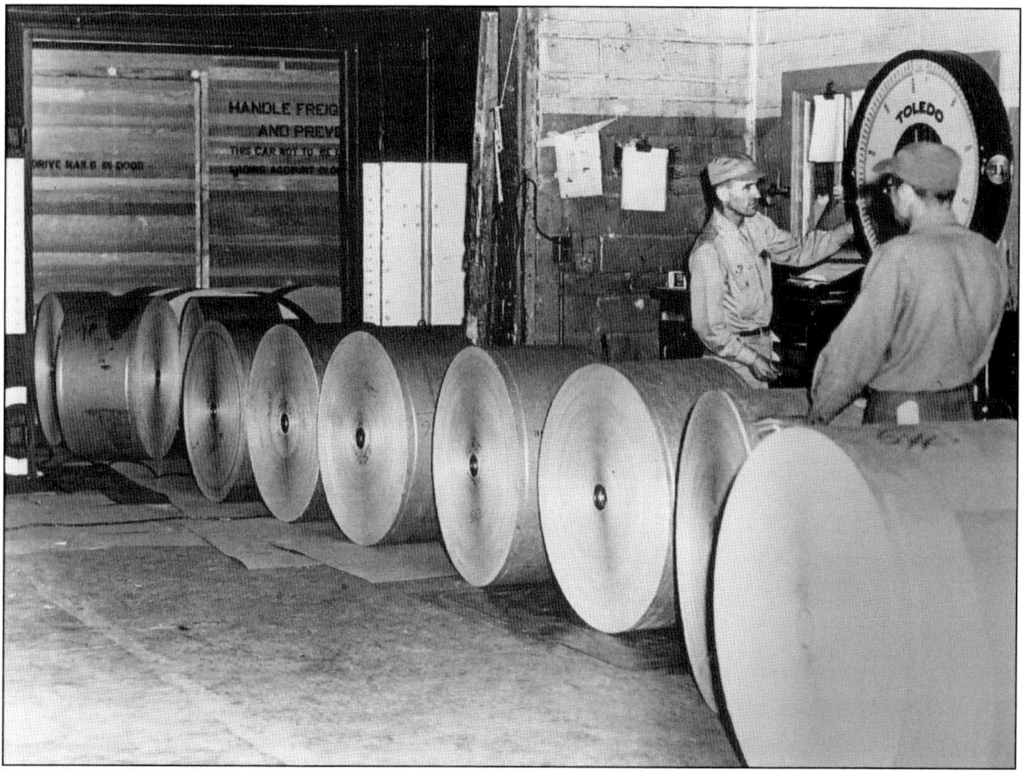

Some of the first paper machines to be used at the Madawaska mill by Fraser Papers arrived in the mid-1920s. Lumber came from both sides of the river as the plant grew and prospered. (Courtesy of the Madawaska Historical Society.)

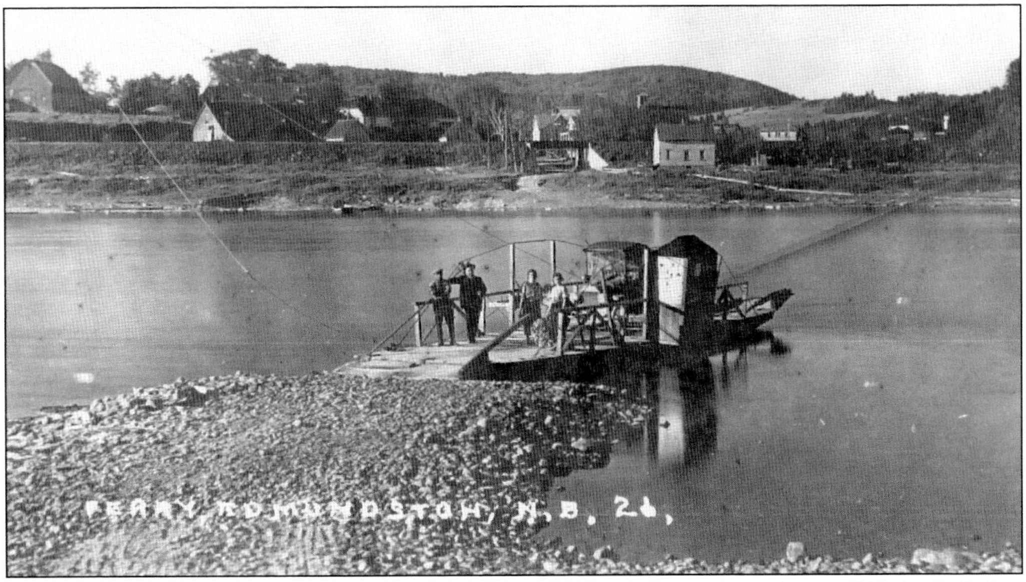

This ferryboat is traveling between Madawaska and Edmundston, Canada, in 1919. Included in this photograph are Solomon Beaulieu (left) and Eugene Bouchard with two unidentified women. (Courtesy of the Madawaska Historical Society.)

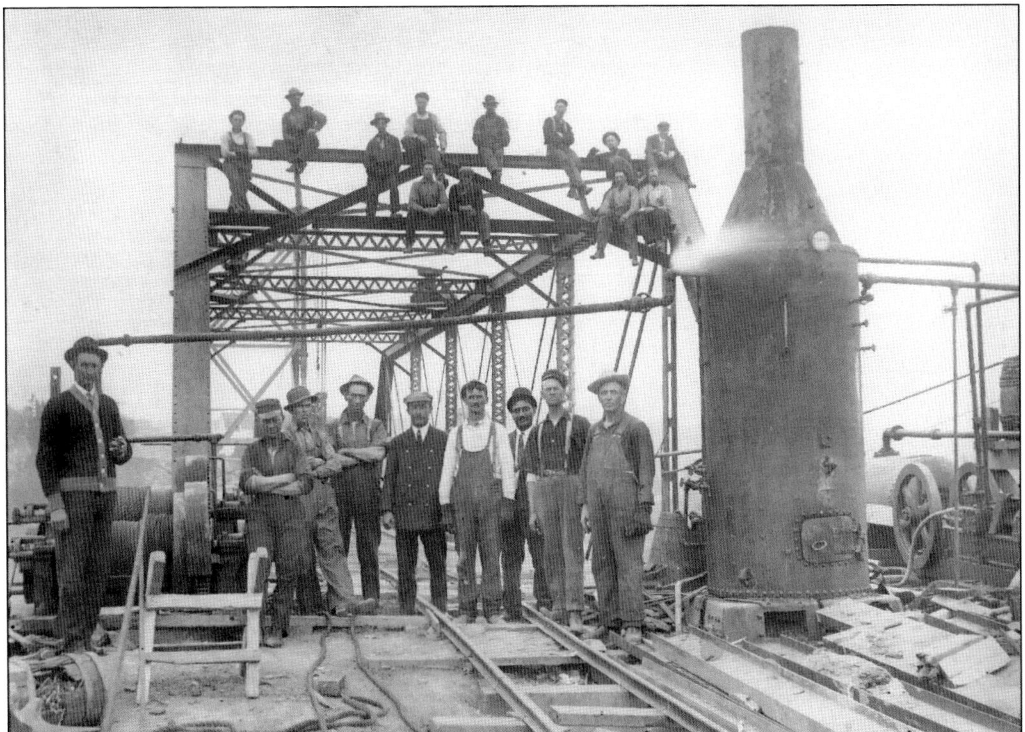

Workmen were building an international bridge between Madawaska and Edmundston in 1921. Today bridges between the two nations feature much security and many customs inspectors. (Courtesy of the Madawaska Historical Society.)

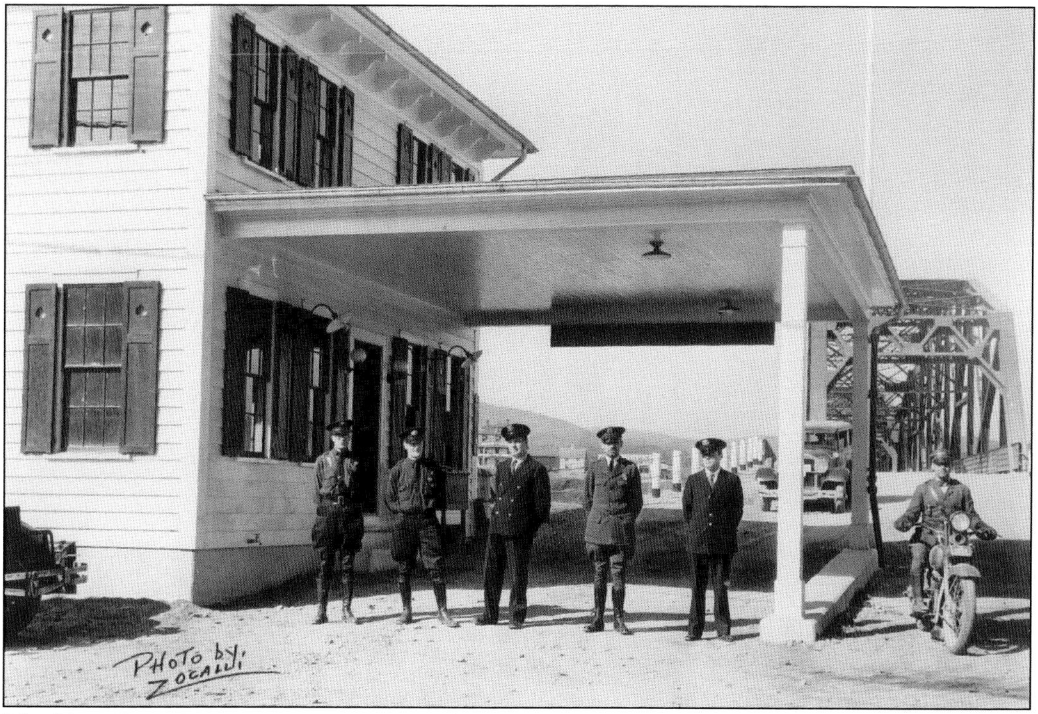

The Fort Kent Custom House is pictured in 1930. Today the custom house has sophisticated devices to detect illegal or dangerous cargo, but this image depicts a simpler era. (Courtesy of the Madawaska Historical Society.)

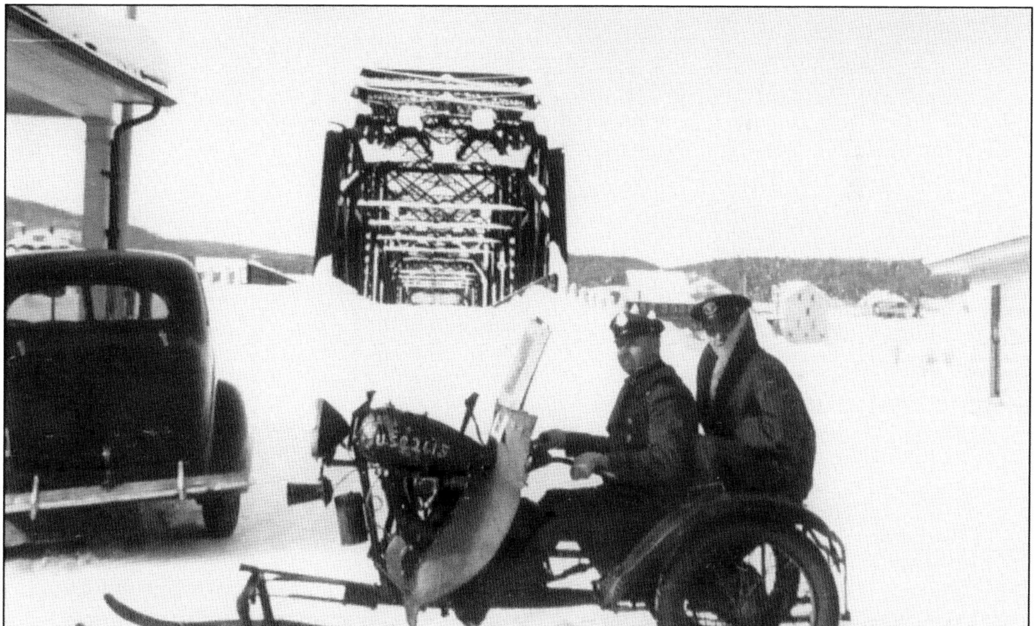

This border patrol team monitored traffic between Canada and northern Maine and was equipped to travel through deep snow if necessary. The men are unidentified. (Courtesy of the Madawaska Historical Society.)

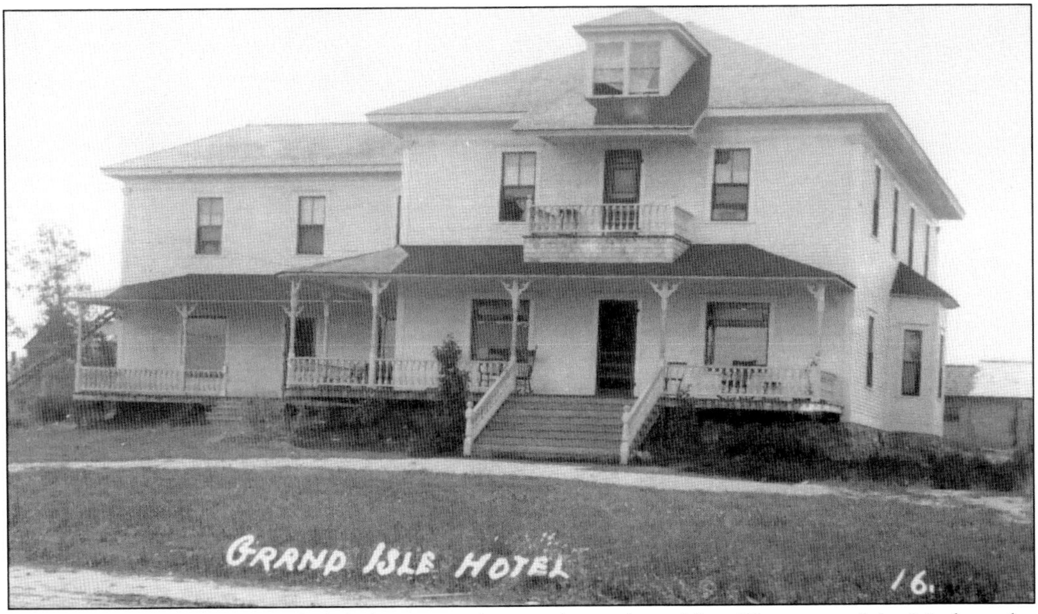

The Grand Isle Hotel provided shelter to workers and travelers alike. (Courtesy of the Madawaska Historical Society.)

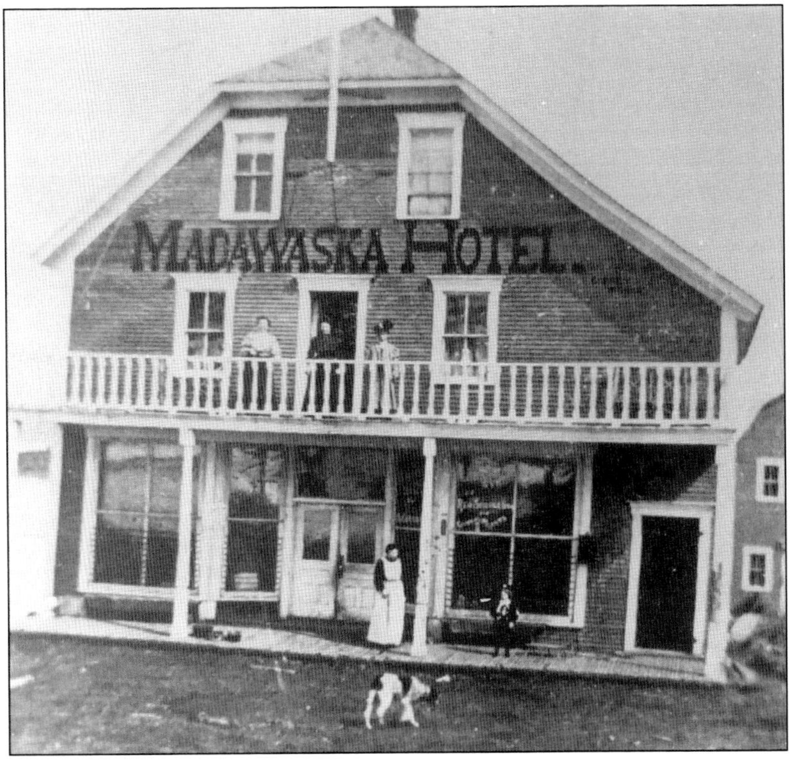

Small businesses often had many roles. This is the Belonie Hebert General Store, Post Office, and Madawaska Hotel, built in the late 19th century. (Courtesy of the Madawaska Historical Society.)

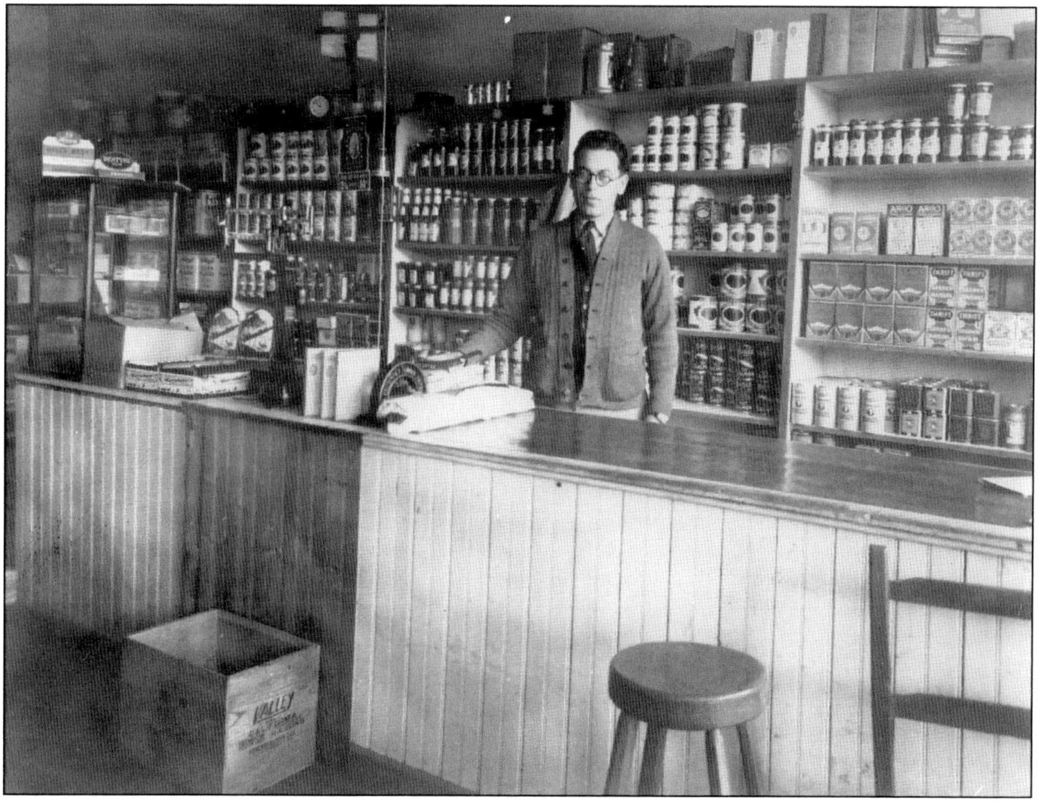

Pierre Dufour, pictured here in 1929, managed the Dufour General Store in St. Agatha. Storekeepers found it difficult to remain open when the Depression took hold in the 1930s. (Courtesy of the Madawaska Historical Society.)

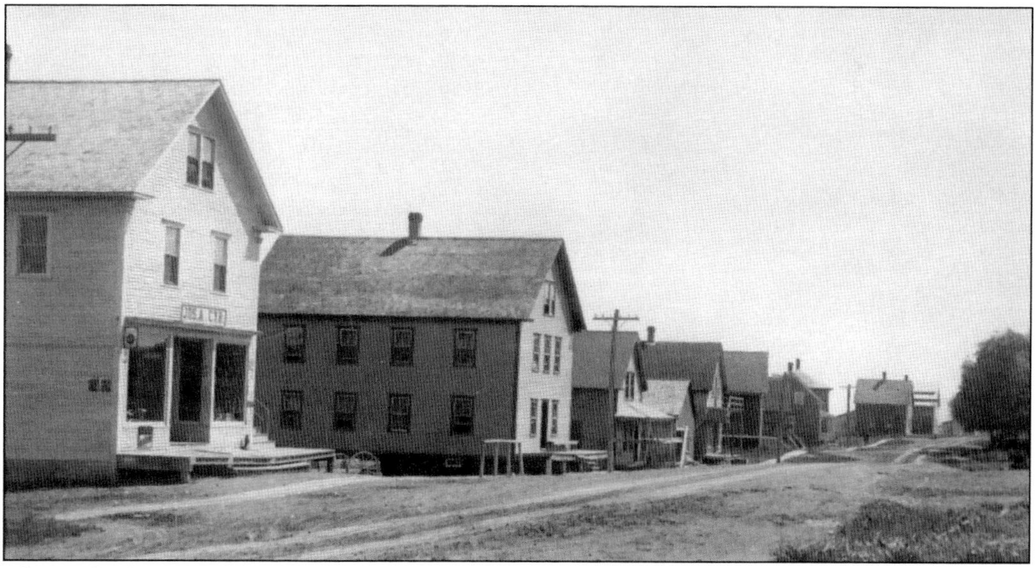

This is the Joe Cyr Grocery Store (left) in Grand Isle, later owned by Gordon Soucy. It appears that hitching posts for horses were still in use in this early-20th-century photograph. (Courtesy of the Madawaska Historical Society.)

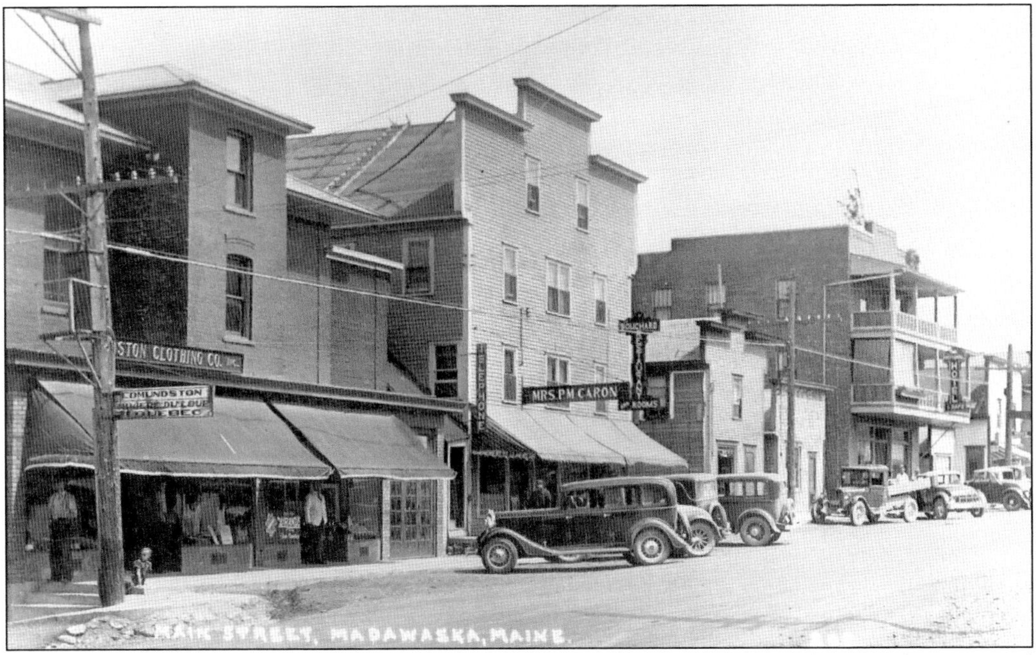

Main Street in Madawaska has hosted a countless number of lumbermen, loggers, farmers, and families over the years. (Courtesy of the Madawaska Historical Society.)

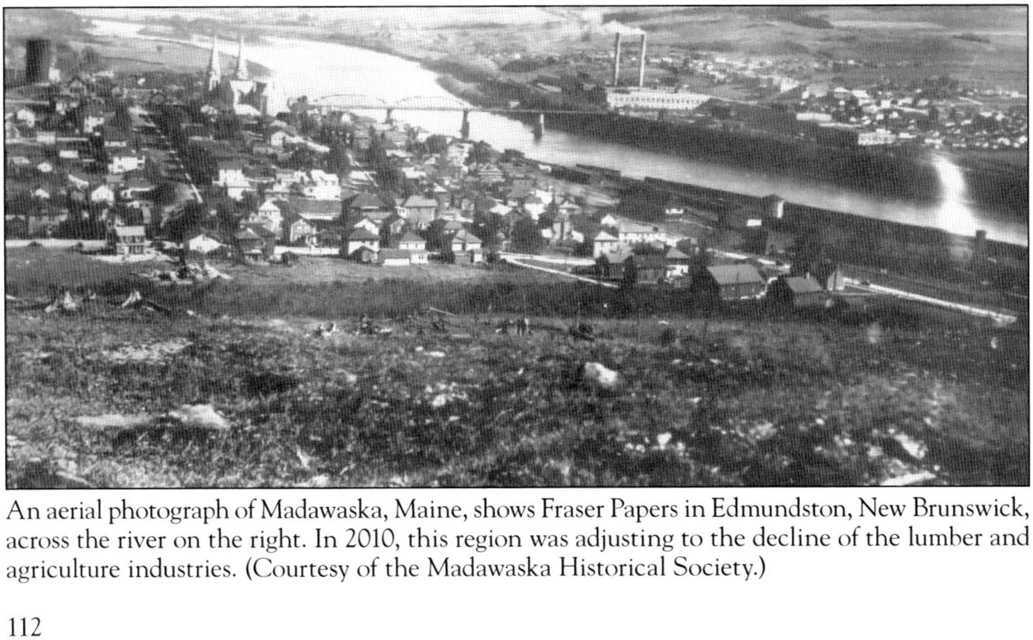
An aerial photograph of Madawaska, Maine, shows Fraser Papers in Edmundston, New Brunswick, across the river on the right. In 2010, this region was adjusting to the decline of the lumber and agriculture industries. (Courtesy of the Madawaska Historical Society.)

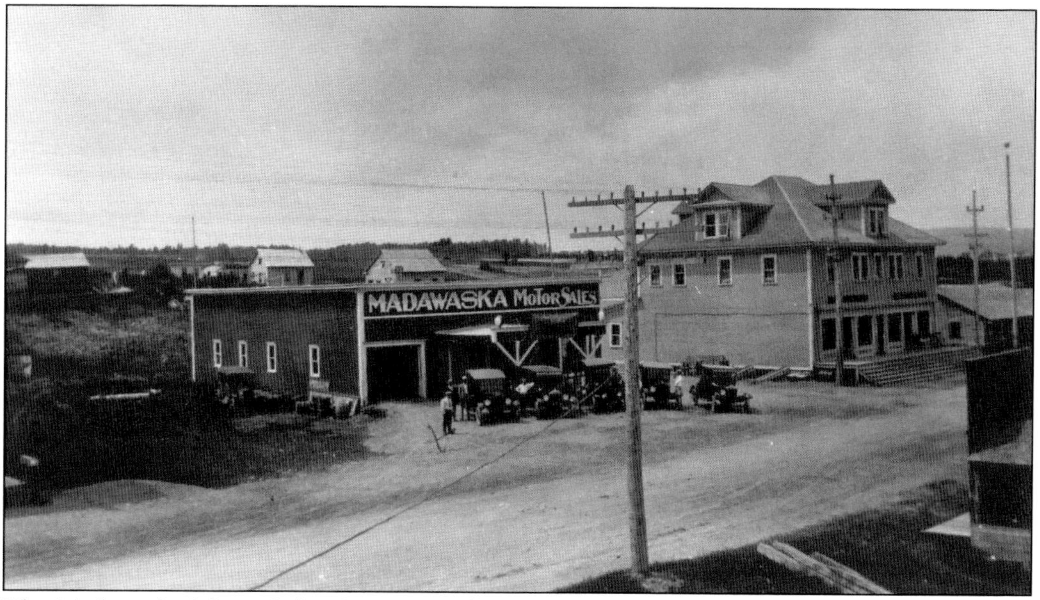

The Madawaska Motor Sales Company offered a variety of cars in 1926. Next to the lot was Arthur Daigle's dining hall and bunkhouse for lumber workers. (Courtesy of the Madawaska Historical Society.)

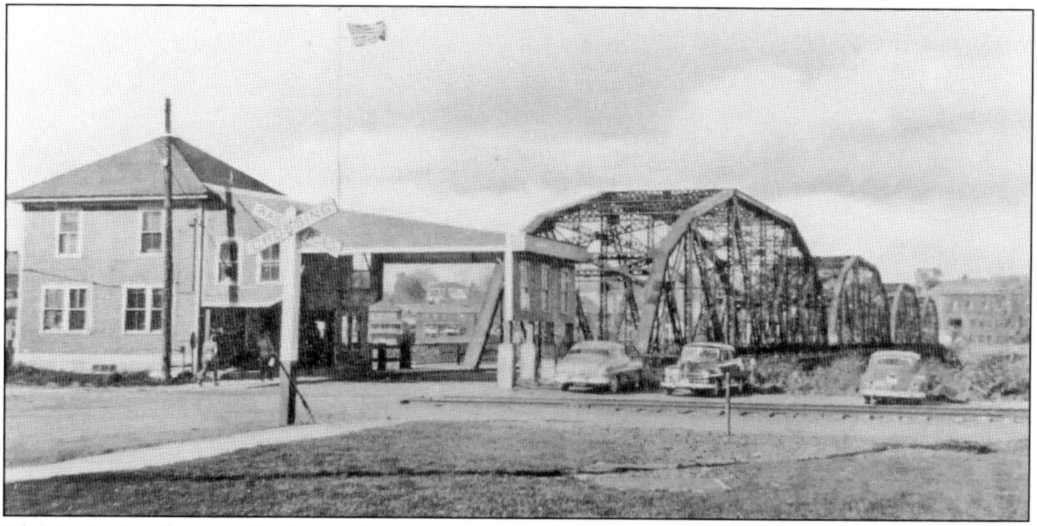

This is the Madawaska Bridge to Canada in 1956. In that era, residents crossed the international border with no constraints, but in recent years, officials have been checking travelers' identification and searching some vehicles. (Courtesy of the Madawaska Historical Society.)

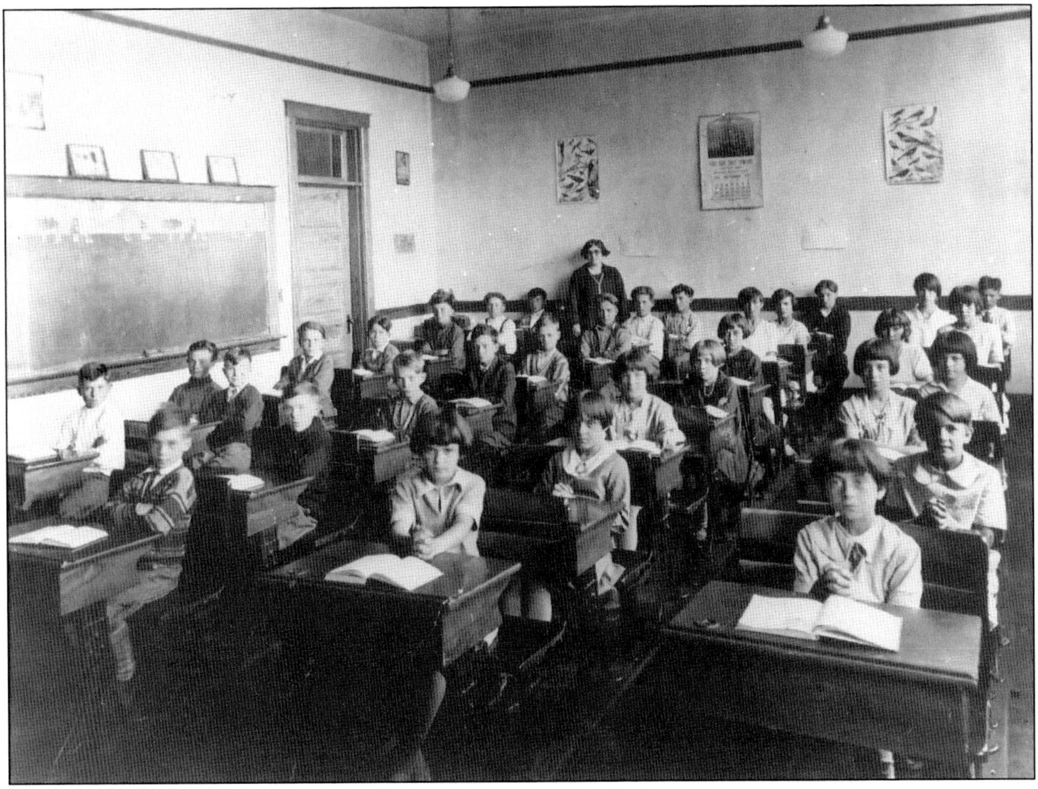

The Madawaska Training School was founded in 1878 by William Dickey, and students were taught in both French and English. This photograph was taken in 1906. (Courtesy of the Madawaska Historical Society.)

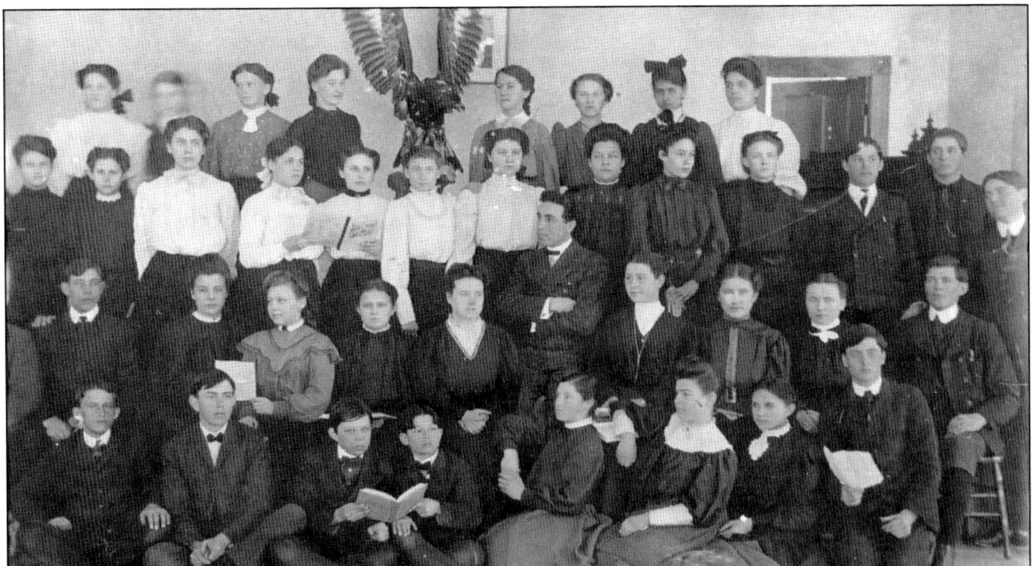

The Evangeline School was named with a nod to history. This class photograph was taken in 1927. (Courtesy of the Madawaska Historical Society.)

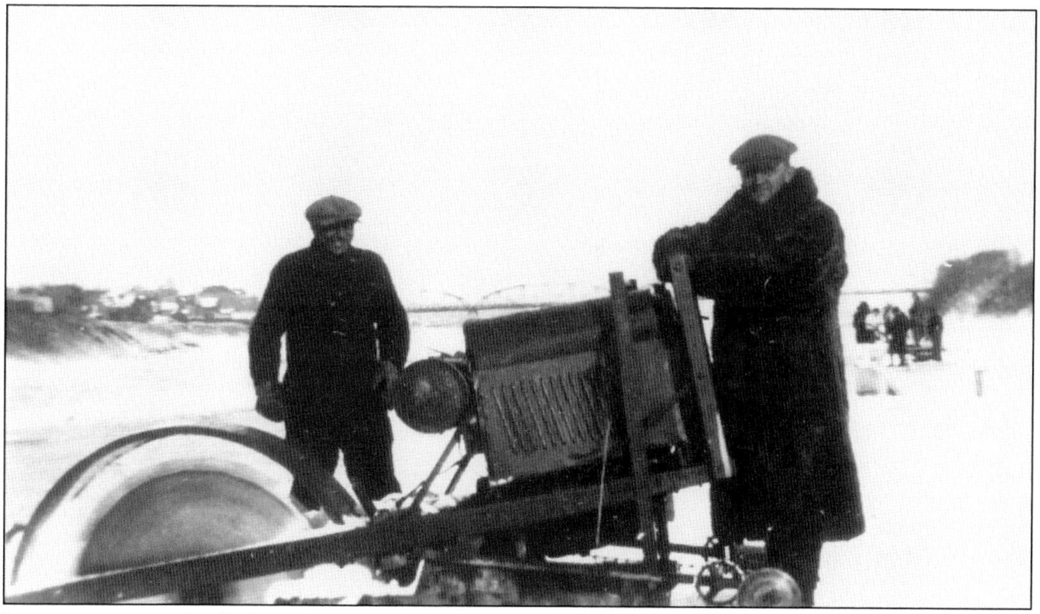

Ice cutting was a lively business a century ago, before electricity came to the St. John Valley. Here are members of the Solomon Beaulieu Ice Cutting Business on the St. John River. (Courtesy of the Madawaska Historical Society.)

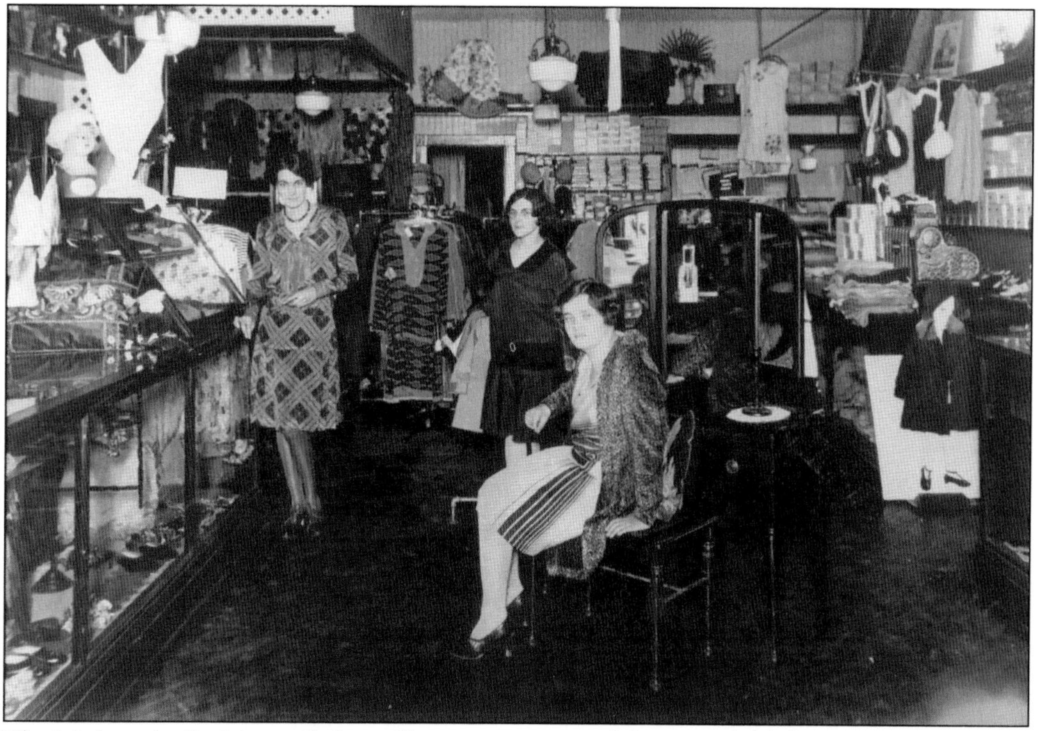

The Madawaska Parisienne Fashion Shop was a center of shopping for fashionable women. This photograph was taken in 1927. (Courtesy of the Madawaska Historical Society.)

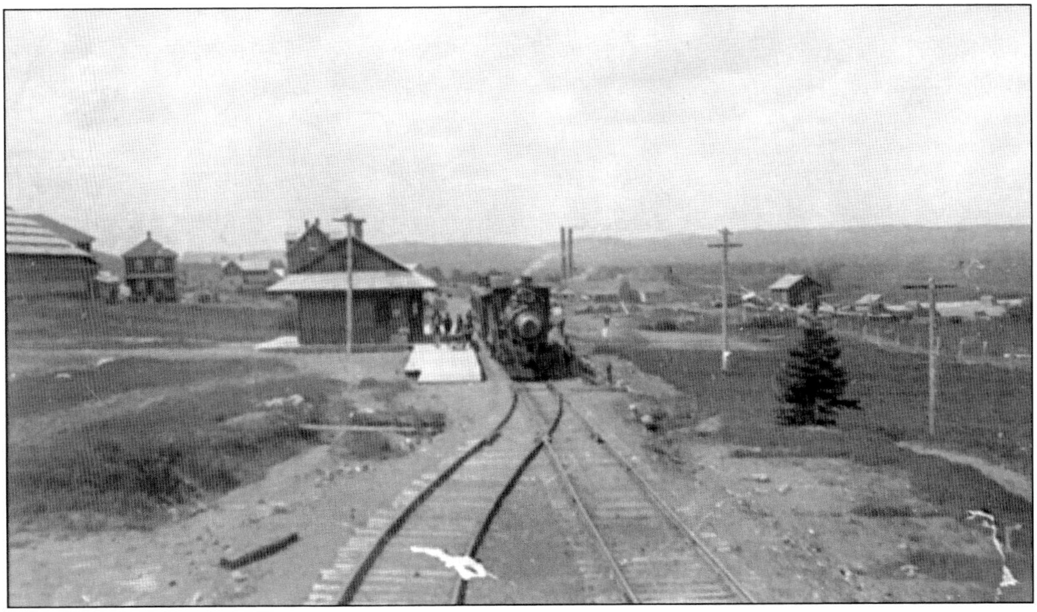

The Grand Isle Railroad line, shown here in 1911, played a key role in commerce. The railroad connected Aroostook County with distant trading markets and was essential to the survival of those in the St. John Valley. (Courtesy of the Madawaska Historical Society.)

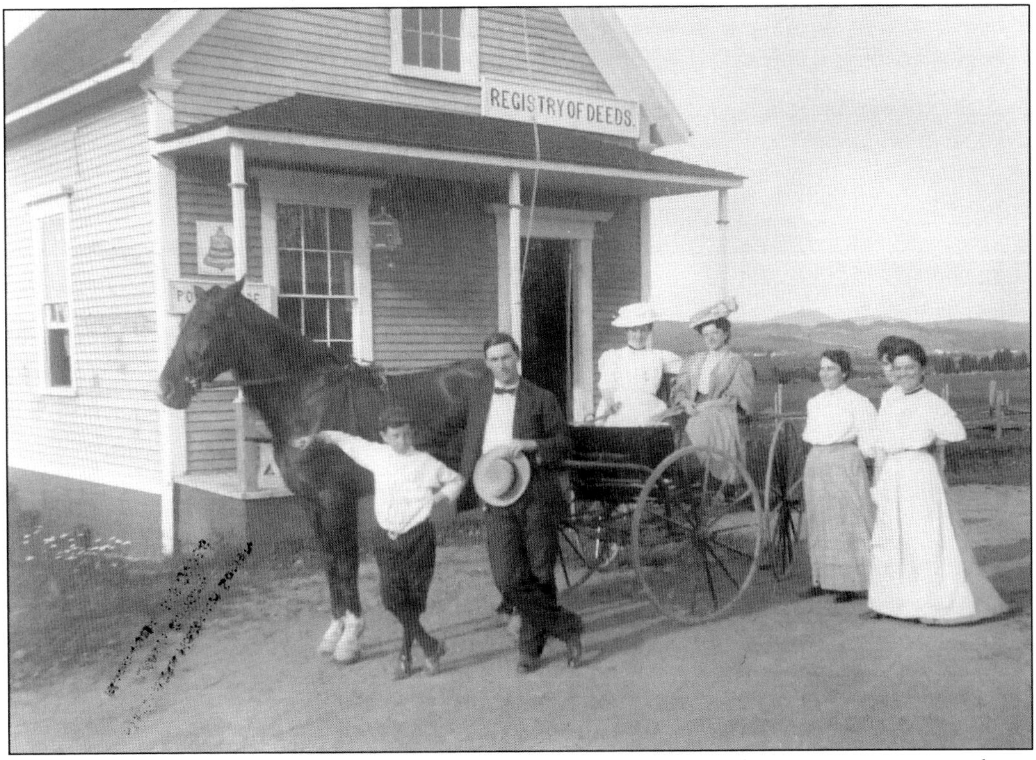

Family members stand outside a registry of deeds in the early 20th century. Many residents in the St. John Valley conducted their business in French. (Courtesy of the Madawaska Historical Society.)

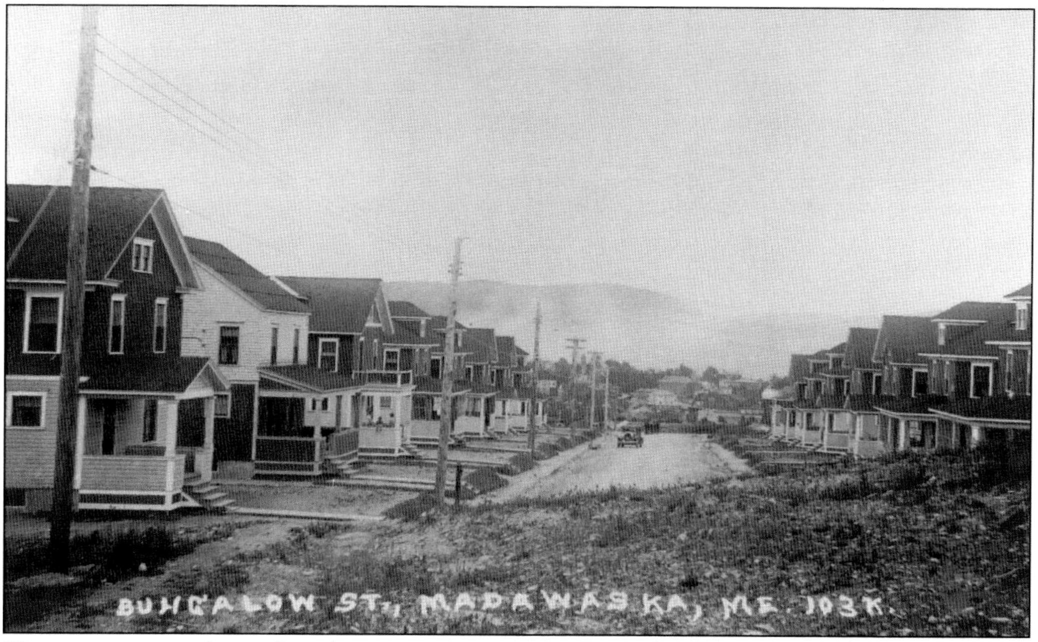

There were many bungalows but not many cars on Bungalow Street in Madawaska in 1938. (Courtesy of the Madawaska Historical Society.)

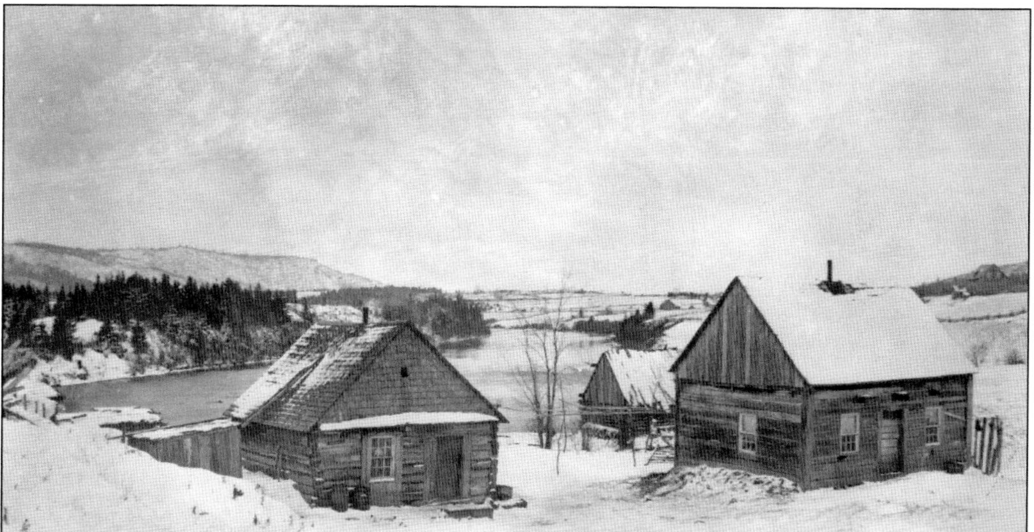

This is what winter looked like to rural Canadians in the late 19th century, for this is a photograph taken in the provinces more than a century ago. Some Canadians moved to Aroostook County, but many more migrated farther south to work in the mills in Maine. (Courtesy of the Madawaska Historical Society.)

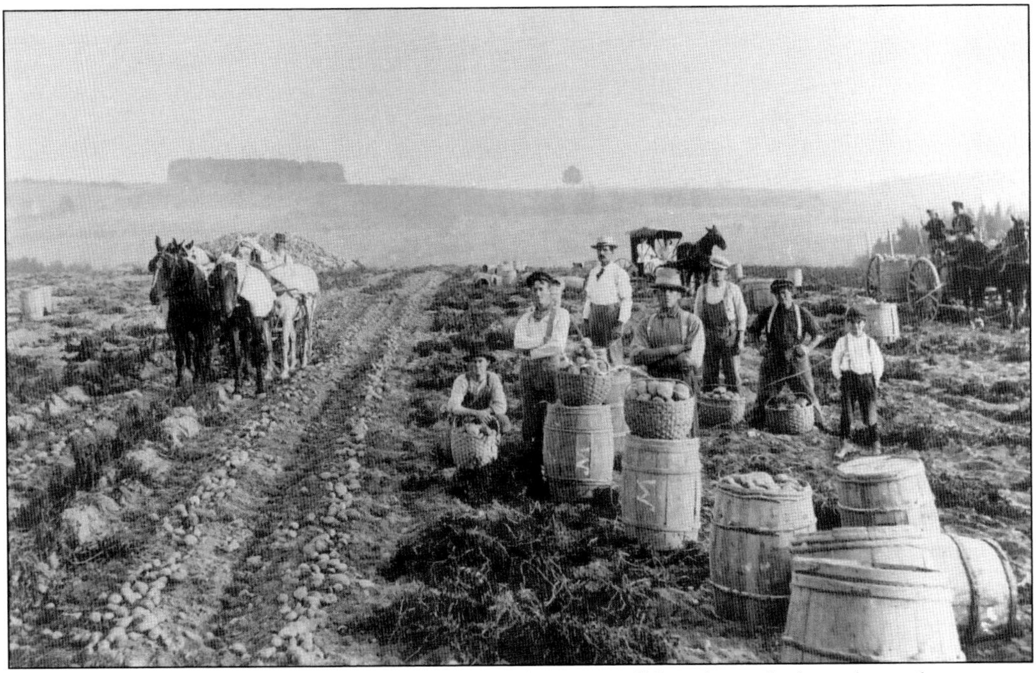

Harvesting potatoes was a family affair, and Acadians put all hands on deck in the early autumn. Males of many ages gathered the crop, and in this photograph, women can be seen in carriages to the rear. (Courtesy of the Madawaska Historical Society.)

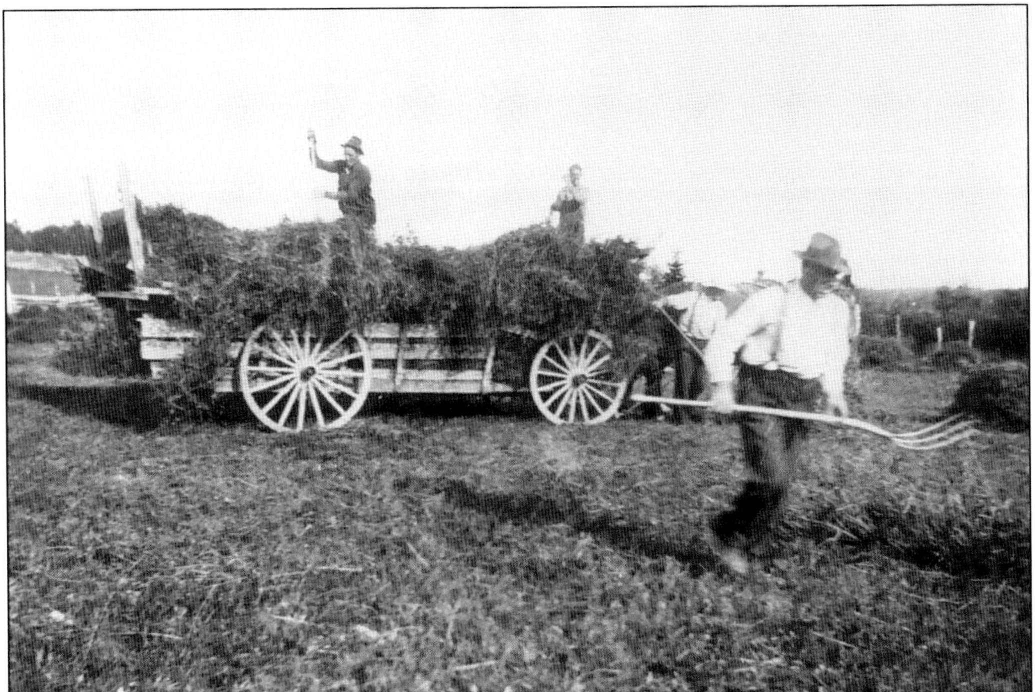

Farmers depended on hay to feed the livestock over the winter, and here a team hustles to bring in the fodder before the cold weather arrives. (Courtesy of the Madawaska Historical Society.)

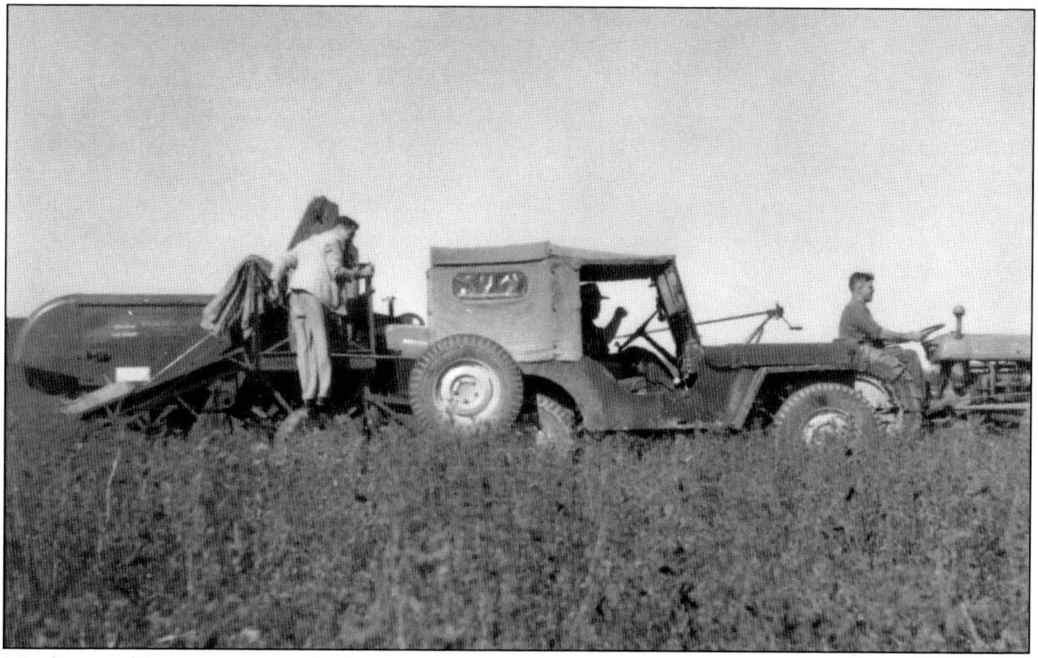

Mechanized harvesting methods came none too soon for those in the St. John Valley, as this image indicates. (Courtesy of the Madawaska Historical Society.)

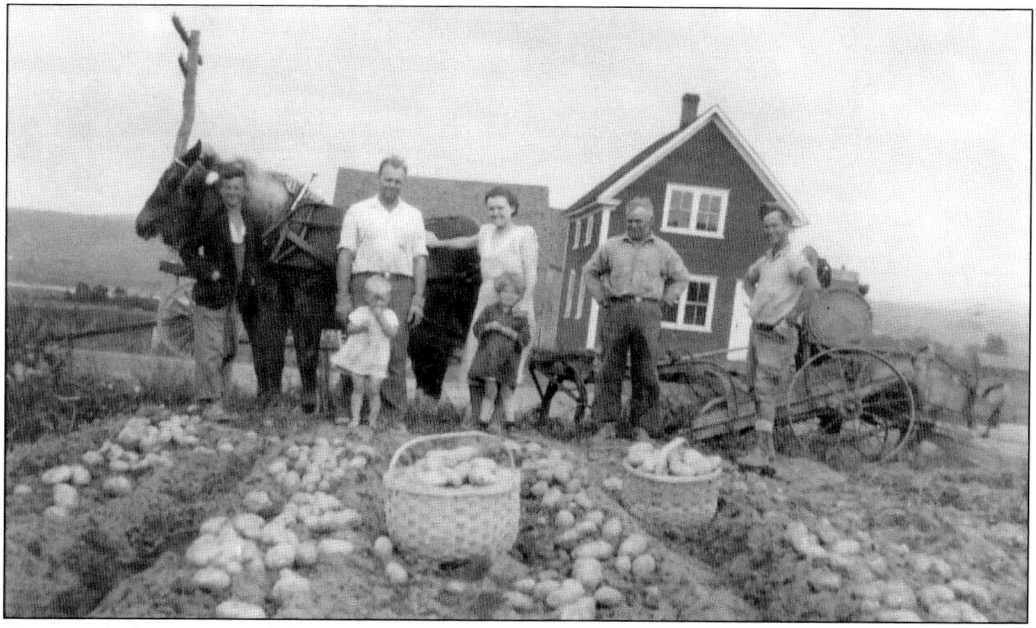

Aroostook County is still known for its potatoes, but days like these, when the crop sustained whole families, are disappearing. (Courtesy of the Madawaska Historical Society.)

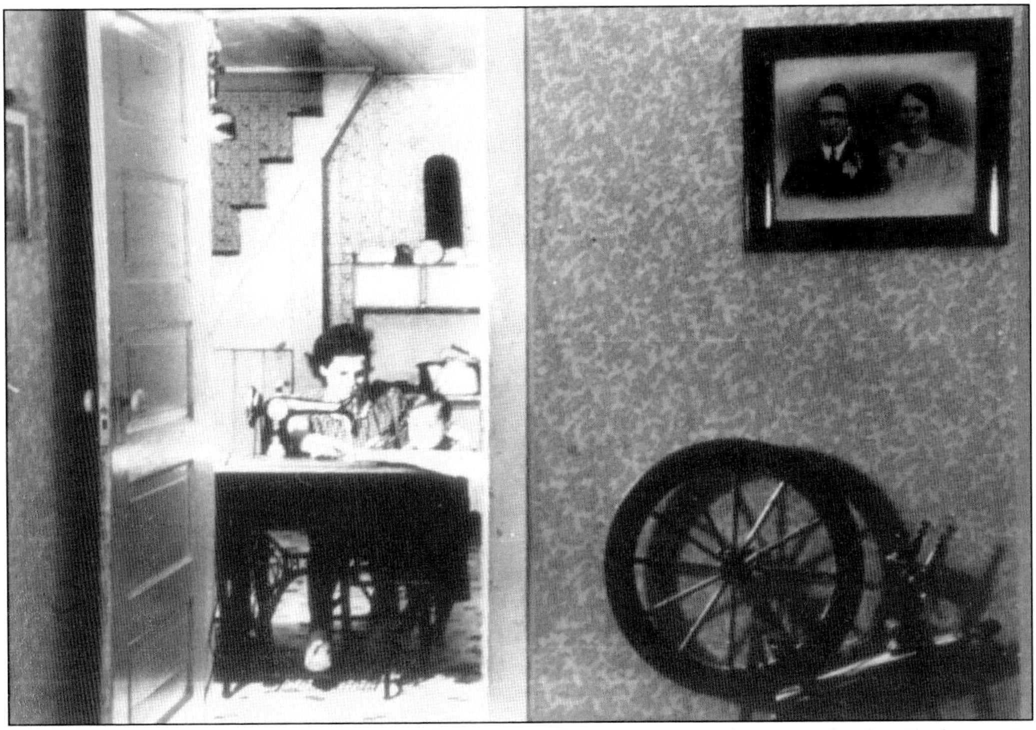

Julie Clavette Gendreau, with son Real is seen at her sewing machine in the family home in 1940. Julie used the wheel in the foreground to spin yarn for knitting. (Courtesy of the Acadian Archives, University of Maine at Fort Kent.)

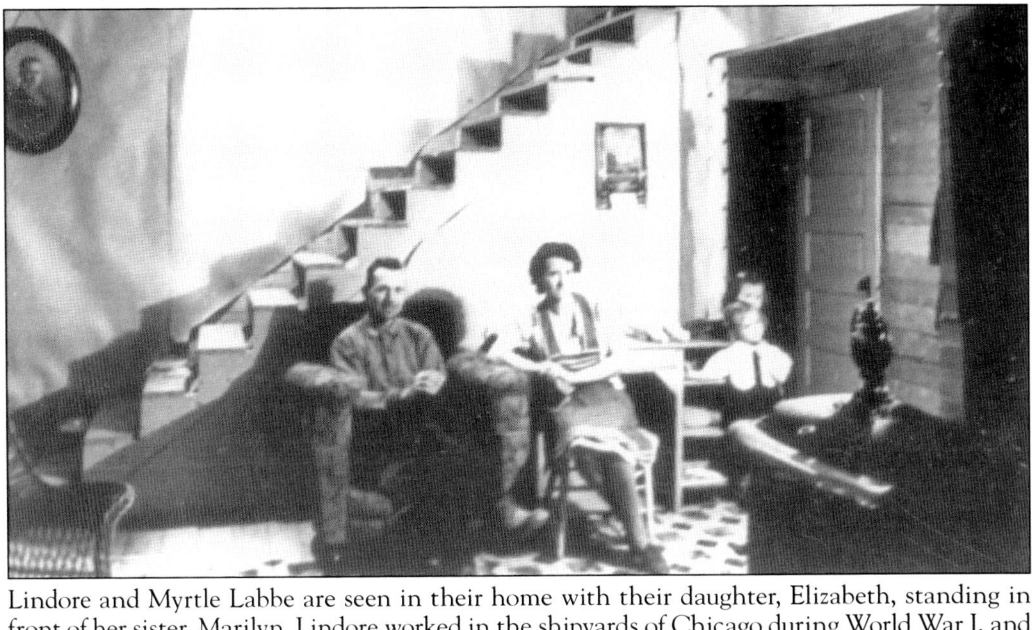

Lindore and Myrtle Labbe are seen in their home with their daughter, Elizabeth, standing in front of her sister, Marilyn. Lindore worked in the shipyards of Chicago during World War I, and Myrtle was a teacher who had attended Castine Normal School. A year after this photograph was taken, in 1940, the family moved to Wallagrass, Maine, to run a small store. (Courtesy of the Acadian Archives, University of Maine at Fort Kent.)

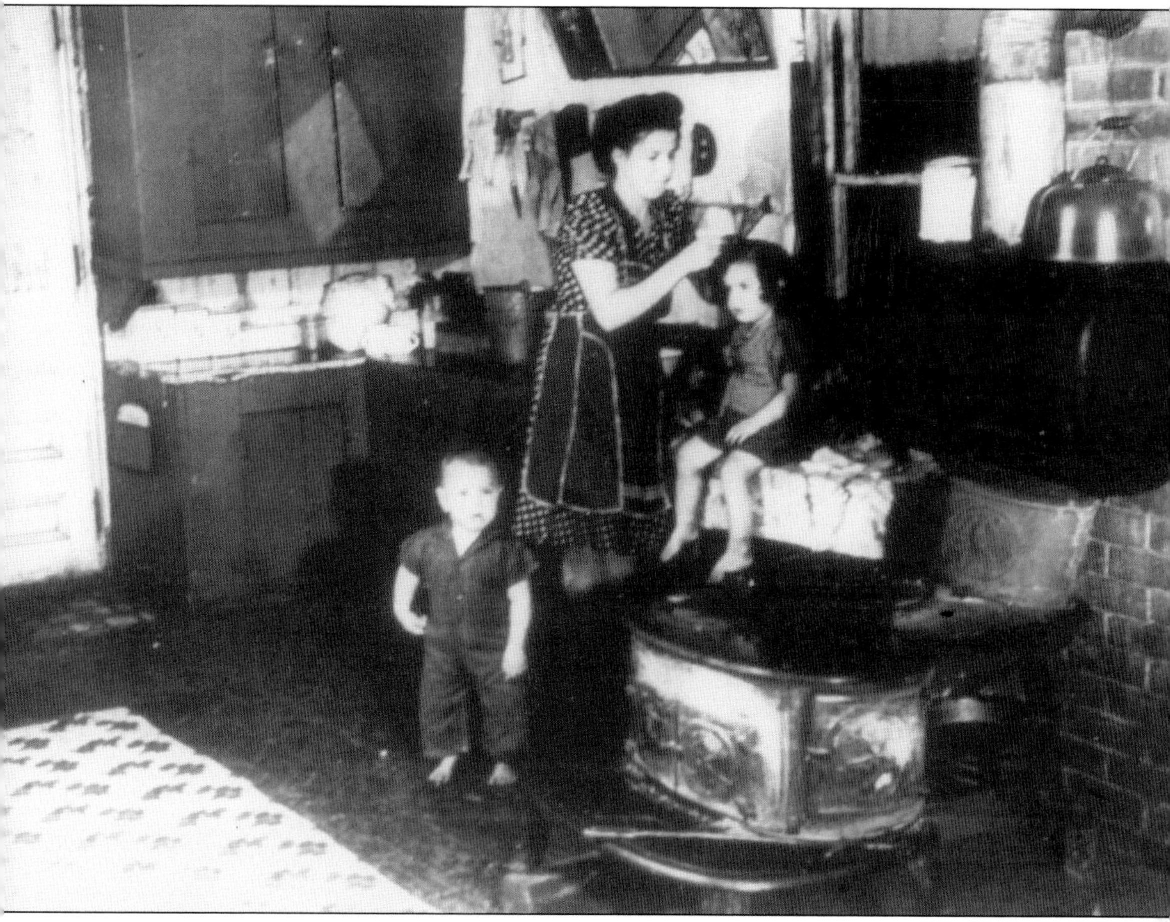

Rita Dumond Cyr (wife of George Cyr) was 18 when this picture was taken in 1940. She was intent upon making her young daughter and son, Geraldine and Gerald, clean and presentable. (Courtesy of the Acadian Archives, University of Maine at Fort Kent.)

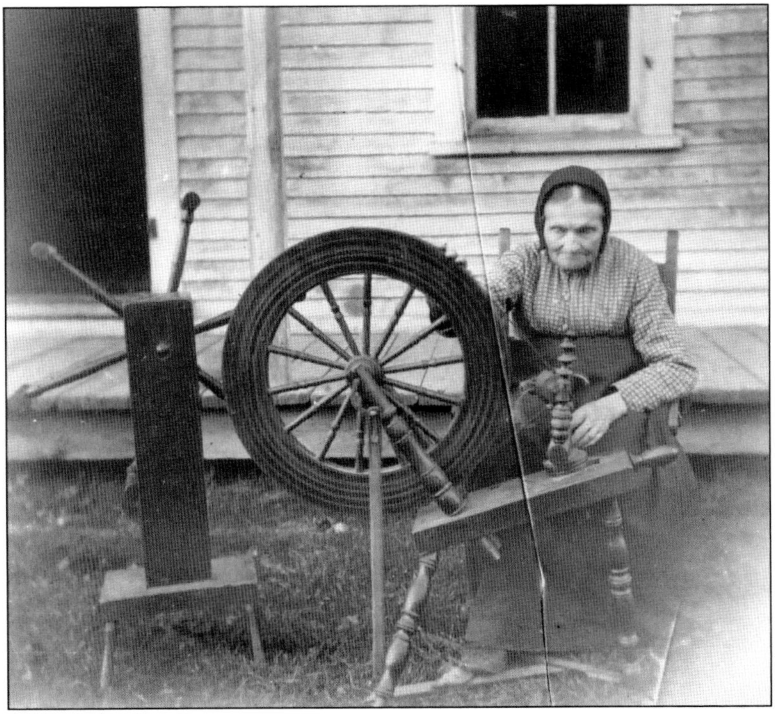

An aging family member continues her efforts to be productive at a farm near Fort Kent. Caring for elders was part of the Acadian ethic. (Courtesy of the Acadian Archives, University of Maine at Fort Kent.)

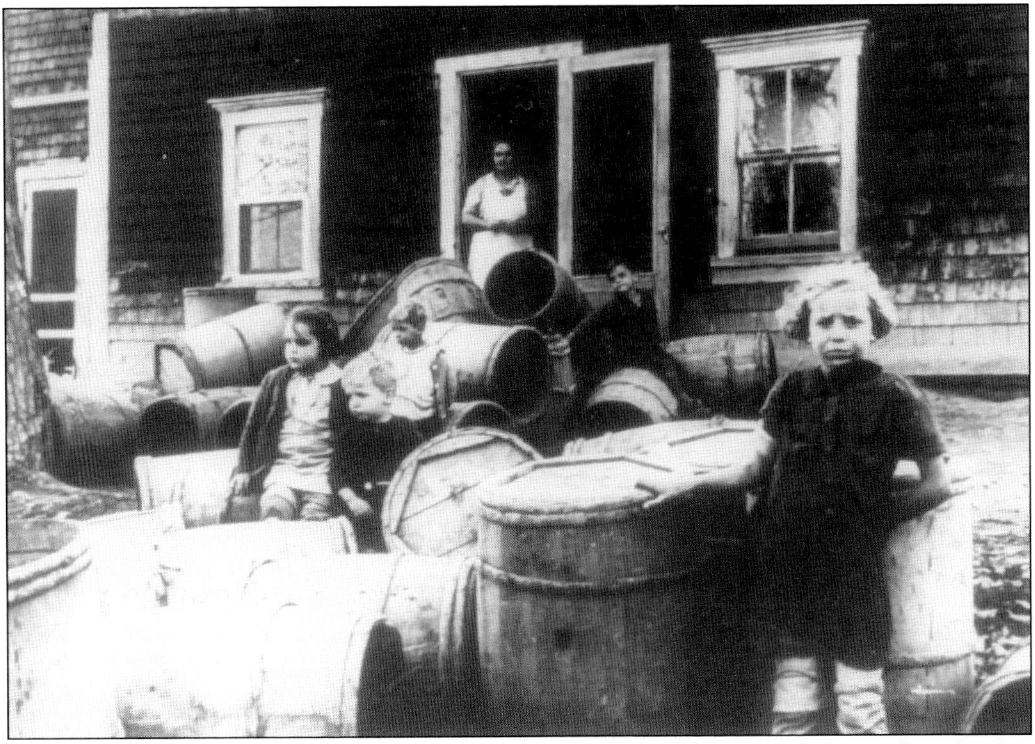

Beatrice Labbe Deprey supervises young children who wander among the potato barrels after adults had brought in the harvest in Soldier Pond. Potatoes would sometimes fill a whole basement. (Courtesy of the Acadian Archives, University of Maine at Fort Kent.)

Youngsters learned crafts early in the St. John Valley. Here, from left to right, Lillian, Therese, and Marie Anne Gagnon are knitting in Frenchville in 1942. (Courtesy of the Acadian Archives, University of Maine at Fort Kent.)

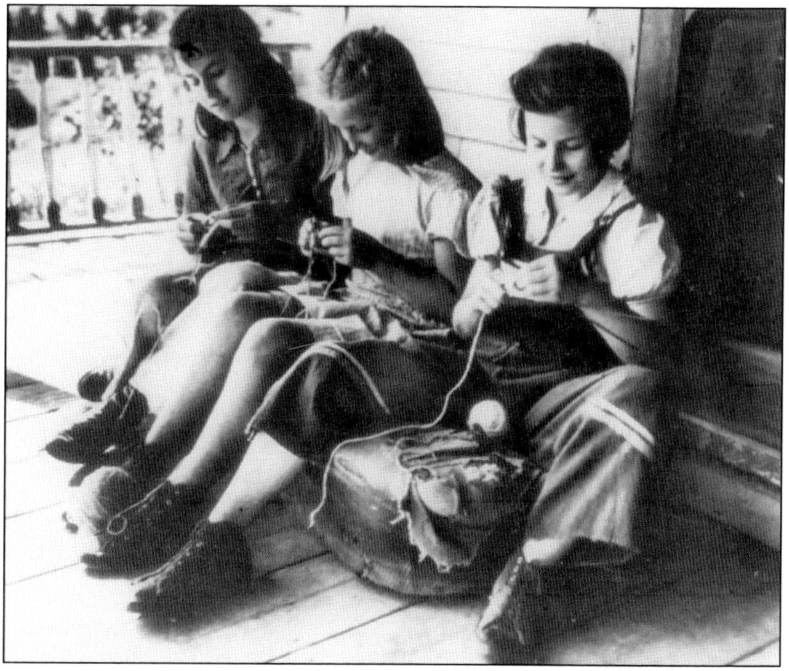

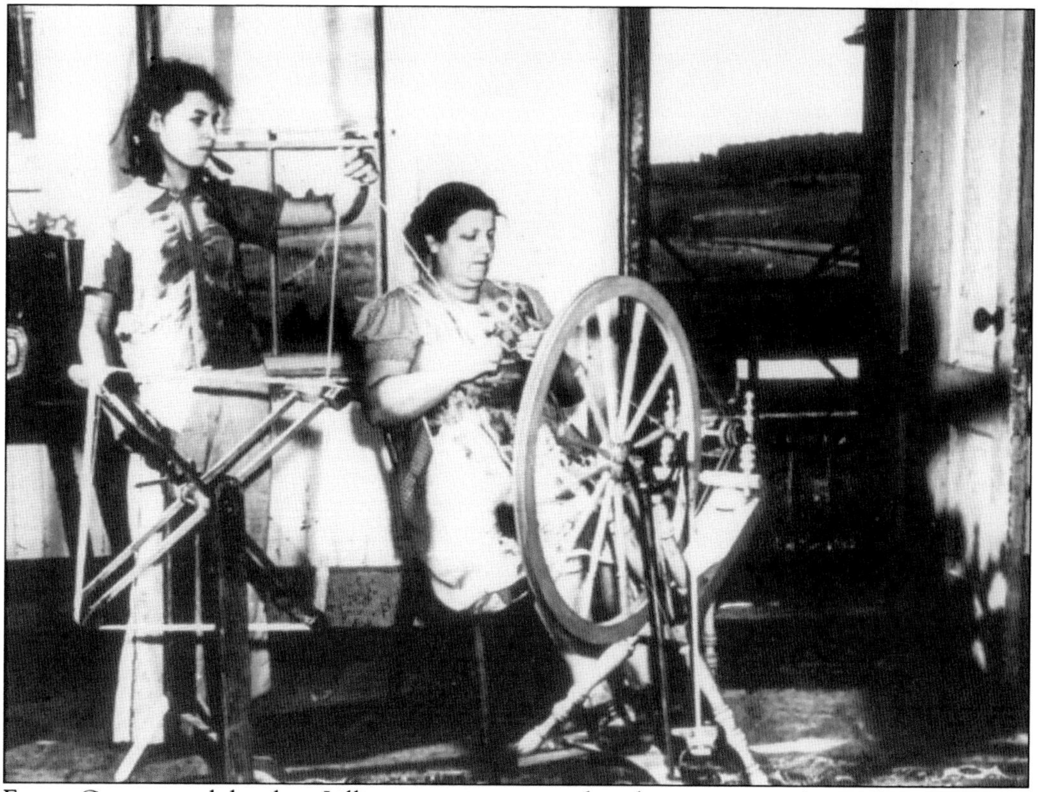

Emma Gagnon and daughter Lillian are spinning in their living room in front of a screen door that overlooks the farm. Many valuable skills were passed on from mother to daughter. (Courtesy of the Acadian Archives, University of Maine at Fort Kent.)

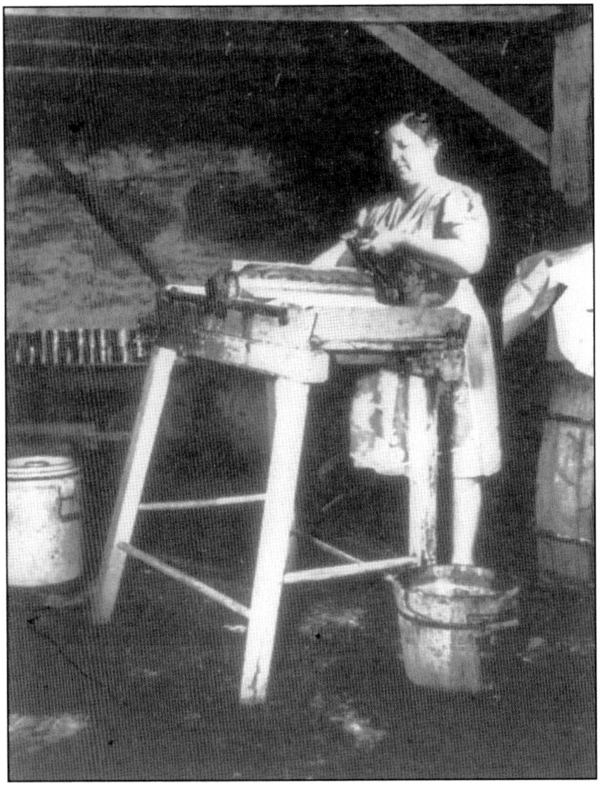

Emma Gagnon wrings buttermilk out of butter after salting it. The butter was often stored in the icehouse until it was needed. ((Courtesy of the Acadian Archives, University of Maine at Fort Kent.)

The women on the farms learned to produce many necessities for their families. Here Emma Gagnon makes butter in Frenchville in 1940. (Courtesy of the Acadian Archives, University of Maine at Fort Kent.)

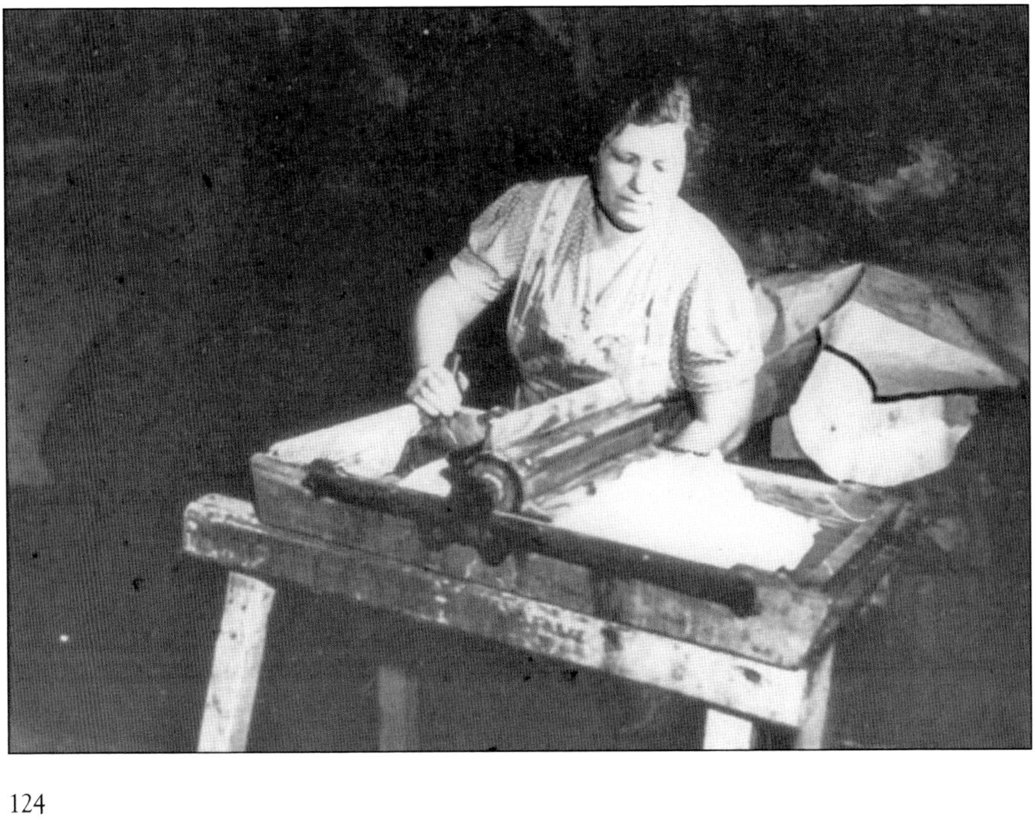

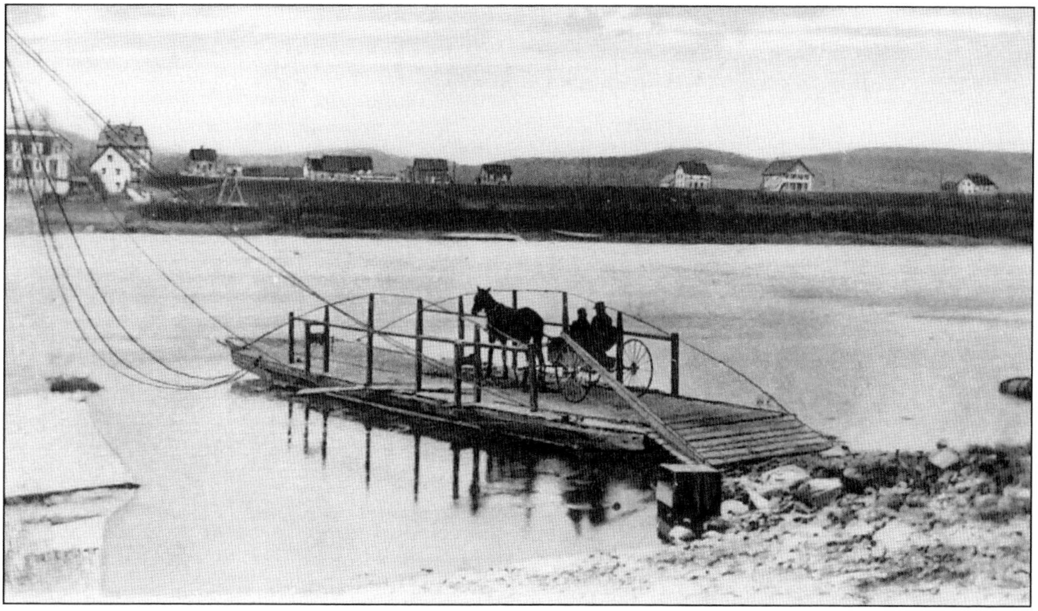

A couple awaits the ferry to take them from Maine to New Brunswick on the St. John River early in the 20th century. (Courtesy of the Madawaska Historical Society.)

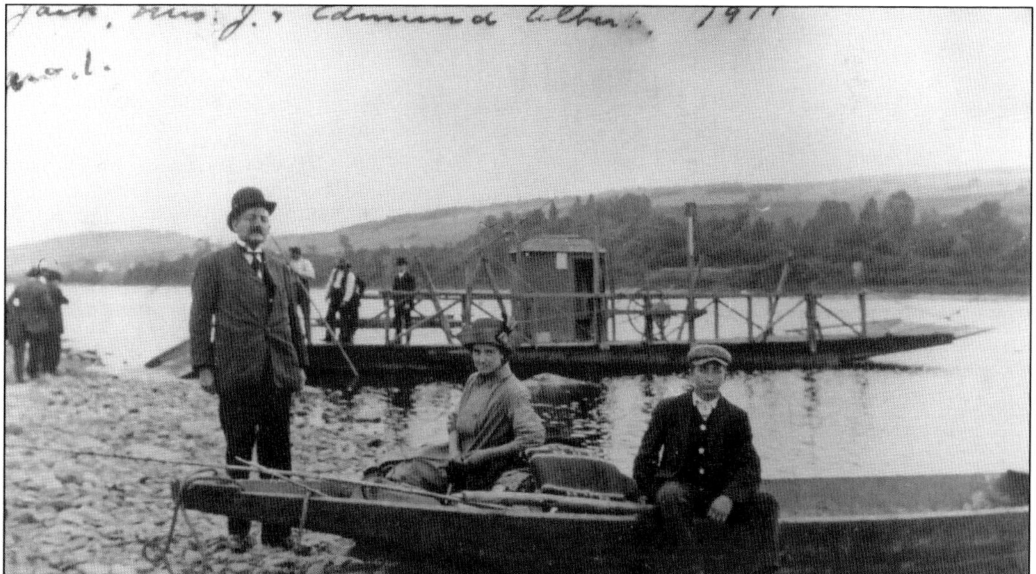

Boaters prepare for a trip on the St. John River in 1911. In the background must be a "modern" craft with the first elements of mechanization. (Courtesy of the Madawaska Historical Society.)

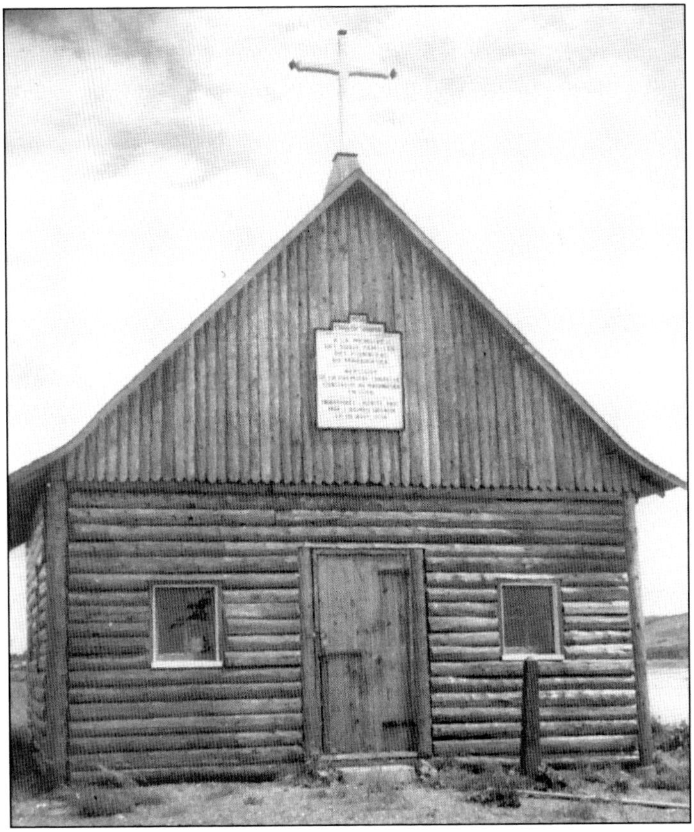

Franco-Americans have always had an appreciation of their ethnic history. In 1956, the community of St. Basile built this replica of a chapel that the Acadians had constructed in 1786. (Courtesy of the Madawaska Historical Society.)

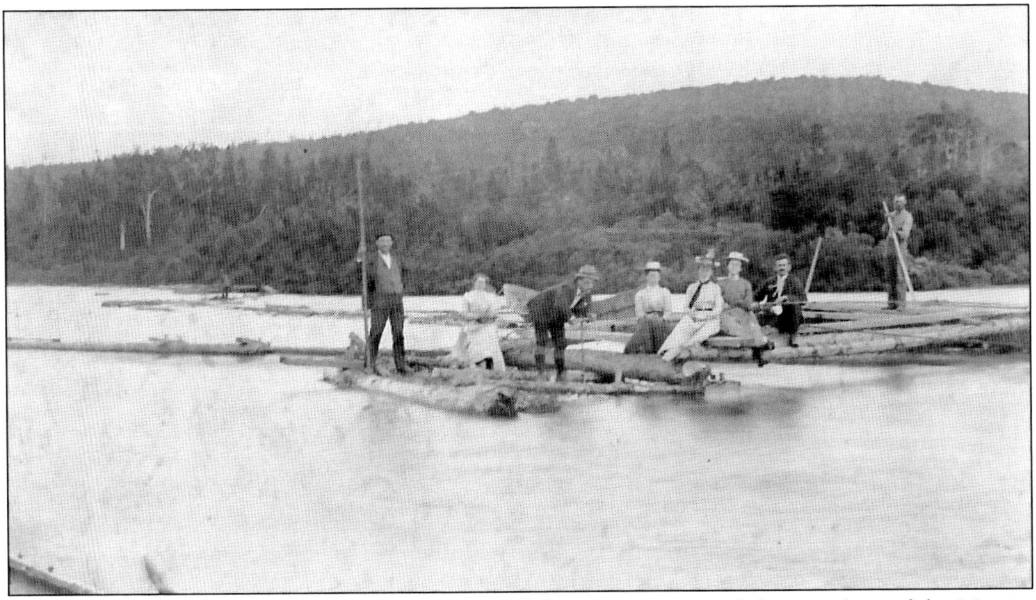

This photograph was taken on a wedding day, and the marriage united the members of the Martin and Michaud families in 1900. One would hope the partiers held off on having a celebratory drink until they exited the rickety—if unique—river-going vessel. (Courtesy of the Acadian Archives, University of Maine at Fort Kent.)

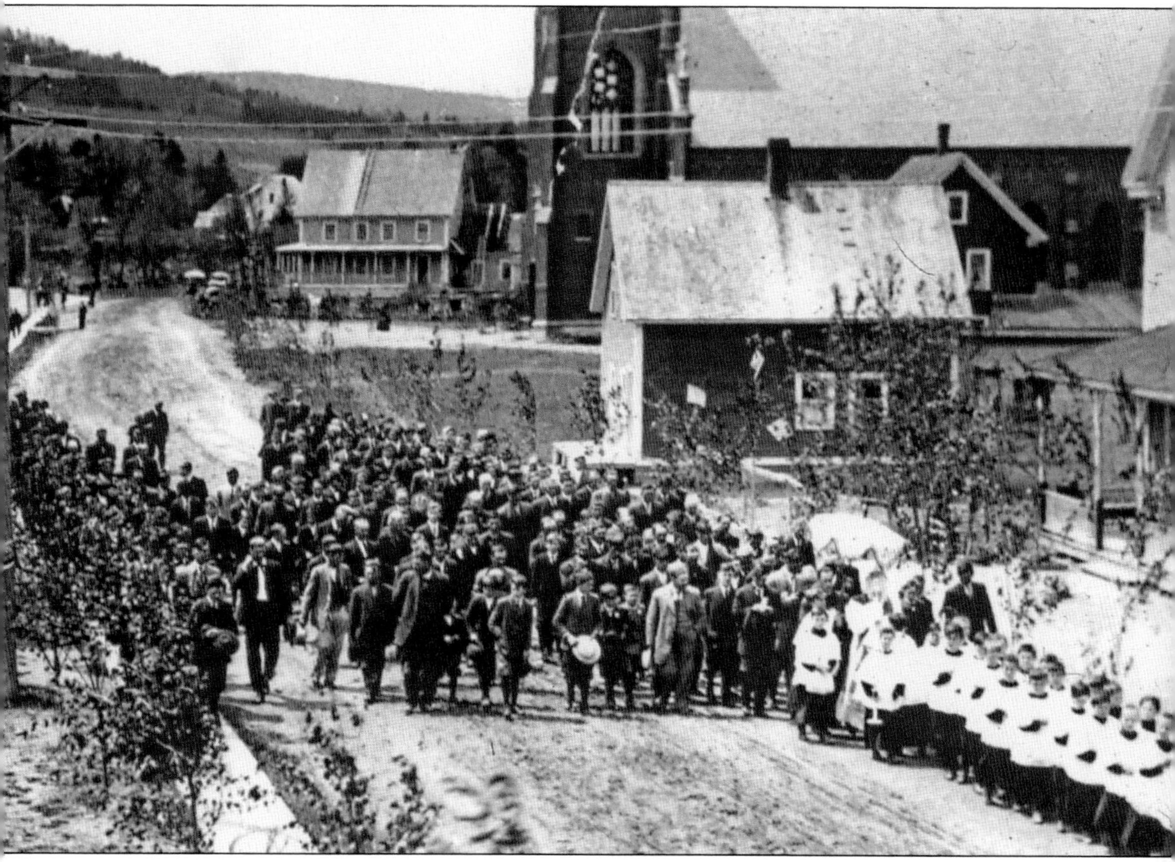

Youngsters and adults walk together in unity during a religious procession in Fort Kent in 1898. The early Franco-Americans had great faith in their church. (Courtesy of Rose Nadeau.)